D1428383

Information Resource Description

Creating and managing
metadata

Philip Hider

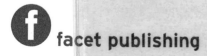

facet publishing

Published by Facet Publishing
7 Ridgmount Street, London WC1E 7AE
www.facetpublishing.co.uk

Facet Publishing is wholly owned by CILIP: the Chartered Institute of
Library and Information Professionals.

British Library Cataloguing in Publication Data
A catalogue record for this book is available from the British Library.

ISBN 978-1-85604-667-1

First published 2012

Text printed on FSC accredited material.

Mixed Sources
Product group from well-managed
forests and other controlled sources
www.fsc.org Cert no. SA-COC-1565
© 1996 Forest Stewardship Council
FSC

Typeset from author's files in 10/14 pt Palatino Linotype and Frutiger by
Facet Publishing Production.
Printed and made in Great Britain by MPG Books Group, UK.

To Lawrence

Contents

List of figures and tables

Figures

Tables

Preface

It is said that we live in an Information Age, that we have access to volumes of information unimaginable in earlier times, and that this access has far-reaching consequences for our society and economy. Most of us who have experienced the world both before and after the world wide web would surely agree that our lives have changed in all sorts of ways, due to our new-found abilities to share information – at work, at home, in our communities. As a result, it might seem as though information is all around us, as abundant as the air we breathe. We access it via our desktop, our laptop and, increasingly, via our smart phones, as well as by more traditional means, such as the physical library or museum.

As with air, the abundance of information does not diminish its importance. If anything, information resources have become all the more valuable, because of the integral role they play in modern life. Also like air, some information resources may be better than others. Their content may be more accurate, more relevant, or more intelligible. This may not always matter so much, but sometimes finding better information can make a big difference, perhaps even a life-changing or life-saving one. The abundance of information resources in today's digital environment, however, can actually make it more difficult for people to access the information that would be of most use to them. This can be an invisible problem: people may be happy with what they find, but they might be less happy if they knew about what they had missed. It is nevertheless a very real problem, and one that many information professionals spend a lot of time trying to address. Two primary ways of addressing the problem are by providing quality information resources and by organizing those resources to facilitate *effective* access to them.

This book is concerned with the second of these activities, that is, with the organization of information resources. In particular, it is concerned with how information resources are organized through their description, providing an overview of both the process and the product (often referred to as 'metadata') as they function in the contemporary information environment. We shall discuss how and why information resource description continues to play a critical role in the provision of information access in a wide variety of contexts. We shall consider what makes for effective resource description, or metadata, whether it is produced by information professionals, authors, users or computers. The book looks at how metadata *works* (or does not work), irrespective of the particular tradition from which it emanates. The approach is descriptive and explanatory, rather than prescriptive; the book is *not* a manual.

The text's broad sweep attempts to place the various practices and results of information resource description into a bigger picture, which is painted with reference to fundamental principles. Other introductory texts in the field tend to focus either on product, particularly in a narrower sense of 'metadata', or on processes, such as library cataloguing and indexing. This book represents an attempt to integrate these two approaches. Its subject matter is tightly focused around resource description and its use in the various tools of information organization. Related fields, such as information literacy (covering the use of the tools themselves) and content-based information retrieval, have their own texts. Similarly, further reading is offered to those who wish to study a particular description practice or standard in more depth. As an introduction to the field, the book is intended primarily for students and practitioners, but may also be of interest to those specialists looking for that bigger picture.

This work is the outcome of a long journey, both intellectually and professionally. I would like to acknowledge all those who have helped me along the way. In particular, I thank Raylee Macaulay, Carla Daws, Liz Mayfield and Rosie Dunnett for the editorial assistance they provided. I am indebted to my employer, Charles Sturt University (CSU), which allowed me to take a sabbatical, despite my administrative responsibilities, and to Professor Toni Downes and Dr Bob Pymm, who covered those responsibilities. I am likewise grateful for the support and input provided by my colleagues (especially Dr Sigrid McCausland and Dr Mary Anne Kennan) and students in the School of Information Studies at CSU, and to all those who continue to enthuse about their work in the field of information organization, even in difficult times. I thank the staff at Facet for their patience and encouragement and, above all, I thank my wife and son, and my parents, for everything.

Philip Hider

Abbreviations

AACR	Anglo-American Cataloguing Rules
AAT	Art and Architecture Thesaurus
AGIFT	Australian Government Interactive Functions Thesaurus
AGLS	Australian Government Locator Service
AIFF	Audio Interchange File Format
AIM25	Archives in London and the M25 Area
ALA	American Library Association
AMIM	Archival Moving Image Materials
ANSI	American National Standards Institute
ANZLIC	Australia and New Zealand Spatial Information Council
APPM	Archives, Personal Papers, and Manuscripts
AVI	Audio Video Interleaved
BC	Bliss Classification
BIBCO	Monographic Bibliographic Record Cooperative Program
BISAC	Book Industry Standards and Communications
BT	broader term
CBIR	content-based image retrieval
CC	Colon Classification
CDWA	Categories for Descriptions of Works of Art
CHIM	Canadian Heritage Information Network
CIDOC	International Committee for Documentation
CILIP	Chartered Institute for Library and Information Professionals
CIMI	Consortium for Interchange of Museum Information
CIP	cataloguing in publication
COMPASS	Computer Aided Subject System
CONSER	Cooperative Online Serials Program
CQL	Contextual Query Language

CRM	Conceptual Reference Model (CIDOC)
CSDGM	Content Standard for Digital Geospatial Metadata
CURL	Consortium of University and Research Libraries
DACS	Describing Archives: a content standard
DC	Dublin Core
DDC	Dewey Decimal Classification
DDI	Data Documentation Initiative
DOI	Digital Object Identifier
DTD	Document Type Definition
DwC	Darwin Core
EAC	Encoded Archival Context
EAD	Encoded Archival Description
EdNA	Education Network Australia
EDRMS	electronic document and records management system
eGIF	eGovernment Interoperability Framework
e-GMS	e-Government Metadata Standard
ERIC	Education Resources Information Center
FAST	Faceted Application of Subject Terminology
FRAD	Functional Requirements for Authority Data
FRBR	Functional Requirements for Bibliographic Records
FRBRoo	FRBR-object oriented
FRSAD	Functional Requirements for Subject Authority Data
GEM	Gateway to Educational Materials
GIF	Graphics Interchange Format
GILS	Government Information Locator Service
HEREIN	European Heritage Network
HILT	High-Level Thesaurus Project
HTML	Hypertext Markup Language
I3A	International Imaging Industry Association
ICA	International Council on Archives
ICOM	International Council of Museums
IEC	International Electrotechnical Commission
IEEE-LOM	Institute of Electrical and Electronics Engineers Learning Object Metadata
IFF	Interchange File Format
IFLA	International Federation of Library Associations and Institutions
IMDb	Internet Movie Database

IPSV	Integrated Public Services Vocabulary
IPTC	International Press Telecommunications Council
ISAAR(CPF)	International Standard Archival Authority Record for Corporate Bodies, Persons and Families
ISAD(G)	General International Standard Archival Description
ISAN	International Standard Audiovisual Number
ISBD	International Standard Bibliographic Description
ISBN	International Standard Book Number
ISMN	International Standard Music Number
ISNI	International Standard Name Identifier
ISO	International Organization for Standardization
ISSN	International Standard Serial Number
ISTC	International Standard Text Code
JPEG	Joint Photographic Experts Group
JSC-AACR	Joint Steering Committee for Revision of AACR
JSC-RDA	Joint Steering Committee for Development of RDA
LC	Library of Congress
LCC	Library of Congress Classification
LCGFT	Library of Congress Genre/Form Terms for Library and Archival Materials
LCRI	Library of Congress Rule Interpretations
LCSH	Library of Congress Subject Headings
MACS	Multilingual Access to Subjects
MAD	Manual of Archival Description
MADS	Metadata Authority Description Schema
MARC	Machine-Readable Cataloguing
MeSH	Medical Subject Headings
METS	Metadata Encoding and Transmission Standard
MODS	Metadata Object Description Schema
MPEG	Moving Picture Experts Group
NACO	Name Authority Cooperative Program
NAL	(US) National Agricultural Library
NISO	National Information Standards Organization
NLM	(US) National Library of Medicine
NT	narrower term
OAI	Open Archives Initiative
OAI-PMH	Open Archives Initiative Protocol for Metadata Harvesting
OCLC	Online Computer Library Center

ONIX	Online Information Exchange
OPAC	online public access catalogue
OWI	OCLC Work Identifier
OWL	Web Ontology Language
PBCore	Public Broadcasting Core
PCC	Program for Cooperative Cataloging
PRECIS	Preserved Context Index System
RAD	Rules for Archival Description
RAK	Regeln für Alphabetische Katalogisierung
RAMEAU	Répertoire d'autorité matière encyclopédique et alphabétique unifié
RDA	Resource Description and Access
RDF	Resource Description Framework
RKMS	Recordkeeping Metadata Schema
RLG	Research Libraries Group
RLIN	Research Libraries Information Network
RSS	Rich Site Summary
RSWK	Regeln für den Schlagwortkatalog
RT	related term
RVM	Répertoire de vedettes-matières
SAA	Society of American Archivists
SACO	Subject Authority Cooperative Program
SCIS	Schools Catalogue Information Service
SEO	search engine optimization
SEPIADES	Safeguarding European Photographic Images for Access Data Element Set
SGML	Standard Generalized Markup Language
SICI	Serial Item and Contribution Identifier
SKOS	Simple Knowledge Organization System
SPECTRUM	Standard Procedures for Collections Recording Used in Museums
SRU	Search/Retrieve by URL
SWD	Schlagwortnormdatei
TEI	Text Encoding Initiative
TGM	Thesaurus of Graphic Materials
TGN	Thesaurus of Geographic Names
TIFF	Tagged Image File Format
UBC	Universal Bibliographic Control

UDC	Universal Decimal Classification
UF	use for
ULAN	Union List of Artist Names
URI	Universal Resource Identifier
UTLAS	University of Toronto Library Automated System
VIAF	Virtual International Authority File
VRA	Visual Resources Association
W3C	World Wide Web Consortium
WAV	Waveform Audio File Format
WLN	Western Library Network
XML	Extensible Markup Language

1

Definitions and scope

This chapter defines the book's scope and aims, and introduces key concepts that will be discussed at much greater length in the following chapters. The book's title and subtitle are explained first, and then how information resource description fits into the modern information environment. This is followed by an outline of the field of information organization and an overview of the book's structure.

Information resources

This book is about the description of information resources. Just about all types of resource can be described, and are. However, this book focuses on *information* resources. We are not so much interested in how vacuum cleaners, for instance, are described by sales people; we are more interested in, for example, how books (including e-books) are described by librarians. On the other hand, we *are* interested in how vacuum cleaners are described by museum curators: as museum objects, vacuum cleaners can provide us with information about, for instance, their mechanical development. Thus, just about everything *can* be an information resource, depending on the context, and so we need to avoid defining information resources too narrowly. We are interested here in the description of all resources that, in the context of their description, are primarily intended to inform.

The word 'primarily' in that last sentence is worth including. A very sophisticated vacuum cleaner could, say, inform its user when the dust bag is full, but, as a cleaning tool, the vacuum cleaner's primary function is to clean, not to inform. As a museum exhibit, however, its primary function would indeed be to inform. Conversely, many resources found in museums, libraries, archives and other 'information agencies' (they are sometimes also referred to as 'memory institutions') may do more than just inform, even in those contexts (they may also entertain, for instance), but a primary function is nevertheless to provide the patron with information.

Ultimately, resources are described as information resources according to the view of the describer, even if they have not been created as an information resource and are not generally used as one. However, those resources that are created primarily to inform and that are mostly used for the information they contain are those most likely to be described as information resources, and so will be given greater coverage. Thus, readers may be relieved to learn, we will talk more about resources such as books than about resources such as vacuum cleaners.

Resources have been created for the purpose of providing information for a very long time. They are essentially communication devices, designed to disseminate messages. Not all communication devices are information resources, however. Many devices, such as the human vocal chords, produce 'live' messages, for a particular moment in time. We are more interested in those devices that contain messages, re-transmittable across time. As such, these resources carry *recorded* information. The information may come in a variety of forms, but whatever its form, it is, at least potentially, re-accessible and re-usable. In today's world of digital information, this functionality may sometimes be taken for granted, but it has underpinned the development of all human civilizations. Many of the inventions that have advanced the recording of information – writing, printing, photography, computers and so on – have had profound effects on human history. Indeed, they have, in a very literal way, made history.

Sometimes recorded information is referred to as recorded *knowledge*; similarly, information resources such as books could be considered and are sometimes called 'knowledge resources'. Indeed, many books in the field of information organization (also referred to as knowledge organization) use the terms 'information' and 'knowledge' interchangeably. Knowledge managers sometimes refer to the pyramid set out in Figure 1.1, with *wisdom* at the top and *data* at the bottom, but for our purposes it might be more useful to view this as a continuum based on the amount of processing carried out in the generation of a message's content. Data may represent very little processing, in which, for example, observations are directly recorded from a science experiment; information may involve an analysis of data; knowledge may represent an integration of different pieces of information and a conclusion; and wisdom may represent a reflection on this conclusion, in the

Figure 1.1 *The 'knowledge pyramid'*

light of other conclusions and experience. As 're-accessible message resources' is a bit of a mouthful, this book will use the term 'information resource' as the generic term to cover all those resources that contain, or represent, data, information, knowledge and/or wisdom. For one thing, 'information' conveys a communicative aspect (to inform) that is not present in the other three terms.

Resource description

We now turn to the other half of the book's title. As we have noted, all kinds of resources can be described, for all kinds of different purposes. Information resources are described, ultimately, for the purpose of facilitating the use of the information they contain. The reasons why describers want this information to be used vary. Authors may want to become famous, publishers may want sales, librarians may want to improve their patrons' knowledge. The various reasons need to be borne in mind, as they may well have a bearing on the nature of the description.

The questions of how and what description might facilitate the use of information resources are addressed throughout the book, but we will make a start here. First, we need to recognize that, as a communication process, resource description involves both describers and recipients. Describers need not be directly associated with the resource, though sometimes they are (as in the case of authors). Describers need not even be human: computers are able to automatically generate descriptions for all kinds of digital information resource. While different describers may have different roles to play, as well as different motives, they almost always intend their descriptions to have recipients. These recipients may be a particular group of people or the population at large or (at least in the first instance) computers. They may even be the describers themselves, as in the case of individuals compiling personal reading lists. The intended audience of a description, as well as the describer, is likely to influence its nature, or at least should do, if the description is to be effective.

Just as our focus is on recorded information, so too is it on recorded description (of that information). The medium in which the description is recorded is also significant, of course. Descriptions recorded on sheets of paper or on index cards are retrieved and used in different ways than are those recorded in online databases. Indeed, the nature of the description may well vary according to the kind of system, not just the medium, in which it is stored. For example, a description is more likely to include certain data elements if the system indexes those elements.

Essentially, descriptions consist of information about different aspects of the thing they describe. We have just referred to these as *data elements*. In the case of information resources, elements may pertain to the information itself (the *content*) or to the *carrier* of this information (all recorded information is dependent on some sort of carrier, such as a book, a roll of film or a computer file) or to both content and carrier. Examples of content elements include subject and language; examples of carrier elements include size and physical location (if there is one).

Information resource descriptions come in all shapes and forms. They may be long or short, containing many elements or very few. Recorded descriptions tend to be textual, or at least verbal, but do not have to be. This book, however, concentrates on those descriptions or elements of description that are primarily used to (effectively) access information resources, as explained in the next section.

Metadata

As a product, information resource description is quite often referred to as *metadata*, which literally means data about data (more definitions are provided by Liu, 2007, 5; see also Greenberg, 2005). We have already given ourselves licence to use the term 'information' for data, and we will likewise use the term 'metadata' as another term for 'information resource description' (and treat it as a singular noun). In this vein, metadata covers data elements that pertain to the carriers of information, as well as those that pertain to the information (content) itself.

We should note, however, that the term 'metadata' is often associated specifically with *digital* information resources and is commonly defined as 'structured' data (about data), which in this context means data that can be processed by computer. In most cases, the metadata covered in this book will operate in the electronic environment and thereby conform, at some level, to a certain structure. However, even the non-electronic metadata dealt with here is likely also to be structured, so that it can be used in some form of non-computerized information retrieval system. For instance, card indexes are structured, with headings at the top and various other data elements set out underneath.

It should also be noted that 'metadata' is sometimes associated with other kinds of resource, apart from information resources, such as other products and services transacted through e-commerce. These do not directly concern us, although they may well influence the ways in which information resources are described, particularly in cross-domain applications.

Various categories of metadata, specifically for information resources, have been identified by different writers. Often metadata is characterized by its function. For example, Haynes' 'five-point model of metadata' (2004, 17) is based on five purposes: resource description; information retrieval; resource management; ownership and authenticity; and interoperability. While all metadata might ultimately be intended to facilitate the use of resources, there is a range of ways in which this occurs. For instance, resources may need to be managed so that they remain usable, hence Haynes' category of 'resource management' metadata. This kind of metadata might be needed to inform, for example, the preservation of a resource. Another term for this category is *administrative* metadata (though sometimes preservation metadata is distinguished from other forms of administrative metadata). Resources, particularly digital resources, may also need to be assembled and rendered for (human) use. The metadata used to facilitate this is often called *structural* metadata. Last, but by no means least, information resources also need to be accessed, i.e. retrieved. In Haynes' model, 'retrieval performance' is supported by 'resource description' and 'information retrieval' metadata. It is the metadata that supports the provision of access to, and retrieval of, information resources that is the focus of this book.

Metadata that facilitates access to information resources is sometimes referred to as 'discovery metadata', although access is a broader concept than discovery. Another term used is 'descriptive metadata', even though all metadata is ultimately descriptive (Caplan, 2003). For our purposes, the generic term will suffice: 'metadata' will be used to mean this specific kind of metadata, unless otherwise indicated. 'Information resource description' will likewise be used in this narrower sense, as it has been in the book's title.

Metadata can support effective access to information resources in several ways. As well as indicating to the prospective user how to obtain them, metadata can help the user decide whether they should be obtained. Moreover, metadata is often used to advise the user of their existence in the first place. It can also be used to provide an overview of a collection of resources by grouping like resources together (otherwise known as *collocation*), allowing the user to 'navigate' it. Similarly, metadata can be used to navigate a single resource, or to facilitate access to particular components of a resource. All of these functions will be investigated.

The metadata discussed in this book is mostly intended for use in *information retrieval systems* of various kinds, designed to facilitate access to collections of information resources (or resource components). As we have noted, these systems constrain the nature of the metadata, including its structure. We shall pay particular attention to those systems developed by information agencies such as libraries and archives, which have been a leading force in the field for a very long time. We shall deal with *personal* information retrieval systems only to the extent that their nature coincides with those intended for wider use.

Finally, it might also be pointed out that 'metadata' is by no means the only other term that can be used for information resource description. Terms such as 'cataloguing', 'bibliographic data', 'indexing', 'archival description' and 'museum documentation' are commonly employed in particular contexts, and will be in this book too.

Elements, values, format and transmission

An information resource can be looked at, and described, in all sorts of ways. There are, in fact, an infinite number of possible *metadata elements*. It may, of course, be more useful to record some attributes of a resource than others. The weight of a book, for instance, might not be particularly helpful for the purposes of resource discovery (people generally don't search for books of a particular weight, unless they are after a door stop); its title, on the other hand, may well be (people often search for books by title). Chapter 2 introduces some of the more commonly recorded elements.

Producing effective metadata, however, is not just about choosing the right elements. It is also about using appropriate *values* to record these elements. Most commonly, these values comprise words, such as the words of a title. Sometimes they comprise numbers (e.g. an International Standard Book Number), or other kinds of representation. Just as there can be any number of possible metadata elements, there can also be many options when it comes to recording their values. For example, the name of an author might be recorded as 'Joe Bloggs', or 'Joseph Bloggs', or 'J. H. Bloggs' etc., while the subject of a resource could be, say, 'Animals' or 'Fauna'. Some values are likely to be more effective than others, and the values used often have a large impact on the quality of metadata, discussed at length in Chapter 5. They need to be accurate, of course (unless one is looking to mislead), but they also need to possess certain other qualities, such as intelligibility.

Further, these values need to be recorded in an appropriate *format*. Importantly, the format needs to be compatible with the information retrieval system for which the metadata is intended. The metadata may also need to be input into the system in a particular way, i.e. using a particular *transmission protocol*.

These different aspects of metadata creation can be illustrated by the analogy of bottles being labelled, filled, stored and delivered (Elings, 2007). The elements of description provide a *structure*: they are the bottles. A catalogue record, comprising various *fields* (one for the title, another for the name of the author, another for the name of the publisher etc.), is an example of such a structure. These bottles are then filled with particular values, i.e. *content*. Note that not all bottles need be filled for a particular description: some fields may not be applicable for particular resources (a resource might not necessarily have an International Standard Book Number, for instance).

Once the bottles have been filled, they need to be stored in boxes. Similarly, the metadata needs to be *encoded* in a particular format. This can be for the benefit of people and/or machines, so that they can read and process the metadata. An example of an encoding scheme is HTML, a mark-up language that can be processed by web browsers. Finally, the boxes may be delivered to a particular place (although they could, alternatively, be taken out of storage and consumed directly). Packages of metadata, typically in the form of computer files, are often fed into other systems through certain protocols that they have been programmed to act upon.

All four aspects of metadata – elements, values, format and transmission – are examined in this book, in some cases simultaneously, as they are not always so readily distinguishable. What is important to note from the outset, however, is that different elements, values, formats and protocols are effective in different information contexts, depending on the characteristics of the users, the technology, the information resources and other environmental factors.

Managing metadata

The subtitle of this book indicates that it covers not only the process of describing information resources, i.e. creating metadata, but also that of managing the metadata once created. There are various ways in which metadata is managed, an activity typically carried out by information professionals.

First, metadata may be obtained from an external source, rather than being created in-house. As we have already noted, not all metadata is equal, and the quality of metadata from different sources, or even the same source, may need to be evaluated.

Second, metadata may need to be fed into an information retrieval system, which may entail converting it into a compatible format and applying certain protocols.

Third, metadata may need to be improved by editing or adding to it. As a process, this is similar to metadata creation, but is even more likely to be done with reference to particular users, systems and costs.

Fourth, metadata needs to be presented to users as effectively as possible. Modern computing enables systems to provide a wide range of user interfaces; different interfaces may suit different users and search contexts.

Fifth, metadata needs to be preserved, if it is to be reused. Rapid technological change has created greater, rather than less, risk to the integrity of data. All too quickly, data can be 'lost', due to the obsolescence of both software and hardware. In today's digital environment, systems and metadata cannot afford to be left behind.

Sixth, the significant costs involved in metadata creation and management can often be reduced through exchange mechanisms, which means giving as well as receiving. When providing metadata to other agencies, it may be necessary to comply with external policies and standards: the efficient sharing of metadata usually requires a degree of standardization, and sometimes data conversion, so that the metadata can be used effectively in other systems. Standardization is a key concern of many metadata managers.

All these areas of metadata management require a detailed understanding of the functions of metadata, in relation to particular user contexts, just as the creation of metadata does. Creating and managing metadata can sometimes be a rather technical business, but decisions and policies should ultimately be made with reference to what works for the end-user.

The contemporary information environment

We have outlined the scope of this book by discussing its title and subtitle. It is important to put information resource description, as a process and product, into context. Metadata is not created and managed in isolation. We have already alluded to some of this context – describers, users, systems and so forth. Clearly, with so many variables affecting information resource description, its relationship with the wider information environment is complex and ever changing. This does not mean, however, that metadata is arbitrary; on the contrary, it is frequently conventionalized and standardized. For example, the nature and format of the metadata presented in and on information resources has evolved into conventions such as title pages, film credits and record labels.

Metadata works only if people understand and use it. Thus, it could be argued that all effective metadata is based on certain social conventions, such as language. When conventions are deemed important enough, they sometimes become *standards*, which are essentially formal agreements to adhere to certain practices. The convention of the title page, for instance, may become a standard if a particular community considers it to be an essential component of a text. Thus, universities require students to include title pages (set out in a particular way) in the theses and dissertations they submit. Over the past century or so, library cataloguing conventions have become increasingly standardized, to the extent that most cataloguers in the English-speaking world now apply the same set of content rules and use the same record structure and encoding system.

Standardization may encourage particular practices, but it does not prevent practices from changing. Just as laws change according to evolving social norms, so metadata standards change according to the evolving information environment. New types of information resource require new conventions and standards. For example, websites do not have title pages, but instead have home pages. Metadata standards for existing resources may also change as new technologies become available. For instance, in the first half of the 20th century, library catalogue records were produced on standard 3 by 5 inch cards. By the end of the century, this standard had become all but obsolete – instead, the vast majority of records were being created according to standards for electronic records. Metadata creation and management, even when conventionalized and standardized, is never insulated from changes in information technology and information behaviour; rather, it is always an integral part of an information *ecology*, in which information agents constantly interact with their information environment.

The contemporary information environment encompasses an extraordinary range of technologies. Older technologies are still widely used: many people still read printed books, newspapers and magazines; historians still visit physical archives; people still hang paintings on their walls. However, the digital technologies developed over the past few decades have transformed the information environment beyond all recognition, both qualitatively and quantitatively. Just about any form of information can now be recorded digitally, and not just by a privileged few but by the empowered many. Personal computers, let alone corporate servers, can now store huge amounts of data, while anyone with an internet connection can disseminate information to millions of people across the world, often in a matter of seconds. Mobile technologies are further increasing the pervasiveness and utility of the online information environment.

Although there are still large parts of the world's population with little or no access to digital technology, it is becoming ever more affordable. In the developed world, creating and using digital information has become an everyday activity for a majority of people. As a result, the amount of recorded information has increased at a mind-boggling rate, with very significant implications for the task of information retrieval.

This information revolution has given rise to information resources with very different characteristics from those based on older technologies. According to Liu (2004), digital resources exhibit greater information density; less longevity; less uniqueness; greater duplicability; greater mobility and fluidity; greater connectivity; and greater integration. Online information resources tend to be far less permanent than their analogue counterparts. Their longevity may depend on just one computer server: if it is disconnected, or a file on it is deleted, a resource may be lost to the world for ever. Digital resources can also be readily manipulated, so that new versions can be made with ease; they can likewise be duplicated at the touch of a button. Information resources published on the web are connected to each other in a very powerful way, through the hyperlink. This enhances both physical and intellectual access to documents, and to components of documents.

These characteristics raise various issues when it comes to the description of digital information resources. Should each version of a website be described? Should the various components of the website be described as resources in their own right? Indeed, who should do the description? Furthermore, which, and how many, of the millions of information resources now available online should be described? Different approaches to information resource description are necessary in the new information world in which we find ourselves.

Digital technologies have already had a profound effect on metadata creation and management. This book examines the new approaches to information resource description brought about by these technologies, but also recognizes the value and continuing validity, in certain contexts, of traditional practices. The digital information revolution does not, of course, constitute a complete break with the past, and it is likely that older technologies and practices will continue to influence the way we describe information resources for a long time to come. Even in the web environment, we still talk of 'pages', for instance. However, it needs to be acknowledged that digital information is not only here to stay, but will become even more pervasive in the future. The book considers the description of all information resources, both physical and online, from this perspective.

Information organization

The practice of information resource description is central to the field commonly known as *information organization* or *knowledge organization*. As such, it is part of the broader field of information management. The term 'organization' is used here to refer to various ways in which information resources are organized so as to improve access to them, and not just to their *physical arrangement*. Clearly, how objects are arranged in physical space has a bearing on the extent to which they may be accessed effectively. The same can be said for how links to digital resources are arranged on a web page. However, when there are a lot of resources and/or a lot of space (either physical or virtual), other organizing techniques may need to be utilized. This applies to resources of all kinds, not only information resources.

In a kitchen, for example, all the spice jars might be placed together on a particular shelf. This arrangement is based on a categorization (spices) intended to narrow down the search for a particular spice. Instead of having to remember where each foodstuff is kept in a random arrangement, the cook just has to remember where the spices are kept.

However, the cook still has to identify which of the spice jars has the particular spice they need. The cook could inspect the contents of the various jars, but it might be easier if the jars were labelled. Again, the aim is to facilitate access to the desired ingredient. *Labelling* is also a common way of organizing information resources. The spines of books, for example, are typically labelled with titles, author names and, in a library, call numbers. Likewise, links to web resources are usually labelled with words that indicate their content. All such labels are metadata, since they describe information resources.

Appropriate labelling, in addition to convenient arrangements, is likely to make for a more organized kitchen, so that the cook can find the things they want more easily. However, this may still not be enough. Instead of a kitchen, suppose the cook is looking for a particular spice in a large supermarket. Perhaps it is shelved in a general 'spices' section, or amongst the 'Asian foods', or in some other section, or perhaps the supermarket does not stock the particular spice. All the jars in the supermarket may be sensibly arranged and clearly labelled, but the cook may not be familiar with the supermarket and may end up spending a lot of time walking up and down the aisles in search of the elusive spice. It might be better to consult a database of all the stock available in the store.

Most databases comprise one or more *indexes*. In the supermarket's database, the spice might be indexed (if it is stocked) under its generic name and brand name. Typically, the user merely types in a name and the computer does the rest, searching the index and displaying the details for the item, including its location in the store. Essentially, an index consists of *representations* of the actual resources, arranged in a way that makes them easier to search through than the resources themselves. In the case of indexes to information resources, these representations may be metadata, such as titles and author names, or they may be derived from the information content itself, such as the words found in a text. They may be viewed as 'conceptual' labels, and the index as an arrangement of labels, combining the two basic organizing techniques.

If indexing can be useful in the supermarket context, it is often vital for the effective use of libraries, archives and other collections of information resources. Most of the tools developed to provide access to these collections, such as library catalogues, archival finding aids, museum registers and search engines, are essentially indexes. Many are also based on metadata. The content of individual information resources, such as books, serials and maps, is also often accessed via indexes.

Whether indexed or not, metadata is very much at the heart of information organization practice. However, we should recognize too the importance of *content-based* indexes in modern information retrieval. Without doubt, these indexes, epitomized by search engines such as Google, cover a far greater number of information resources than do the traditional tools based on metadata, and in many situations are very effective. Although this book does not cover content-based information retrieval per se (it is generally regarded as a separate field), its continuing advance is reflected upon in later discussion concerning the value and future of metadata-based information retrieval.

The field of information organization deals with information packaged up as resources, which are also commonly referred to as *documents*, even when they contain non-textual information. Information organization is thus concerned with *document retrieval*. Most information retrieval is essentially document retrieval of one kind or another, although it also covers efforts to provide information that answers particular questions much more directly than would a whole document, or even a section of a document. These efforts are on-going and represent an interesting area of research, but are beyond the scope of this book.

There are a couple more terms that need to be explained in relation to the field of information organization. *Bibliographic control* and *bibliographic organization* generally refer to the practice of information organization in libraries. Although the term 'bibliographic' literally pertains to books, librarians tend to use it in a more general sense, for all information resources provided by libraries. A primary mode of bibliographic control is library cataloguing. However, although some books on information organization concentrate on this activity, it should already be apparent that it is by no means the only mode of information resource description, and this book aims to cover the field much more broadly. In recent times, many writers have distinguished the traditional bibliographic approach embodied in library cataloguing from newer forms of information resource description represented by the term 'metadata'. There are certainly differences, but, as Howarth (2005, 37) argues, there are also sufficient similarities 'to warrant a confluence in terminology and definition'.

Overview of this book

The next chapter discusses the nature of metadata in terms of its likely elements. The discussion is based on a consideration of why metadata is needed and used. The third chapter then looks at an important part of the context surrounding its use, namely, the various systems and tools dedicated to information retrieval. Chapter 4 considers another critical contextual aspect, the creators of the metadata. We then turn our attention back to the users: how does information resource description best serve their needs? Chapter 5, therefore, looks at metadata quality. Chapter 6 returns the discussion to the systems utilizing metadata and examines how they go about sharing metadata. Standardization is a key quality of effective metadata, as well as of system interoperability, and metadata standards are surveyed at length in Chapters 7 and 8. First, standards that focus on elements, format and transmission are examined, and then the vocabularies used for values. The final chapter considers the future of information resource description through a discussion of the prospects for the different approaches to information retrieval. A list of selected resources for further reading is provided at the end of the book, followed by a list of the metadata standards covered.

References

Caplan, P. (2003) *Metadata Fundamentals for all Librarians*, American Library Association.

Elings, M. W. (2007) Metadata for All: descriptive standards and metadata sharing across cultural heritage communities, *VRA Bulletin*, **34** (1), 7–14, www.vraweb.org/seiweb/readings-prep/MetadataforAll_Elings-Waibel.pdf.

Greenberg, J. (2005) Understanding Metadata and Metadata Schemes, *Cataloging & Classification Quarterly*, **40** (3/4), 17–36.

Haynes, D. (2004) *Metadata for Information Management and Retrieval*, Facet Publishing.

Howarth, L. (2005) Metadata and Bibliographic Control, *Cataloging & Classification Quarterly*, **40** (3), 37–56.

Liu, J. (2007) *Metadata and its Applications in the Digital Library: approaches and practices*, Libraries Unlimited.

Liu, Z. (2004) The Evolution of Documents and its Impacts, *Journal of Documentation*, **60** (3), 279–88.

2

Information resource attributes

Introduction

In the previous chapter, we talked of *metadata elements*, the building blocks of information resource description. Each element describes an aspect, or *attribute*, of the information resource. Its title, author, subject, size, publication date and so on – all are attributes that could be described if applicable to a particular resource. As was mentioned, there are countless ways in which one could look at, and therefore describe, an information resource. Clearly, some attributes are more relevant in the provision of information access than are others. This chapter will discuss which attributes are likely to be more important, and why.

In some more technical discussions, a resource's attributes are distinguished from its *relationships* to other entities. In such a model, a book's size might be considered an attribute, whereas its author might be considered another entity with an 'authorial' relationship to the book. The distinction will not be pursued here, however, as ultimately it is one of expression: any attribute could be expressed as a relationship between two entities (e.g. the concept 'folio' might have a 'size' relationship to a book), and any relationship could be expressed as an attribute (e.g. of authorship). Nevertheless, expressing and presenting metadata in the form of relationships can be a very effective mode of description, as we shall later observe.

Describer and user contexts

Information resource description is inevitably biased: it is influenced by the motives, situation, limitations and world-view of its creator. This is true regardless of how much the creator wishes to assist prospective users. Even information professionals, who may profess a 'neutral' position, will invariably have a particular take on how best to serve users' needs. The field of information organization has developed various policies and standards that are generally regarded as 'good practice', but no one would seriously contend that any of them were perfect solutions (even in a particular context). Nevertheless, metadata creators should all start with the same fundamental question: what metadata will most help users to obtain the information they are looking for?

The question begs another, of course: who are the users? We should distinguish here between users of the metadata itself and users of the resources that the metadata represents. They are not always the same. For instance, a parent might use metadata to find a suitable story book for their child. Or a reference librarian might interrogate a catalogue on behalf of a patron. In such cases, the metadata creator needs to keep both kinds of user in mind, end-user and intermediary.

Most metadata creators, like most information resource creators, have only a generalized notion of their audience. There may even be quite unintended, or at least unexpected, recipients, particularly when metadata is transmitted to other systems. Nevertheless, most metadata is created with some sort of audience in mind. Authors may think of the people likely to read their work, library cataloguers of their patrons, website managers of their prospective visitors and so on. The more metadata creators know about their users, the more effective the metadata is likely to be. This is true even when the same resource is being described: people may use it in different ways, so that different metadata elements may be needed. For instance, public library users may be less interested than academic library users in whether or not a book contains a bibliography, but more interested in its cover picture. Different user groups may also require different metadata values. For example, database users in China will generally prefer abstracts written in Chinese than in English.

An important preliminary activity for information resource description, therefore, once the target user group has been established, is often *user research*. Information professionals, in particular, need to know about their clients' information needs and behaviour. Studies carried out over the past several decades have identified all sorts of information-seeking styles and goals. People seek information for work purposes, course assignments, recreational activities, health reasons or simply for the joy of learning. They may seek information on a confidential basis, to share with others or on behalf of others. We cannot possibly enumerate all motivations here, nor all the ways in which information resources can be used; suffice it to note that how and why people use information resources is going to influence what they need to know about them. Similarly, how they use (or don't use) information retrieval systems and the metadata they contain is of critical importance to those concerned with the provision of information access, or at least it should be.

Information resource contexts

Nevertheless, despite the wide range of user contexts, it is possible to identify, at a basic level, ways in which various kinds of information resource are generally used. This is because particular information resources are, almost always, designed for particular uses. Maps are designed to be read for navigational purposes; patient records are designed to be looked up for medical purposes; recipes are designed to be followed for culinary purposes. To a certain extent, therefore, metadata creators can anticipate how resources will be used, irrespective of who uses them. This means that, even in cases where no specific user group is targeted, metadata can still be effective, if not necessarily so effective.

Information resources can, in fact, be viewed in even more basic ways. We have already observed how all information resources are carriers of content. This perspective has led to the development of a model involving four different *levels* of information resource, originally set out in a report published by the International Federation of Library Associations and Institutions (IFLA) entitled *Functional Requirements for Bibliographic Records*, otherwise known as FRBR (IFLA, 1998). The four levels represent what are termed *items*, *manifestations*, *expressions* and *works*, and comprise the so-called 'FRBR hierarchy'. We shall talk more about FRBR in due course.

As an item, an information resource is an individual object, with some kind of physical form, such as a copy of a printed book or a website rendered on a computer screen. As a work, on the other hand, an information resource consists of content, such as a novel, picture, law or news report. It may also be an aggregation of component works, such as an anthology. In between items and works come manifestations and expressions. An expression of a work is a construct based on how a work is 'expressed'. For example, a novel might be expressed in different languages, through translation. Expressions may be thought of as versions of a work. In contrast, a manifestation of a work (and of an expression) is a particular version of the *carrier* of that work (or expression). For instance, it may be a particular printing of a book.

Sometimes, a manifestation is represented by a single item; other times, by thousands of copies. Similarly, an expression may be represented by one or more manifestations; and a work by one or more expressions. Items, manifestations, expressions and works clearly have different characteristics, and these will be reflected in the different elements used to describe them.

The functions of metadata

We have discussed briefly the context of information resource and metadata use. In the first chapter, we set out the scope of information resource description in terms of a general purpose, i.e. to provide effective *access* to information resources. We shall now consider further what we mean by this. As it happens, FRBR also identifies a set of four basic tasks that users may carry out when searching for information resources through the library catalogue. As such, these tasks represent the *functions* of library catalogue.

The four FRBR *user tasks* are:

- find
- identify
- select
- obtain.

First, the catalogue is searched in order to find a resource, or set of resources. The term 'find' here is used in a conceptual, rather than physical, sense, that is, the user discovers a resource's existence by finding a record for it. The ultimate goal, of course, is to obtain the resource itself. In between the two tasks of *find* and *obtain* is a decision to proceed. This occurs when the resource, on the basis of its record, is *identified* as the resource being sought, or when a resource is *selected* on the basis of its being useful. Whether a user identifies or selects is ultimately dependent on the user's search goal: if they are looking for a predetermined resource, then it needs to be identified; if they are looking for resources with certain attributes, then they need to be selected.

It turns out that these four functions of bibliographic records can, in fact, be applied to many other kinds of metadata and information retrieval tools, and provide a good basis for our discussions about the attributes of information resources that users (and not just library users) most need to know about, so that they can access the resources they need. Svenonius (2000,

20), however, has added a fifth function, namely, *navigate,* which she defines as 'to find works related to a given work by generalization, association, or aggregation; to find attributes related by equivalence, association, and hierarchy'. In Chapter 1 we noted how metadata can be used to navigate resource collections, as well as information resources themselves, allowing for the collocation of like resources. Systems of collocation, such as classification schemes, provide *structures* for users to navigate. In a sense, navigation constitutes looking at, rather than for, resources. Nevertheless, its ultimate goal is the same as that of the FRBR functions: to access useful information. We shall add it to our own list of functions.

Finding resources

To determine the most important attributes of information resources for metadata's finding function, in the FRBR sense of 'finding', we must start by considering the ideas people have of what they are looking for when they start searching an information retrieval system. In many cases, their search goal is, at this point, going to be somewhat vague, such as 'material' on a particular subject. In other cases, it is more concrete, such as a particular edition of a textbook from a reading list. In all cases, however, only certain attributes of the sought-after resource will be thought of, and even these may not be thought of very clearly. For instance, only part of a title might be recalled.

Search goals are not the same as search *strategies*, either. A user's search query is unlikely to involve all the attributes they can think of. For example, they may know that a specific resource they are looking for is written in English, but they are unlikely to search on language. Rather, they will search on an attribute that pinpoints the resource much more precisely. The most precise attribute for this purpose is an *identifier*, which frequently takes the form of a number, uniquely assigned to a particular resource. Another attribute that serves to identify a resource is its *name*. This can be more descriptive than an identifier, but may not be totally unique. Nevertheless, it often does the job and is more likely to be remembered than an 'artificial' identifier.

We shall look further at identifiers in the next section, and concentrate here, instead, on names, which are probably the most common means for people (if not computers) to search for resources, including information resources. Names, like identifiers, are *assigned*, and these assignations have to be adopted by the wider community if they are to be effective. Various conventions and standards have been developed to facilitate the adoption of names. Common nouns, once established, are recorded in dictionaries. Babies' names are assigned by parents and recorded on birth certificates. Place names are recorded in gazetteers. In the case of information resources, however, it is slightly less straightforward.

Earlier in this chapter, we noted four different levels of information resource: items, manifestations, expressions and works. As information seekers, people are generally most interested in resources as works and expressions, that is, in their information content. Nevertheless, they may, for a variety of reasons, prefer a particular manifestation of a work, or even a particular item. We shall continue our discussion by considering how names might be used at these different levels.

An item could, just like any other object, qualify for a name (a proper noun), yet most items are not assigned their own names. A particular copy of a printed book, for instance, almost never has a name, or at least not one that is established in the community. (One might refer to, say, 'Joe's copy' in certain, restrictive situations.) Some items do get named, though, including most original works of art. The *Mona Lisa*, for example, exists as a singular object: it hangs in the Louvre, in Paris. Many *copies* of the work also exist, but, as items, they usually go unnamed (though they may be numbered); it is the *original* item that is named. In the electronic world, however, original items are very hard, if not impossible, to identify, let alone name.

A manifestation of a work, such as a particular printing of a book, is also unlikely to be named, except in very generic terms, such as 'third printing' or '2003 release'. This sort of metadata may be used in the identification or selection process, but it is seldom used to find the resource. A user may choose between a PC and a Mac version, or prefer an earlier printing if they are a literary scholar.

Expressions of works tend to be of greater interest to users, and may have more specific, and descriptive, names. A student may wish to read the 'Butler translation' of Homer's *Odyssey*; a Christian may be looking for the *Good News Bible*; a musician may want Thomas Wood's piano arrangement of 'Waltzing Matilda'. Many expressions, however, like many manifestations, are named in very simple terms, such as 'revised edition', and most expressions are not named at all, as they are the only expression of a work (a book almost never calls itself the 'first edition').

The work, on the other hand, is the primary objective of information seekers, and is quite likely to have a fairly descriptive name. The names of works are, of course, commonly called *titles*. However, works exist at a fairly high level of abstraction, which can make them 'slippery', that is, they do not always stick very firmly. This can lead to multiple titles for the same work. For example, a novel by Isaac Asimov has been published under the title, *The Man Who Upset the Universe*, but the work is much more widely known as *Foundation and Empire*.

Although most works have only one known title, when different manifestations of the same work are issued under different titles it is important for information retrieval systems to index all the titles that the work might be searched under. In some systems, the titles might be assigned to different levels of the resource: one title might be treated as *the* title for the work, while the other titles might be regarded only as titles for particular manifestations or expressions. (This is an exception to the general observation that manifestations seldom have descriptive names.)

Instead of multiple titles, some works have the opposite problem: they have no title, or at least not one presented to the outside world. Many unpublished resources, including archival and pictorial materials, do not come with a title. Occasionally, users may learn of an externally assigned title (e.g. 'Dead Sea Scrolls'), but mostly there is simply no title to index – the title attribute is not applicable.

Titles are by no means the only attribute users think of when trying to find works. Another important attribute is *creator*. Partly for the purposes of precision, works are conventionally referred to by both author and title (e.g. 'Dante's *Inferno*'). In some cases, people may forget, or not know, the title, but know the author. They may, for example, be looking for Philip Roth's 'latest novel' or Einstein's 'paper on the theory of relativity'. Or they may be looking for all the works by a particular person. As a construct, every work has one or more creators, although, like titles, they may not be known, or they may be known by more than one name.

A complex category of authorship worth mentioning here is what librarians refer to as *corporate* authorship. In some bibliographic traditions, this category barely exists, since it is considered that only people can create works. The English-speaking tradition, on the other hand, interprets notions such as a company's annual report or a pop group's song in an 'authorial' way. That is, it regards groups of people as capable of collective authorship, at least in some circumstances, in the same way as publishing companies can collectively disseminate manifestations.

Quite often though, people are not looking for a specific work, or works by a particular creator. Rather, they are looking for works (i.e. information) on a particular *subject*. The provision of subject access to collections of information resources is thus a major component of information organization, and many information retrieval systems index terms intended to represent the subject attribute. Unlike titles and author names, however, subject terms are often not assigned by the creator or publisher of the resource, and can be even more slippery and fuzzy. One user's 'soccer' may be another user's 'football'. A user may disagree that a resource is even about the game. The challenge of assigning values to the subject attribute is discussed in later chapters.

Identifier, title, author name and subject are just four of many attributes that may come to mind when users try to find records and other metadata that might lead to helpful information resources. Different search contexts will affect the applicability and significance of different attributes. One way of identifying key finding attributes is to analyse search queries, although one needs to bear in mind how users' knowledge of a system may influence their inputs. Chen (2001) examined image database queries and compiled the following list of attributes for pictures: location, literal object, art historical information, people, colour, visual elements, description, abstract concepts, content/story, external relationships and viewer response. On the other hand, Jansen (2008) ended up with a different list for users of web images. The specific context can make a big difference.

Table 2.1 lists the most important attributes and relationships for the finding function, as identified in the FRBR report. The list compilers focused, of course, on library resources.

Identifying resources

After an information resource description, such as a record in an information retrieval system, has been found, the next step is for it to be considered, so that a decision can be made about whether or not to obtain (or try to obtain) the resource that the description represents. As we noted earlier, there are two ways in which this decision can be made. If the user has an idea only of the kind of resource they want, they *select*, or reject, a particular resource. If, on the other hand, the user has an idea of the specific resource they are after, they *identify* the resource as the correct one, or they reject it is as not the correct one.

As with finding, the identification and selection functions pertain, strictly

Table 2.1 *Attributes and relationships of 'high value' for the finding task (IFLA, 1998)*

	Find			
	Work	Expression	Manifestation	Item
Attributes/relationships of a work				
Title of the work	■			
Dependent component	■			
Independent component	■			
And persons/corporate bodies responsible for the work	■			
And entities treated as subject of the work	■			
Attributes/relationships of an expression				
Dependent component		■		
Independent component		■		
And persons/corporate bodies responsible for content		■		
Attributes/relationships of a manifestation				
Title of the manifestation	■	■	■	
Manifestation identifier			■	
Attributes/relationships of an item				
Item identifier				■

speaking, to the metadata, rather than the resources themselves. Users looking for particular resources need sufficient and accurate description to act upon. A description cannot be comprehensive (otherwise it would be the resource); instead, it needs to do a reasonable job of representing the resource. (The concept of *representation* is an important one in information organization; records are sometimes referred to as resource *surrogates*.) How much and what metadata constitutes a 'reasonable' representation very much depends on the nature of the retrieval system. If the resource itself cannot be accessed directly via the system, the description may save the user significant amounts of time and effort; if, on the other hand, the resource can be inspected immediately, via a hyperlink, the description may be less critical.

We noted above that numbers and other character strings are often assigned as *identifiers*. Because it is more straightforward to assign an identifier to something tangible, items and manifestations are more conducive to systems of identification than are works and expressions, particularly in the analogue world.

At the item level, information resources may be assigned product numbers by publishers, and item numbers by libraries. Recorded in bar codes, these identifiers are more for inventory purposes than to assist end-users.

Particular manifestations of a work may also need to be identified, by both collection managers and end-users. A prime example of a systematic identifier is the International Standard Book Number (ISBN). Through the co-operation of publishers and ISBN agencies, which operate at a national level, most (published) books and e-books end up with a unique ISBN for each of their manifestations. Thus the ISBN for the hardback version of *Far-Out Guide to the Moon* is 9780766031890, and for the paperback, 9781598451849. Examples of identifiers for the manifestations of other kinds of resources include the International Standard Serial Number (ISSN), the International Standard Music Number (ISMN), the Digital Object Identifier (DOI) and the Serial Item and Contribution Identifier (SICI).

Large-scale systems of identification for works and expressions are still under development, including the International Standard Text Code (ISTC) and the International Standard Audiovisual Number (ISAN), for textual and audiovisual works, respectively. Also of note is the OCLC Work Identifier (OWI), devised by the Online Computer Library Center (OCLC), which hosts a database of library catalogue records representing millions of information resources, generally at the manifestation level. The aim of the OWI is to facilitate the grouping together of these manifestations into their respective works. This is by no means a straightforward activity, however, since works are ultimately constructs dependent on human judgement rather than computer algorithm.

Nevertheless, some smaller-scale systems of work identification are well established. In the field of classical music, for example, composers tend to assign their own identifiers in the form of *opus* (Latin for 'work') numbers. One reason for this, of course, is that many musical works are not assigned titles. Some famous composers of the past have also had numbers assigned to their works by musicologists. For instance, each work by Mozart has a *Köchel number*, based on a 19th-century catalogue of Mozart's music compiled by Ludwig Ritter Köchel (thus Mozart's unfinished requiem is identified as 'K. 626').

Systematic identifiers are not, of course, the only means of identifying resources. Information about any attribute may help. Titles, even if not necessarily unique, are often a fairly good bet for the identification of works. To be more confident, the author's name may also be checked. Sometimes the user may be reassured by a summary of a resource's content. If a particular expression is sought, the user will usually first establish that they have the right work; then, they may look for something that specifically identifies the expression, such as an edition statement (e.g. 'third edition'); if they cannot find this, they might consider various other elements of the description, such as dates (particularly copyright dates), and names of editors. Similarly, if a particular manifestation is required and there is no systematic identifier such as an ISBN to check, the user will typically start by identifying the work and then look at attributes pertaining to the carrier, especially publication and format. At the item level, users may consider attributes such as *provenance*, i.e. the item's custodial history, to identify, for example, a piece of art or an archival file.

Clearly, some of the attributes used for identifying resources, such as titles and systematic identifiers, are also those frequently used to find them. This should not come as a surprise, as the act of identification is to some extent a re-enactment of finding specific resources. Thus a title search finds a record with a particular title; that title is checked and the resource is thereby positively identified. However, identification may also involve other attributes not typically involved in the finding process. A particular version of a resource may be identified, but the user is unlikely to enter 'third edition', for example, as part of their search query. There are two reasons for this. First, the user may be confident that they will retrieve a manageable set of results without having to search on all the attributes they can think of. Second, the user may not be confident that certain elements will be of much use when searching a particular retrieval system. The edition statement, for instance, may not be indexed, or the user may not know how it is indexed. Table 2.2 lists the attributes and relationships that the FRBR report deems to be the most important for identification purposes in the library cataloguing context and that, as such, might also be prioritized in resource description, along with those elements in Tables 2.1 and 2.3.

Selecting resources

Selection takes place when the user does not have a specific resource in mind. After finding one or more descriptions, the next step is to select or reject. This is done by considering particular attributes. These may already have been thought about when the user started searching, but not always. On reading the resource descriptions, the user may be influenced by other elements that

Table 2.2 *Attributes and relationships of 'high value' for the identifying task (IFLA, 1998)*

	Identify			
	Work	Expression	Manifestation	Item
Attributes/relationships of a work				
Title of the work	■			
Intended termination	■			
Co-ordinates (cartographic work)	■			
Dependent component	■			
And persons/corporate bodies responsible for the work	■			
Attributes/relationships of an expression				
Form of expression		■		
Language of expression		■		
Other distinguishing characteristic		■		
Expected frequency of issue (serial)		■		
Type of score (musical notation)		■		
Medium of performance (musical notation or recorded sound)		■		
Dependent component		■		
And persons/corporate bodies responsible for content		■		
Attributes/relationships of a manifestation				
Title of the manifestation	■	■	■	
Statement of responsibility		■	■	
Edition/issue designation		■	■	
Publisher/distributor			■	
Date of publication/distribution			■	
Series statement			■	
Form of carrier			■	
Manifestation identifier			■	
Foliation (hand-printed book)			■	
Collation (hand-printed book)			■	
Numbering (serial)	■	■	■	
Attributes/relationships of an item				
Item identifier				■

they realize are relevant to the selection process.

The kind of resource people want, when they do not have a specific resource in mind, often relates to the subject of its content. Elements of description that indicate what a work is about are thus frequently of interest to users when selecting information resources. For instance, users may read abstracts in periodical databases to gain a better idea as to whether particular articles address the topic they are interested in. Titles may also provide a good indication of subject, as may direct extracts of content, such as the snippets displayed in search engines' hit lists. Many library catalogue records include tables of contents, or plot synopses in the case of movies and novels, as well as separate subject terms assigned by cataloguers.

Other aspects of a resource's content may also be of interest to selectors. For example, users may well be interested in its *quality*, in which case reviews and ratings can be helpful. The *currency* of content may also be a factor to consider, and the user may look for a date. Likewise, the *amount* of content (e.g. the number of words) may have a bearing. The *form* of a work could also be relevant. It may be 'about' Japan, but it may be a map, website or film documentary. It turns out, then, that information content can be described in many different, and sometimes unanticipated, ways.

Some selection criteria may also pertain to information resource levels other than that of the work. Faced with records for several expressions of a work, the user may, for example, select the most recent edition, or the English translation. Users may also select resources on the basis of carrier attributes. For instance, they may prefer electronic to print, or a CD rather than a cassette. Some carrier attributes are also clues to aspects of content. For example, the publication year may, in some cases, provide a good indication of when the content was created; similarly, the number of pages can be a fairly good indicator of the amount of text. Even a particular item, or copy, may be selected, often because it is easier to obtain (e.g. it is held in the local branch library, or is accessible online).

In the field of information retrieval, the attributes used to select resources are referred to as *relevance criteria*. It has been well established that there are many of them, including those complied by Schamber (1994), listed below.

Aboutness
Accuracy (truth)
Aesthetic value
Authorship
Credibility
Difficulty
Diversity of content
Importance
Informativeness
Interesting content

Level of condensation
Logical relevance
Novelty
Pertinence
Publication source
Recency
Scientific 'hardness'
Specificity/amount of information
Style
Subject matter
Textual attributes
Usefulness

Different criteria will be important in different information contexts. Effective information retrieval is not always just about *topical relevance*, although the subject of a document is, as we have noted, a very important criterion in many cases.

Complicated computer algorithms have been developed so that search results are displayed in what, it is hoped, is the optimal order, from most to least relevant. It should be pointed out, however, that the *utility* of a resource is not quite the same as its relevance, as it may be contingent on what has already been used or selected for use. (This is why search engines tend not to list pages from the same website one after the other, but instead group them together as a unified entry.)

The *relevance rankings* of information retrieval systems are mostly based on analysis of the resources themselves, though some external data may also be used (Google's PageRank algorithm, for example, counts the hyperlinks made to resources). Rankings can also be improved through iterative processes, in which user feedback is taken into account. The amount of traffic on today's search engines would suggest that the ranking algorithms get it at least roughly right a lot of the time. However, since different people typing in the same search query are not always going to have the same relevance criteria in mind, it is impossible for search engines to get it right all of the time; even when a system is trained to build search profiles of individual users, it cannot always get it right, as humans are, alas, often unpredictable. Thus users still need to make their own selections, a task that needs to be supported.

Attributes commonly considered for the purposes of selection are sometimes different from and sometimes the same as those used for finding and identifying information resources. It can be difficult to conduct research into their relative importance, particularly in a naturalistic setting, as the selection process essentially occurs inside the user's head. One method employed to investigate selection criteria is think-aloud protocol analysis, in which users are asked to verbalize their responses to search results. Some key attributes and relationships, according to the FRBR report, are listed in Table 2.3.

Obtaining resources

In today's online world, users often need very little by way of metadata in order to *obtain*, or gain access to, an information resource – just a label on a hyperlink that indicates that, by clicking on it, they will retrieve the described resource. On the other hand, if the description is not linked to the resource, information about how to obtain it would obviously be very helpful. An attribute that is critical in this regard, of course, is the resource's *location*, whether physical (e.g. in a particular archival file) or virtual (e.g. at a particular URL). As a manifestation, expression or work cannot be obtained without also obtaining an item, it is at the item level that this function primarily operates.

Even when they are not linked to their resources, descriptions do not always include much in the way of obtaining information, however. Some indexes, for instance, simply cite manifestations, without pointing to particular items. Such tools are usually based on a particular category of resource, such as a subject, rather than a specific collection of resources. We shall return to some of them in the next chapter.

Navigating resources and collections

While finding resources can involve the collocation of similar resources, *navigating* a collection of resources largely depends on collocation. Metadata creators are able to facilitate collocation and, more broadly, the co-ordination of resources by recording metadata values consistently, as well as by describing explicit relationships between resources. The navigation of a single resource can be supported by co-ordinating its component parts in much the same fashion.

Resource attributes important for navigating collections are likely to include some of those considered important for finding, identifying and selecting resources, such as subject and author. To establish that resources are

Table 2.3 *Attributes and relationships of 'high value' for the selecting task (IFLA, 1998)*

	Select			
	Work	Expression	Manifestation	Item
Attributes/relationships of a work				
Title of the work	■			
Form of work	■			
Co-ordinates (cartographic work)	■			
Referential successor	■			
Referential supplement	■			
Referential complement	■			
And persons/corporate bodies responsible for the work	■			
And entities treated as subject of the work	■			
Attributes/relationships of an expression				
Form of expression		■		
Language of expression		■		
Other distinguishing characteristic		■		
Use restrictions on the expression		■		
Expected frequency of issue (serial)		■		
Type of score (musical notation)		■		
Medium of performance (musical notation or recorded sound)		■		
Scale (cartographic image/object)		■		
Revision		■		
Arrangement (music)		■		
Translation		■		
Referential successor		■		
Referential supplement		■		
Referential complement		■		
And persons/corporate bodies responsible for content		■		
Attributes/relationships of a manifestation				
Statement of responsibility		■	■	
Edition/issue designation		■	■	
Date of publication/distribution			■	
Form of carrier			■	
Reduction ratio (microform)			■	
Presentation format (visual projection)			■	
System requirements (electronic resource)			■	

similar with respect to a particular attribute, the values for this attribute must be the same. In addition, relationship 'attributes' can be recorded: 'translation of', 'based on', 'accompanied by', and so forth.

From attributes to elements

We have outlined some of the attributes that users most want to know about when finding, selecting, identifying, obtaining and navigating information resources. Of course, what people want and what they get are two different things. There are several reasons why attributes may not end up by being described. They may not be considered so important by the metadata creators, or they may not be applicable to a particular resource, or their values may not be readily ascertainable. Moreover, there may not be a metadata creator in the first place. We shall look at sources of metadata in Chapter 4. First, however, we shall consider the tools and systems in which metadata is typically used.

References

Chen, H.-L. (2001) An Analysis of Image Queries in the Field of Art History, *Journal of the American Society for Information Science and Technology*, **52** (3), 260–73.

International Federation of Library Associations and Institutions (1998) *Functional Requirements for Bibliographic Records: final report*, K. G. Saur.

Jansen, B. J. (2008) Searching for Digital Images on the Web, *Journal of Documentation*, **64** (1), 81–101.

Schamber, L. (1994) Relevance and Information Behavior, *Annual Review of Information Science and Technology*, **29**, 3–48.

Svenonius, E. (2000) *The Intellectual Foundation of Information Organization*, MIT Press.

3

Tools and systems

Introduction

In the previous chapter we talked about how the various attributes of information resources might be of interest to users, and are thus described as metadata for use in information retrieval systems. These systems bring together metadata for multiple resources and help the user to negotiate the information universe and gain access to what they need. While some information retrieval systems are based on the content of information resources, this chapter looks at those based on metadata, and which are central to the field of information organization.

In Chapter 1 we noted the three basic ways in which information resources can be organized in order to improve (effective) access to them: they can be arranged, labelled and indexed. These operations are by no means mutually exclusive, and many information retrieval systems make use of all three techniques. However, we shall begin by considering those systems that do not involve any form of index, and that are based solely on the arrangement and labelling of the items themselves.

Arrangements

Things have been arranged by people for many thousands of years, and information resources have been arranged for as long as there have been collections of them. For our purposes, arrangements are designed to help people look for information resources and look through information resource collections. Just as information resources have countless attributes that can be recorded in any number of ways, so too are there all sorts of ways to arrange them. Critically, users need to know in which way resources have been arranged.

Most sophisticated arrangements of information resources make use of labels. Both groups of resources and individual items can be labelled. In a library, there might be a 'fiction' section, a 'sport' section and so on. For more precision, however, each resource will have a label that indicates its place within the relevant section. This could be a ready-made label, such as an author's name on the spine of a book, or one assigned by the arranger, such as a library call number. In the online environment, labels are used on hyperlinks to describe (briefly) the target resource; together, these labels may be arranged to form, for example, a menu for a website or an online directory.

Labels can describe a particular resource attribute either literally or symbolically. For instance, they may spell out the subject of a resource (e.g. 'cricket') or employ notation intended to stand for that value (e.g. '796.358'). We shall consider why such notation might be used in a moment. Sometimes, labels consist of symbols that are not even characters. For example, a library might use colours to represent different subjects, perhaps for their simplicity.

Arrangements can be made across one, two or three dimensions. A very common system of arrangement is of a certain *order*, across one dimension, as in 'by author'. Many arrangements involving letters, numbers and other textual characters also adhere to conventions and standards that specify their order precisely, independently of any particular set of values. Simplest of all is the convention of numerical order, which might be used to arrange resources by, for example, their acquisition number. For most alphabets, there is likewise a conventional letter order. The A–Z order has been established in English for several centuries. Not all writing systems are based on an alphabet, of course.

Alphabetical and numerical order does not, however, solve all sequencing issues involving letters and numbers. Do numbers come before or after letters? What about hyphens and other punctuation marks? Also problematic is the ordering of word strings. Should the terms

Computer terminals
Computers

be ordered as above, or the other way around? If the order is based on the first word, then the above order is correct; but not if the order is based on letters, and not words. We thus have a choice between word-by-word and letter-by-letter order, and both systems are used. There is no 'right' or 'wrong' system; what is important is that only one system is used to arrange a particular set of word strings. This can be achieved by a standard being established and followed. For instance, for the (original) purpose of arranging library catalogue cards, the American Library Association (ALA) issued its *Filing Rules* (1980) so that everyone who filed the cards did so in the same order. Nowadays, computers often do the filing and ordering on behalf of humans, and generally do a very good job of it, but they too need a set of rules to begin with.

We mentioned just now how some arrangements involve symbolic notation. Prime examples are library classification schemes, such as Dewey Decimal Classification (DDC). The notations are still filed in numerical and alphabetical orders, but the result is an arrangement based primarily on subject, with resources on similar topics placed close to each other. This is known as a *classified* order. For instance, in DDC, the notation for tennis is 796.342, while the notation for badminton is 796.345. If the literal words 'tennis' and 'badminton' were used, resources on the two sports would most likely be located a very long way apart. However, in an artificial 'language', such as DDC notation, any character string can be used to represent any particular concept. This allows similar concepts to be assigned notations that file close to each other. We shall look more closely at library classification schemes in Chapter 8.

Classified arrangements are not always based on artificial notation, though, particularly when labels can be arranged independently of their resources, as is the case online. Thus website menus typically consist of links to constituent pages arranged in some sort of 'logical' order, based on the meaning of the labels rather than the words themselves. Such an order may make more sense to the user than an alphabetical one based on natural language, and should not cause cognitive overload as long as the list is reasonably brief. An extension of the website menu is the *online directory*, which typically provides links to external web resources. A directory's initial list of labels is often based on subject, or some other aspect of content, which may be arranged in a classified order. Both menus and directories are also likely to be arranged *hierarchically*, so that the labels on the initial list link to sub-lists of second-order links and so on.

We noted earlier how indexes were essentially arrangements of labels connected conceptually, rather than physically, to their resources. Logically arranged website menus and online directories can, therefore, be considered indexes, although the term is more typically applied to lists designed to be 'looked up', and arranged alphabetically or according to some other standardized order. Another non-alphabetic 'index' is the *site map*, which arranges links to constituent pages according to their structural location. The analogue equivalent of this might be the *table of contents* found in many printed resources, which sets out the titles of sections and subsections in order of appearance. We shall start, however, by looking at 'indexes' as they are more commonly conceived.

Indexes and databases

The basic tool of information organization is the index, comprising metadata that can be arranged independently of the resources it represents. This independence has two key advantages over labels attached to resources.

First, it allows for multiple *access points* to a resource, with multiple descriptions all pointing to a particular resource. These descriptions may link directly to online resources, or contain information about the location of physical resources. The more access points there are, the more likely it is that the searcher will find the resource. Many modern retrieval systems offer a range of access points, such as title, author name, institutional name, subject, series title, identifiers etc.

Second, as metadata is generally more compact than its resource, a set of independent descriptions can usually be viewed more efficiently and effectively than can the set of resources that they represent. For example, a user may find it easier to look through a list of titles than to walk up and down the stacks. Or they may find it easier to consult an index than flip through the pages of a large book.

Indexes have been used in information organization since long before the advent of computers, and remain prevalent in both physical and electronic form. They are the basis of a wide range of information retrieval systems, including library catalogues, periodical databases, archival finding aids and search engines – all are essentially indexes, or sets of indexes, to particular collections of information resources.

An index can, of course, be created for single resources as well as for collections of resources, providing access to a set of resource components. Indeed, the type of index that first comes to many people's minds is probably the *book index*. It normally consists of a list of terms, arranged alphabetically, that refer to page numbers, or *locators*, and to other terms in the list. Each term that refers to one or more page numbers is called an *entry*, i.e. a term entered in the list. Terms that merely refer to other terms are, not surprisingly, called *references*. Index entries can comprise lengthy descriptions consisting of many elements, but in the case of book indexes, they are generally very brief and comprise just one element, most often pertaining to subject.

Indexes printed in books are usually the product of *closed* indexing, that is, one-off treatment of a static resource or collection. More flexibility, however, is required for an (*open*) index to a growing collection of resources. In the online environment, this is less of an issue, as the computer can readily insert a new entry into a list or file. In the physical environment, one solution is the loose-leaf file, into which pages containing descriptions for new resources can be entered. Another solution is the *card index*, in which resource descriptions, or *records*, are written, typed or printed onto cards and entered (i.e. filed) in runs according to the *heading* at the top of each card. Thus the record is also known as an *entry*, and the heading under which it is entered is a kind of access point. A large card index might comprise several drawers of cards, or even several cabinets. A prime example of a card index is, or was, the library card catalogue.

Electronic indexes work on much the same principles as physical ones. However, they have a number of distinct advantages. They can store huge numbers of records in very small amounts of space; and they can be searched by computers, instead of humans, and thus far more quickly. *Computer databases* play a critical role in today's information environment. Almost all are based on indexes, organized in ways that enable the efficient processing of search queries. Typically, records are assigned a number and divided into *fields* that hold the various elements of description. Separate indexes are then compiled for different fields or combinations of fields. (Some fields may not be indexed at all, but they may still be displayed.) The contents of a field are entered into a file, known as an *inverted file* (see Figure 3.1), along with the corresponding record number. When the file (i.e. index) is searched by the computer and a match on an entry is made, those records with the numbers assigned to the entry are retrieved (or the numbers are combined with other numbers from other parts of a search to produce the final set of record numbers for retrieval).

Because modern computers search very large files extremely quickly, every word in a field can be individually indexed. For example, all the words of a title can be indexed to provide for a 'title keyword search'. (A few words, called *stop words*, such as 'a', 'the' and 'and', may not be indexed, however, as they would retrieve too many records, due to their high frequency.) It would simply not be practicable for a card index to provide this depth of access. A library card catalogue that indexed every word in a bibliographic record would require whole buildings full of card cabinets.

(a) Document records

Document no. 1
Author: Cunningham, M.
Title: File structure and design
Publisher: Chartwell-Bratt
Year: 1985
Keywords: File structure; File organization

Document no. 2
Author: Tharp, A.
Title: File organization and processing
Publisher: John Wiley
Year: 1988
Keywords: File structure; File organization

Document no. 3
Author: Ford, N.
Title: Expert systems and artificial intelligence
Publisher: Library Association
Year: 1991
Keywords: Expert systems; Artificial intelligence; Knowledge-based systems

Document no. 4
Author: Charniak, E.; McDermott, D.
Title: Introduction to artificial intelligence
Publisher: Addison-Wesley
Year: 1985
Keywords: Artificial intelligence; Expert systems

(b) Index file

4 40 1 1 ADDISON-WESLEY
3 60 1 2 ARTIFICIAL INTELLIGENCE
4 60 1 1 ARTIFICIAL INTELLIGENCE
4 20 1 1 CHARNIAK, E.
1 40 1 1 CHARTWELL-BRATT
1 20 1 1 CUNNINGHAM, M.
3 60 1 1 EXPERT SYSTEMS
4 60 1 2 EXPERT SYSTEMS
3 30 1 1 EXPERT SYSTEMS AND ARTIFICIAL INTELLIGENCE
1 60 1 2 FILE ORGANIZATION
2 60 1 2 FILE ORGANIZATION
2 30 1 1 FILE ORGANIZATION AND PROCESSING
1 60 1 1 FILE STRUCTURE
2 60 1 1 FILE STRUCTURE
1 30 1 1 FILE STRUCTURE AND DESIGN
4 30 1 1 INTRODUCTION TO ARTIFICIAL INTELLIGENCE
3 60 1 3 KNOWLEDGE-BASED SYSTEMS
3 40 1 1 LIBRARY ASSOCIATION
4 20 1 2 MCDERMOTT, D.
2 20 1 1 THARP, A.

Figure 3.1 *Documents and inverted file (source: Chowdhury, 2010)*

Computer databases can store all kinds of data, not just metadata. Their records can thus not only represent information resources; they can *be* information resources. Patient records, student records, business records – they can all be digitally created and managed in computer database systems (often referred to by records managers as *electronic document and records management systems* or EDRMS). All sorts of information content can be stored in database management systems. However, we shall focus in the following sections on those systems that provide access to information resources, either directly or indirectly, through metadata.

Bibliographic databases

Bibliographic databases are commonly employed in the library domain, and in related domains such as bookselling. Information resources, mostly at the manifestation level, are described in bibliographic records, broken down into various fields that represent different bibliographic elements. Typically, a bibliographic database might provide a general keyword index, containing words found in many of the fields, a title keyword index, an author keyword index, a subject keyword index, an ISBN index and perhaps several other indexes.

The most common kind of bibliographic database, by far, is the library catalogue, which is the subject of the next section. There are, however, other kinds of bibliographic database, including those provided by commercial services. Figure 3.2 shows the search interfaces for the bibliographic database Bowker's Global Books in Print, which is aimed at publishers and booksellers, as well as librarians.

Library catalogues

Libraries have provided catalogues to their collections for hundreds of years. In the days when library collections consisted mostly of books, catalogue records were literally *bibliographic*. Some of the earliest catalogues were lists of manuscript books housed in the monastic libraries of medieval Europe. As university libraries and other major collections started acquiring large numbers of printed books, their catalogues became more organized and more systematically constructed. They also became primarily *retrieval* tools rather than inventories.

As libraries continued to expand, there was an increasing need for their

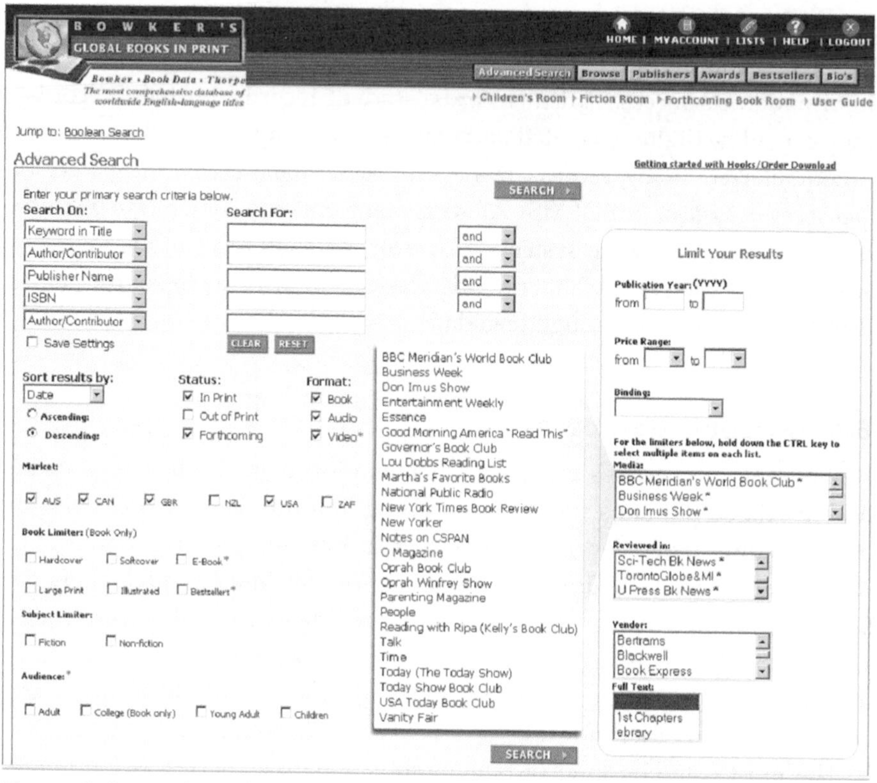

Figure 3.2 *Bowker's Global Books in Print (source:*
www.bowkersupport.com/library/pdfs/Slick-GBIP-P.pdf)

catalogues to accommodate new acquisitions, so that the list eventually gave way, in the 19th century, to physically separate records, between which new records could be interfiled. These records were initially written on loose sheets of paper, but by the mid-20th century they were mostly produced on cards.

The advent of the library card catalogue coincided with the standardization of library cataloguing. Not only were catalogue records set out in a way that was consistent with other records in the catalogue, they were also consistent with those in other catalogues. Standards were established partly to ensure best practice, but primarily for economic reasons, that is, to allow for the *sharing* of records amongst libraries.

Both the heading and the rest of the description on library catalogue cards were subject to standardization. Typically, there were three types of heading used as access points: author, title and subject. These headings were sometimes interfiled; other times they were filed in separate indexes. In an *author–title catalogue*, a library resource, such as a book, might be represented by three or four records, entered, for instance, under the name of the first author, that of a co-author and the title. The resource might also be represented by two or three headings in a complementary *subject catalogue.* Alternatively, a *dictionary catalogue* would combine author, title and subject headings in one alphabetical sequence. Another alternative to the (alphabetical) subject catalogue was the *classified catalogue* (or *classed catalogue*), which arranged records in a classified order using the artificial notation of a library classification scheme.

In the world of the card catalogue, time and money were saved by making one of the records for a particular resource the so-called *main entry.* This record would contain the full description, whereas the other records for the resource would include only a brief citation, plus a reference to the main entry. These other records were called *added entries.* The main and added entry system is not so useful in the modern digital environment, however, since computers can display as much of the record as the user wishes for no significant additional cost.

The *online public access catalogue* (OPAC) began to replace card catalogues in the 1970s and 1980s. The process was a major undertaking for most libraries, particularly for those with very large collections. Bibliographic data from hundreds of thousands, or even millions, of cards had to be transferred to the library's automated management system. These exercises in *retrospective conversion* were usually carried out with the assistance of external databases of electronic records, in a standard format known as MARC (Machine-Readable Cataloguing), that were downloaded into the local system and edited as required. Most library management systems are still based (at least for now) on the MARC standard, which is discussed in Chapter 7.

An important aspect of the OPAC is its *integration* with the library system's circulation module, enabling it to advise patrons not only of a resource's existence, but also of the item's availability. The OPAC's functionality and interface have gradually evolved, along with the rest of the library management system. Most of the development work has been undertaken by commercial companies specializing in this product.

The first generation of OPACs was menu driven and offered a limited number of search options (e.g. by title and author). Then, in the 1990s, a second generation took over, providing more options, including keyword searching. With the emergence of the internet, a third generation connected OPACs to the outside world, providing users with access from the comfort of their homes and offices, even when the physical library was closed. They also provided, and continue to provide, additional features, such as different display options, hyperlinks to 'similar' records (e.g. sharing the same subject heading), the inclusion of dust jacket images, 'shopping carts' that compile lists of records the user is interested in and online reservation and renewal facilities.

The OPAC has transformed access to library collections. It provides many more access points than the card catalogue, accommodates more sophisticated search techniques, such as Boolean searching and truncation, and can be accessed both simultaneously and remotely. Despite this, many librarians have expressed concern that third-generation OPACs are now outdated, contrasting them with search engines such as Google, and online bookstores such as Amazon, which have evolved considerably faster and provide, it is contended, a more satisfying user experience (Fast and Campbell, 2004; Šauperl and Saye, 2009). In response to these concerns, the 'next generation' of catalogues is now being developed (Breeding, 2010). Typically, the new OPACs feature Google-like, single-search-box interfaces, automatic query reformulation ('do you mean this?' etc.), relevance ranking and more three-dimensional displays of result sets. They are often 'layered' over the top of existing library management systems. Pioneering catalogues of note include the University of California's Melvyl Catalog and the OPAC developed at the University of Bradford.

A key characteristic of next-generation catalogues is their facilitation of new forms of user–system interaction. For instance, retrieved records may be organized under different metadata elements, referred to as *facets*, for the user to explore. Figure 3.3 shows an interface offering *faceted navigation*, in which the content of various facets, such as creator, format and topic, is listed on the left. A user might, for example, click on 'Audio' to browse the 112 sound recordings within the current result set. Instead of looking through a flat list of records, the user has the option of drilling down within a particular facet (in effect, *limiting* the search).

The metadata values might also be presented in interesting ways. For example, terms found in records are sometimes arranged into a tag cloud (Figure 3.4). The larger the term's font size, the more times that term has been linked to the record, or to a set of records. Various bibliographic

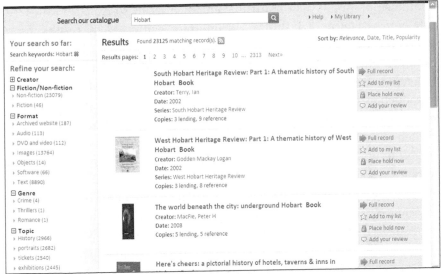

Figure 3.3 *Facets (on the left) of results from a search on the State Library of Tasmania catalogue (source: http://catalogue.statelibrary.tas.gov.au)*

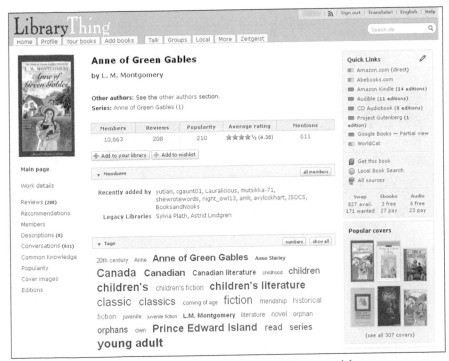

Figure 3.4 *Tag cloud at the bottom of a LibraryThing record (source: http://791linkeddata.blogspot.com.au/2011/04/librarything.html)*

relationships might also be displayed, such as in so-called 'FRBR-ized' catalogues. Figure 3.5 shows an interface with search results for a particular *work*. Systems that retrieve works are relatively rare. An example outside of librarianship is the Internet Movie Database (IMDb).

Even more dynamic forms of user interaction are afforded by the introduction of certain 'Web 2.0' features, such as user tagging and user rating, where the library patron contributes metadata. End-users may be invited to add their own index terms or *tags* to records, to supplement the subject terms assigned by library cataloguers. Similarly, they may be invited to rate a resource, or even write a review of it, for the benefit of other users. We shall discuss the phenomenon of 'social' metadata in the next chapter.

Another possibility is for circulation records to be used to automatically generate *recommendations* based on what patrons who borrowed a particular resource also borrowed. (Such relationships of resource 'use' are akin to those established in citation analysis, between resources that are *co-cited* in the same document.)

Despite all the work that has gone into next-generation catalogues, many

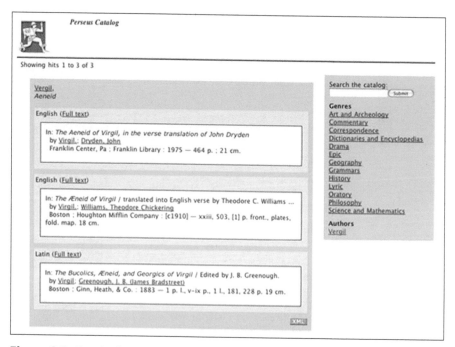

Figure 3.5 *Results from a 'work' search on the Perseus Digital Library catalogue (source: www.perseus.tufts.edu/hopper)*

librarians remain unconvinced and many users are voting with their feet (or hands), visiting the likes of Google as the first port of call and the library catalogue as a last resort. One issue is the quality and applicability of the metadata on which next-generation features depend. Relevance-ranking algorithms based on bibliographic data may be considerably less reliable than those based on the content of the resources themselves, where there is much more data to go on. Likewise, the capacity of catalogues to 'FRBR-ize' may be limited by the lack of detail provided in MARC records (Carlyle, Ranger and Summerlin, 2008). Library users may also be disinterested in taking the time to tag or even to rate, or they may do so unreliably.

Perhaps an even greater issue, however, is the scope of library catalogues. Nowadays, they represent only a small proportion of information resources provided by the library, and only a tiny proportion of resources available in the online environment as a whole. As Ruschoff (2010, 62) argues, 'more lipstick on our catalogs is not going to make our OPACs the search engine of tomorrow'. Since it is clearly impossible for libraries to catalogue all the useful resources now available on the internet, the way forward appears to be for OPACs to be integrated into the larger online environment – if they can't beat the likes of Google, they need to join them. Singer (2008, 140) points out that library catalogues 'are still relatively closed-world silos intended to index MARC records … What we have now are systems that ape Amazon's look and feel with a minute fraction of the kind of data that makes Amazon compelling.' What libraries need to do, Singer (2008, 142) urges, is 'disintegrate the bibliographic data from the inventory control system, let it incorporate and display however it wants or needs to, and leave the circulation, purchasing, and serials prediction to the back-office application. Like it or not, it is the direction the current crop of catalog replacements are taking us anyway; it is time to shed the trappings of the card catalog and reconfigure our assets to work with the Web instead of around it.'

A first step in this direction is for the OPAC to be integrated into the library's own website. Librarians are therefore looking to provide a single search facility that covers all of their library's online databases, including the catalogue. Many library websites now offer a *federated search* interface that sits, as a 'discovery layer', on top of the OPAC and other databases, including those providing access to periodical articles. Instead of having to interrogate multiple databases successively, the user enters a query that is relayed to the specified databases simultaneously. We shall return to these applications in the section after next.

Federated search systems are themselves silos, however, when their contents remain hidden from users of the search engines that cover the web at large. While proprietary databases cannot be made publicly accessible, for obvious reasons, most libraries would very much like their catalogues to receive as much exposure as possible. They have thus started providing companies like Google and Yahoo! with catalogue records for their search engines to index. The sharing of metadata is discussed further in Chapter 6.

Periodical databases

Databases offered by commercial indexing and abstracting services complement library catalogues by providing access to information resources at a deeper level. Whereas library catalogues index periodicals as a whole, these databases index periodical articles. Similarly, they may index conference papers, rather than the proceedings. Nowadays, many periodical databases also provide direct, online access to the articles themselves, or at least to some of them (especially if they appear in journals published by the service provider). The largest providers, such as EBSCOhost and ProQuest, *aggregate* records from multiple sources to create very large databases that have become key academic reference tools.

Most records in periodical databases include an abstract of the article. This is generally provided by the author, but in some cases it may be created (and indirectly charged for) by the service. A typical record in a periodical database is shown in Figure 3.6.

Federated search systems

Increasingly, people are coming to expect *service convergence*, particularly on the web. 'One-stop shopping' is especially popular when it comes to information seeking. Library websites sometimes offer access to scores of databases; most end-users are reluctant to search them one by one. Thus, many libraries have been keen to turn their websites into *portals*, metaphorical windows that provide a point of entry to disparate resources (Butters, 2003). Some portals may provide just a directory of links, but many also offer a federated search option covering multiple databases. Sometimes the result sets from the various target databases are integrated (records for the same resource may even be de-duplicated); other times, they are simply displayed alongside each other.

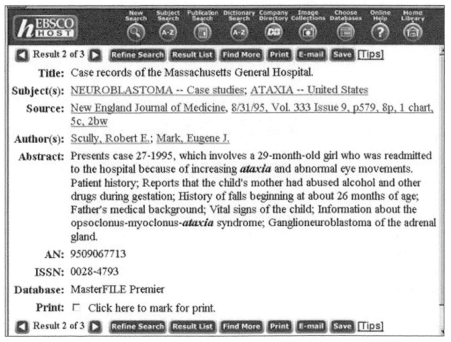

Figure 3.6 *An EBSCOhost record*

Creating federated search applications that can 'talk' to different database systems is the challenge of *interoperability*. Unfortunately, the various systems may not talk the same 'language'. This can be a problem at different levels: syntactic, functional and semantic. Systems may not use the same syntax (for example, the query 'paper industry' might be treated as a phrase in one system, but as two separate words in another); systems may not support the same functions (such as 'scan' and 'sort'); and systems may not define metadata elements in the same way (as in 'title search' or 'author search'), nor indeed their values (such as 'football', which may or may not mean 'soccer'). The main solution to these problems is *standardization*, but this is not so likely to occur across databases built by, or aimed at, quite different communities. As a result, federated search applications may be limited to a somewhat more basic level of functionality than in the individual database systems they cover.

Libraries are by no means the only institutions to have developed federated search systems, but their efforts in this area have been significant. A good example is Trove (Figure 3.7), which provides integrated access to the National Library of Australia's collections. Many libraries have implemented

Figure 3.7 *The Trove home page (source: http://trove.nla.gov.au)*

systems that allow for most of their periodical databases, at least, to be linked together. Some federated search systems operate across multiple institutions. A case in point is the *union catalogue* hosted by the InforM25 consortium of academic libraries located in and around London in the UK (www.inform25.ac.uk).

Archival finding aids

Like libraries, archives normally provide tools to support information access. As physical access to archival materials is usually restricted, and online access is less likely, these tools are particularly important. Indexes to archival collections are commonly referred to as finding aids. Whereas a single catalogue might cover all of a library's collections, archives tend to create different finding aids for different collections.

Also in contrast to library catalogues, archival finding aids describe few, if any, details about *individual* resources. This is because archive users often do not know exactly which items they are looking for and because there are often just too many items to describe. Instead, the basic unit of description tends to be the *file*. This consists of multiple records or documents that were consigned to the archives as a 'set' (e.g. a set of personal papers, a set of minutes from the meetings of a committee, or a set of military service records from a regiment).

A file may be stored in one or more physical containers. Files connected in some way may be organized in a *series* (e.g. files covering different time periods). A collection, or *fond*, generally comprises all the files and series emanating from a particular body or person or family. Files, series and collections are all described in finding aids, which are therefore structured hierarchically, allowing users to 'drill down' to more specific materials. Figure 3.8 shows how a finding aid can provide access to multiple levels of records or documents.

Archival resources are not only described as collections, they are also stored as such (a principle known as *respect des fonds*), with their contents usually kept in *original order*, that is, the order in which they were received by the archives. Again, this differs markedly from library practice, in which items are usually arranged according to a particular classification scheme. Similarly, archival description pays far more attention than does library cataloguing to the history or *provenance* of resources and to their *function* in the organization in which they were created. Conversely, archival description pays less attention to the 'subject' of the resources, which will depend very much on the point of view of the archives user.

Finding aids used to be printed on paper or cards, but many have been uploaded to the web in recent years so that prospective users can ascertain with more confidence whether a trip to the archives would be worth their while. In addition, digital finding aids are usually more searchable, since more of their content is indexed. Furthermore, multiple finding aids can be searched simultaneously, if they conform to particular standards, just as multiple library catalogues can.

Museum registers

Whereas library and archival resources are described primarily so that end-users can gain access to them, this is less the case with museum and gallery resources, which traditionally are listed in inventories, or registers, primarily for the benefit of curatorial staff. The information included in these descriptions thus supports resource *management* as much as resource access. Although curators also provide descriptions of the artefacts they exhibit, for the benefit of the visitor, these are more for educational than for organizational purposes. Both management and educational functions of information resource description are outside the scope of this book.

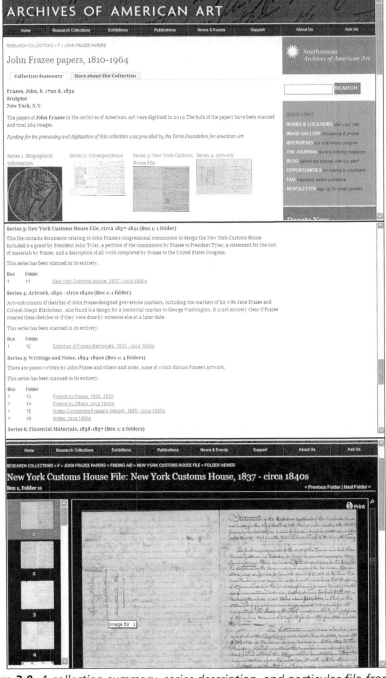

Figure 3.8 *A collection summary, series description, and particular file from the Archives of American Art (source: www.aaa.si.edu)*

However, metadata to support retrieval by end-users is now being created as museums and galleries move online. An important point about this metadata is that it describes not only the original physical artefact, but also its digital surrogate (usually an image or set of images). The database systems that store these digital collections often provide more sophisticated access than the traditional register and are revolutionizing museum resource description. An example of an online museum's search interface is shown in Figure 3.9. Visitors can access images of the artefacts stored in the collection, independently of their exhibition.

Digital collections

The online museum is one of many kinds of database system that manages information content, and not just metadata. Collections of digital information resources are to be found all over the web, and on many intranets. They vary enormously in nature and size. Their content may be textual (e-books, electronic theses etc.) or audiovisual (images, videos, audio recordings etc.) or multimedia. Their retrieval systems may utilize very little metadata, or they may be heavily reliant upon it.

Many libraries, as well as museums, have developed collections of digital

Figure 3.9 *Search interface of the online Smithsonian American Art Museum (source: http://americanart.si.edu/collections/search)*

resources hosted either on their own servers or externally. University libraries may also manage the digital *repository* of their institution's research outputs. However, most digital collections are not managed by libraries or museums, but by a wide range of other types of organization, or even by individuals.

The design and functionality of the database systems that host digital collections likewise vary widely. The nature of the metadata used (if any) is partly dependent, of course, on the nature of the information resources, with different elements used for different kinds of collection. The extent and quality of the metadata is also dependent on its availability. Professional indexing is frequently too expensive for large collections, and so managers may have to rely on those who create, contribute or even use the resources. We shall discuss these sources of metadata in the next chapter.

Many digital collections are managed using generic database management applications, which, like library catalogues, frequently form part of the 'hidden web', that is, the part that is not indexed by external search engines. One solution has been to make the metadata (if not the resources) available for *harvesting*, and thus indexing in other search systems. We shall look at this approach to metadata sharing in Chapter 6.

Some of the digital collections managed by 'memory' institutions, such as libraries, museums and archives, have served as laboratories for the development of metadata standards and various strands of research in information retrieval/organization. One area of study, for instance, is concerned with *visualization*, which considers how information is presented. Although most metadata is textual, it can still be displayed on the screen in innovative and graphical ways. For instance, search results might be set out as a two-dimensional 'map', or a collection might be displayed as virtual bookshelves (e.g. in a next-generation library catalogue) or as a subject 'tree'; digital archives might be displayed as a function 'tree' (Allen, 2005). A 'visual' search interface for a children's digital library is shown in Figure 3.10. Visualization becomes even more of a challenge when the information resources are mixed, for example, of different media.

Another area of digital library research is personalization (not to be confused with customization). Its aim is for the system to anticipate a particular individual's information needs and behaviour based on their history of interactions with it (identified through, for example, their login or their computer's Internet Protocol (IP) address).

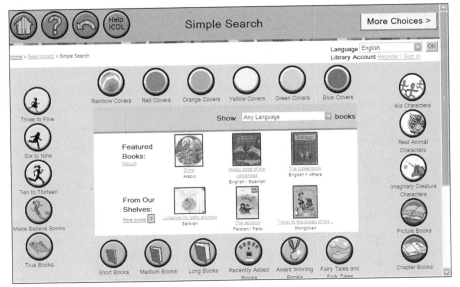

Figure 3.10 *Search interface for the International Children's Digital Library (source: www.childrenslibrary.org/icdl/ SimpleSearchCategory?ilang=English)*

Search engines

Indexes to resources in more 'open' digital collections are compiled by search engines. Although they mostly index content, rather than metadata, they are discussed here because of their great importance in modern information retrieval. The largest, including Google and Yahoo!, provide access to many millions of online resources and have become the first port of call for most people looking for information on the web. As Dawson and Hamilton (2006, 308) observe, 'Google is extremely fast and reliable, it works on a massive scale, it provides useful results much of the time, it searches the full text of documents, it indexes multiple document types, including HTML, PDF and Word documents, it generates contextual summaries that are often useful, it is constantly updated, it has many advanced features for those who can be bothered to use them, it is very simple to use, and it is entirely free to users worldwide.'

While the likes of Google attempt to index the whole web, or as much of it as they can, other search engines aim to cover a particular part of it (for example, web resources on a particular subject, in a particular medium or format, from a particular country or in a particular language). Some search engines do not cover the internet at all, but rather, a particular organization's intranet.

Whatever their coverage, most search engines are effective because they are able to index copious amounts of content. As Dawson and Hamilton (2006, 308) also point out, 'there are many reasons for the success and public acceptance of the market leader Google, but metadata is not one of them'. The key to success of retrieval tools such as Google is their organization of search results. Ordering a million hits by alphabet would not be helpful; instead, they are typically arranged in *relevance order*, as we noted earlier. The techniques used to create this order have been introduced into other retrieval systems, such as next-generation library catalogues. As they primarily belong to the field of information retrieval, however, we shall not dwell on them here.

Search engines are by no means perfect retrieval tools. They may not suit the scholar looking to carry out a comprehensive investigation, or the information seeker with only a vague idea of what they want. In Miller's view (2004), 'faced with a focused request to retrieve richly structured information such as that to be found in the databases of our memory institutions, hospitals, schools, colleges or universities, Google and others among the current generation of Internet search engines struggle. What little information they manage to retrieve from these repositories is buried among thousands of millions of hits from sources with widely varying degrees of accuracy, authority, relevance and appropriateness.'

Unfortunately, indexing more metadata, as well as content, would not necessarily make search engines more effective. Even when the metadata is available (and often it is not), it is not always reliable. Less scrupulous website managers sometimes indulge in so-called *spam tagging*, providing keyword terms that are frequently searched on, but that do not reflect their site's content, in an effort to raise the site's relevance ranking.

Finally, we should note that many search engines are commercial. One way in which the companies running these search engines make a profit is by accommodating sponsored search results, so that the resources represented on the first page of hits are not always even what are estimated to be the most relevant (though the sponsored results are usually demarcated as such).

Online directories

An alternative way of finding resources on the web is by using another kind of index, namely, an online directory. The best-known example is probably the Yahoo! directory (Figure 3.11). Instead of the computer looking up a search query, users are invited to search through lists of resources (or links to

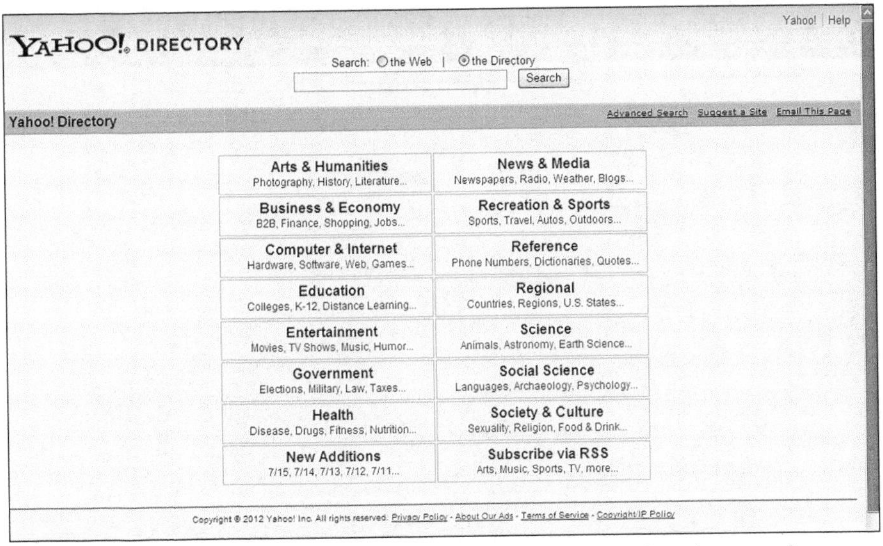

Figure 3.11 *Yahoo! Directory home page (source: http://dir.yahoo.com)*

resources) for themselves. This may seem regressive, but if the user does not have a specific resource in mind, or cannot express it very precisely, the directory may be the most effective retrieval tool. Directories can be arranged in a classified order or alphabetically. The online directory also has an advantage over its print equivalent, in that it can present the hierarchical structure of a list in linked layers, so that users can drill down to the particular type of resource they are interested in.

Many online directories present lists of topics, under which resources from across the web are collocated. They are, in a way, the online equivalent of library stacks, supporting less focused finding and selection, otherwise known as *browsing*. Those which cover a particular field of study are sometimes called *subject gateways*. An example is shown in Figure 3.12.

The ever-growing number of quality web resources has made the compilation of large-scale online directories and gateways ever harder work, and some have fallen into disrepair. As a result, their popularity has fallen off somewhat, in contrast to that of search engines. In many cases, they are combined with search engines on a common interface, giving users more options.

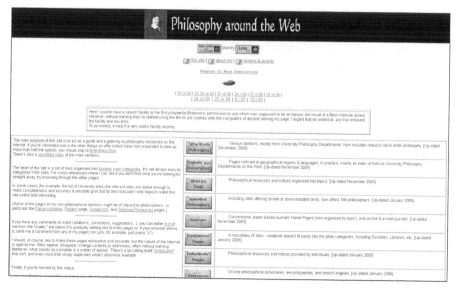

Figure 3.12 *Philosophy around the Web subject gateway (source:*
http://users.ox.ac.uk/~worc0337/phil_index.html)

Bibliographies

The bibliography is literally a list of books, but its meaning has been
extended to include other forms of information resource, although lists of
non-book materials may also be referred to in other terms (e.g.
'discography'). Whereas a catalogue represents resources in a particular
collection (whether physical or virtual), a bibliography is usually based
on a different kind of attribute, such as subject or authorship. Indeed,
many bibliographies, in their description of physical resources, do not
refer to particular items at all. Instead, they typically describe
manifestations, leaving it up to the user to locate and obtain a copy. A
simple form of bibliography, of course, is the *reference list*, based on the
resources cited in a text. More elaborate bibliographies have been
published as independent works, compiled by librarians, booksellers,
scholars and other bibliographers.

As the proportion of information resources available online continues to
climb, bibliographies are increasingly turning into subject gateways and
other forms of online listings, providing direct access to the resources
themselves. Traditional bibliographies are, however, still extensively used in
some quarters, such as by those dealing with rare and antiquarian books. It is
also worth noting that the practice of *enumerative bibliography* (i.e. the

compilation of bibliographic lists) has, historically, influenced other forms of information resource description, including library cataloguing.

Citation databases

Finally, we should mention one other form of index, based on reference lists. In citation databases it is the relationship between citing and cited resources that is of interest, rather than the resource description itself. The premise is that this relationship represents some sort of similarity: if the citing document is relevant, so is the cited document, and vice versa. Of course, documents are cited for all kinds of reasons, and documents that are not linked through citation may nevertheless be relevant. However, citation databases do offer an alternative, and often fruitful, way to search for 'related' materials, especially for materials that are not explicitly related by topic.

Citation databases are based on the work of authors, but the other information organization tools we have discussed in this chapter are based on metadata provided by a wide range of sources, which we shall survey next.

References

Allen, R. B. (2005) Using Information Visualization to Support Access to Archival Records, *Journal of Archival Organization*, **3** (1), 37–49.

American Library Association (1980) *ALA Filing Rules*.

Breeding, M. (2010) *Next-Gen Library Catalogs*, Facet Publishing.

Butters, G. (2003) What Features in a Portal? *Ariadne*, **35**, www.ariadne.ac.uk/issue35/butters.

Carlyle, A., Ranger, S. and Summerlin, J. (2008) Making the Pieces Fit: Little Women, works, and the pursuit of quality, *Cataloging & Classification*, **46** (1), 35–64.

Chowdhury, G. G. (2010) *Introduction to Modern Information Retrieval*, 3rd edn, Facet Publishing.

Dawson, A. and Hamilton, V. (2006) Optimising Metadata to Make High-value Content More Accessible to Google Users, *Journal of Documentation*, **62** (3), 307–27.

Fast, K. and Campbell, D. (2004) I Still Like Google: university student perceptions of searching OPACs and the web. In *Proceedings of the 67th Annual Meeting of the American Society for Information Science and Technology (ASIST)*.

Miller, P. (2004) Towards the Digital Aquifer: introducing the Common Information Environment, *Ariadne*, **39**, www.ariadne.ac.uk/issue39/miller.

Ruschoff, C. (2010) New Areas for Cataloging Research, *Library Resources & Technical*

Services, **54** (2), 62–3.

Šauperl, A. and Saye, J. D. (2009) Have We Made Any Progress? Catalogues of the future revisited, *Journal of Documentation,* **65** (3), 500–14.

Singer, R. (2008) In Search of a Really 'Next Generation' Catalog, *Journal of Electronic Resources Librarianship,* **20** (3), 139–42.

4

Metadata sources

Introduction

Information retrieval systems can use metadata only if it is available. People or computers first have to create it. Some metadata is created along with the resources it describes; other metadata is created after the resources have been created and disseminated, by intermediaries or even by the end-users themselves. An information resource description may include metadata from several different sources, directly or indirectly. In this chapter we shall look at various kinds of metadata creator, and their motives.

Resource creators

It is generally in the interests of the creator of an information resource to provide some basic metadata at the point of creation. Often this forms an integral part of the resource. Its location may be governed by convention. For example, a title is normally included at the top of a manuscript, or on its own title page, or at the bottom of an art work, or at the beginning of a film and so on. In many instances, one might expect the creator to record their name, a title and perhaps a date of creation. They may also include some metadata pertaining to components of the resource, such as headings and page numbers.

In most cases, creators produce information resources, and their associated metadata, intentionally. However, this is not always the case. For instance, a document in an archive might have originally been created as a memo from one official to another but, once deposited in the archive, it becomes a *record* of this communication, with a different function from that of the original document. Nevertheless, metadata included by the memo's author (e.g. its date) may still be useful.

Computers and the internet have made it far easier for people to disseminate metadata as well as information resources. Desktop publishing applications allow them to *tag* (i.e. label) titles and other metadata elements included in the text of a web page, or to *embed* metadata in a document by inserting *meta tags* (see the section on mark-up languages in Chapter 7). As creators of resource carriers, computers can, of course, also add metadata themselves (e.g. file size).

Although many digital resources are created with minimal amounts of metadata, standards have been established for resource creators to apply, should they choose, or be required, to do so. For example, many academic journals stipulate that authors include, as part of their submissions, abstracts and keywords, as well as titles. Companies may likewise require their staff to add 'keywords' to accompany the documents they contribute to their intranet's content management system.

Publishers

Traditionally, information resources are published on behalf of their creators by publishing houses, record companies and the like, mostly on a commercial basis. These publishers may add their own metadata (such as a 'blurb') to that supplied by the resource creators. It is generally the publishers' responsibility to disseminate the metadata along with the resource. For example, book publishers distribute metadata to retailers and libraries, while journal publishers pass on metadata to database providers. Nowadays, publishers are also entering into arrangements with search engine companies. The emerging model of Google Books allows content, as well as metadata, to be indexed and retrieved as extracts; the user then decides whether they wish to purchase and read the whole book (Schnittman, 2008).

In the online environment, resource creators are far less dependent on publishing companies, and in many cases elect to self-publish. They can establish their own website or blog, or they can contribute resources to hosting sites, such as Flickr and YouTube. This has revolutionized both publishing and information resource description. Individuals have much more scope to add whatever metadata they choose. In the space of just a few years, indexing, as well as publishing, has become an activity that everyone (with access to the internet) can participate in. Furthermore, individuals can even publish content that they did not create, and can likewise tag resources that have been published by others. We shall consider end-users as metadata creators later in the chapter.

Information professionals

In a world so full of information, some might wonder why people need help finding it. The more information there is, however, the more difficult it is to find the best information. It is the job of information professionals to assist their clients in this quest. They do this by first of all ensuring that particularly useful information resources are available. They can also do this by helping users to help themselves, that is, by improving their information-seeking and literacy skills. However, even if the best resources are available and users become expert information seekers, they will still not necessarily find what they need, for it also requires the provision of effective information retrieval tools.

In contrast to resource creators and publishers, information agencies are often responsible for thousands, if not millions, of resources. In pre-internet times, all of these resources were physically collected in one place, for more convenient use. Librarians, archivists and curators were, and still are, the custodians of these collections, greatly adding to their value by enhancing access to them through their catalogues, finding aids and other forms of index. Online resources, on the other hand, are not necessarily collected in physical terms, though they may be archived to a particular site. Nevertheless, they can still form a virtual collection, and still need to be described so that they can be found, identified, selected, obtained and navigated.

Not all information professionals focus on resource description. In some information agencies metadata creation and management may be a relatively small part of operations. In larger organizations, resource description may be assigned to specialists. Some metadata specialists may not even be hired directly by an information agency. For example, cataloguers might be hired by the suppliers to libraries of 'shelf-ready' materials. Many book and database indexers work on a freelance basis, as do many information architects.

While agencies such as libraries have a *mission* to provide information, almost all organizations *generate* information for their staff and clients. In this sense, virtually all organizations could be regarded as 'information agencies'. The pervasive use of digital technologies means that many organizations now produce vast amounts of information, and it is often critical that this information is managed effectively. Document and records managers work in many different organizational settings, but in all cases one of their key functions is to ensure that information is accessible to those who need it.

Similarly, information architects are engaged by a wide range of organizations to improve the *usability* of their websites and intranets, so that content is more findable.

Those who specialize in information organization do so in different contexts of information use. Although the ways in which information professionals improve access to information resources are often quite similar, it is also the case that they benefit from first-hand knowledge of the domain in which they work. For instance, archival description is best carried out by archivists, rather than by librarians. Even within a single professional field, such as librarianship, there are significant contextual differences. For instance, school library cataloguing may need to be approached a little differently from, say, cataloguing in a university library. Nevertheless, information organization skills are transferable across domains, as long as those who move across learn about their new environments.

Most metadata specialists are qualified members of a broader profession, such as librarianship. Some are also formally accredited as metadata specialists, but many are not. They will, or should, have been taught the principles of information organization as part of their professional qualification, but, in many cases, they will have learnt a lot of the necessary skills and knowledge on the job. There can be much knowledge to learn, and the skills likewise take some time to acquire. A metadata specialist might become an expert only after years of practice.

This expertise is rarely developed in isolation. Those employed in larger information agencies may be fortunate enough to work with colleagues who can assist directly, as supervisors and mentors. There may also be other forms of support available, such as workshops, professional groups, online resources and so forth. The various metadata specializations have established their own communities of practice, and these are outlined below.

Library cataloguing

The creation and maintenance of library catalogues is essentially a special form of indexing. The term 'catalogue', however, has been used from the outset (in the English-speaking world) for indexes to library collections, and 'cataloguer' is a very well-established job title. Indeed, full-time cataloguers have been employed in some of the largest libraries for hundreds of years. Before the 20th century, every library with a catalogue needed its own cataloguers, as there were no external record sources. Over the course of the

20th century, the mass production of record cards, and then the advent of electronic copy, allowed for an increasing *centralization* of cataloguing, with the cataloguing departments in the larger libraries supplying a growing proportion of records needed by other libraries.

Nevertheless, there was, and still is, a need for some 'original' cataloguing in many libraries, when unique or rare materials are acquired, for which record copy cannot be obtained. The knowledge and skills associated with cataloguing thus remain relevant to a large number of librarians. Recent surveys (e.g. Primary Research Group, 2011) suggest that, at least in academic and research libraries, sizable numbers of librarians are still involved in cataloguing. Groups and forums for cataloguers, such as those co-ordinated by the American Library Association (ALA) and the Chartered Institute for Library and Information Professionals (CILIP), remain active.

However, the days of the full-time cataloguer, outside of a few elite libraries, may be numbered. Yee (2009, 74) laments that 'today cataloguing is practiced [in North America] mainly at the [Library of Congress] and by a tiny corps of librarians primarily located in large research libraries'. The centralization of cataloguing has taken its toll, as has the bypassing of the library catalogue in favour of search engines and other retrieval tools. When library budgets need to be cut, cataloguing departments are especially vulnerable. Banush and LeBlanc (2007, 98) are realistic: 'The necessary expenditures to support it, even in an environment of shared bibliographic databases, co-operative cataloguing and more techno-logically sophisticated cataloguing tools, often fail the cost-benefit test in the eyes of many decision makers.'

It is therefore not surprising that many cataloguers are taking on new duties, and in some cases are redefining their positions altogether. Some have taken on more management responsibilities, while others have got involved more in 'systems' work and have started to deal in other kinds of metadata, used for digital resources not covered by the traditional catalogue (Boydston, 2005). Consequently, a growing number of cataloguers have become *metadata librarians* (Lu, Marion and Park, 2009).

Metadata librarianship

While the internet is enabling libraries to incorporate all sorts of new resources into their digital collections, providing access to these resources presents a number of challenges. There may well be no catalogue records for them; indeed, there may not be much metadata for them at all; and if there is metadata, the elements, values and format are likely to be quite different from those of traditional cataloguing. One solution might be to create 'proper' catalogue records for these resources, but in many cases their sheer quantity makes this an unrealistic proposition. Furthermore, traditional cataloguing standards may not be particularly appropriate. An alternative solution is for librarians to work with, and perhaps even create, metadata in non-traditional forms, for use in retrieval systems outside of the catalogue.

Metadata librarians are typically responsible for several retrieval systems, which might include the library catalogue. They may also be involved in the integration of these systems by working on their interoperability and developing federated search systems. Thus they are involved in 'a much broader suite of metadata implementations [than are cataloguers], demanding familiarity (if not also experience) with an array of formats, standards, schemas, tools and best practices' (Han and Hswe, 2010, 137).

An analysis of library job advertisements from the past decade, carried out by Han and Hswe (2010), neatly shows the transformation from cataloguing to metadata librarian. The job titles in 2000 were mostly 'cataloguing librarian'. By 2008, the numbers had been reversed, with the majority of new jobs advertised as 'metadata librarian' (Table 4.1). New forums are emerging to cater specifically for this new breed of metadata specialist, such as the *Journal of Library Metadata*.

Cataloguers should be well placed to move into this broader role, although it may mean more than learning new metadata standards: it may also require a different approach. Metadata librarianship tends to focus on the management of metadata, more than on its creation, and this is likely to involve the heavy use of computers. Indeed, some metadata librarians are even writing their own computer programs, a task that would have been contemplated by few cataloguers a decade or so ago.

The approach of metadata librarians also tends to be more pragmatic. While cataloguers are sometimes accused of an unhealthy (and unaffordable) obsession with the 'perfect record', metadata librarians focus

Table 4.1 *Jobs posted in Han and Hswe's survey (2010)*

Year	Metadata librarian	Cataloguing librarian
2000	5	19
2001	6	19
2002	7	10
2003	5	8
2004	2	10
2005	8	5
2006	10	7
2007	24	3
2008	19	4
Total	86	85

more on 'solutions', which vary according to the circumstances and nature of each digital library.

Indexing and abstracting

Those who identify themselves as professional 'indexers' perform two different kinds of indexing. They may contribute index terms to databases covering multiple resources, such as periodical articles; or they may index individual resources, especially books and serials. In practice, many indexers do both, as the amount of work available is not so vast. Indeed, indexers, who tend to work on a freelance basis, often supplement their income by taking on other activities, such as abstracting, copy editing and technical writing.

Wellisch's table (Table 4.2) outlines some of the differences between book and database indexing. Whereas book indexing is a one-off ('closed') activity carried out by a single indexer, database indexing is generally carried out on a continuing ('open') basis, often by teams of indexers.

Database indexing is, in fact, very similar to the subject indexing performed by library cataloguers. Usually, a *controlled vocabulary* of subject terms (called *descriptors*) is applied; we shall look at how and why this is done in the next chapter. Here we shall consider for a moment the more distinct craft of book indexing.

Some books are more in need of indexes than others. Large, scholarly

Table 4.2 *The continuum of verbal texts and features of their indexes (source: Wellisch, 1994)*

Form of text		Terminology		Index production		Form of index		Publication	
		Uniform	Non-uniform	By a single indexer	By a team	Published with text	Separate from text	Printed	Electronic
Books	By single author	■		■		■		■	
Books	By multiple authors		■	■		■		■	
Periodicals	One bibliographic volume		■	■		■	■	■	
Periodicals	Cumulated volumes		■	■	■		■	■	■
Periodicals	Current issues		■		■		■	■	■

tomes usually come with an index, as do reference works covering a wide range of topics, and other kinds of book where content is likely to be *looked up*. Novels and pictorial works, on the other hand, usually do not come with indexes. Conventionally, of course, *analytic indexes* (as opposed to, say, tables of content) are placed at the back of the book. They typically provide access to topics, listed alphabetically, via one or more page numbers. Some books include more than one (analytic) index to cover different categories of subject, such as people, places and materials, as well as 'concepts'.

Unlike a full-text index, the analytic index lists only the key topics likely to be of most interest to the reader, as identified by the indexer. The terms used for these topics may also need to be selected, as many topics can be represented by a variety of terms. The indexer usually selects terms that occur in the text, but may also include other terms that they think could well be looked up by readers. More than one term can be included for a given topic, either by providing the same page numbers under each term, or by listing the page numbers under one of the terms and providing *cross-references* from other terms to that term, as in the example below.

Films *see* **Movies**
Movies 12, 17–19, 46

Indexers may also need to be selective when listing the page numbers for a topic, as it could be merely mentioned in some places, but covered in much more depth in others (where it might not, in fact, be explicitly mentioned at all). Selecting the topics, terms and pages for the index requires considerable judgement and skill.

Book indexing also requires decisions about the arrangement and presentation of index entries. Narrower topics could be entered under broader topics, e.g.:

Movies 12, 17–19, 46
    Acting 15, 103
    Directing 79

or they could be entered directly, e.g. as 'Movie acting'. Words could be given in various forms (e.g. singular or plural). Particular pages could be emphasized (e.g. by using bold font) to indicate their greater coverage or a specific kind of coverage (e.g. pictorial). Importantly, these decisions should be made consistently within a given index.

Indexing has been an established occupation since the middle of the last century, if not before. The UK's Society of Indexers was founded in 1957; its journal, *The Indexer*, was first issued the following year and has remained a major reference source for the profession to this day. The American, Australian and Canadian societies were founded in 1968, 1976 and 1977, respectively (Bell, 2008).

As Browne and Jermey (2007) observe, the demand for database indexing has been in decline, with end-users increasingly reliant on authors' keywords and computers' search algorithms. However, professional indexers are still employed by those indexing and abstracting services that remain, especially when controlled subject vocabularies are applied. Periodical indexing is also less in demand, as aggregating databases have greatly reduced the use of indexes to individual serials. Publishers and authors continue to commission book indexes, although in the future they may be less inclined to commission indexes for e-books, given their full-text search functionality. Just as cataloguers have suffered from cuts in library budgets, indexers have suffered from the economic squeeze experienced in the publishing industry. More than ever before, they need to promote the value that an analytic index adds to a text, and that a controlled vocabulary adds to a database.

Professional abstract writing is an even rarer occupation than indexing. While some indexers are paid to provide abstracts as well as index terms for a database, most abstracts for journal articles, conference papers, etc. are supplied by their authors. Although both indexing and abstracting involves summarization, and the content of abstracts is usually indexed, abstract writing is a quite different skill from the assignment of discrete terms, since abstracts are used not only to find resources, but also to select them. Different kinds of abstract support access in different ways. *Indicative* abstracts point to the main topics of the resource; *informative* abstracts go further, summarizing the content in an 'objective' manner; *evaluative* (or *critical*) abstracts, on the other hand, advise the reader not only of what the resource is about, but whether it is worth looking at.

The quality of author-written abstracts varies considerably. Research has suggested that those abstracts written by authors who have taken extra time to 'polish' them are greatly improved as a result: they are more readable and more informative (Betts and Hartley, 2008). Some outlets request that abstracts are submitted in a set structure, which can likewise improve their effectiveness. Janes (1991) has argued that abstracts can increase recall and precision (measures of effectiveness we shall look at later) much more than titles and keywords can, and that more attention should probably be paid to their creation. Economics dictate, however, that most will continue to be written by authors, although this may not necessarily be such a bad thing: abstracting requires a high level of content knowledge, as well as metadata and writing expertise.

Archival description

Resource description is a key part of archival work. Most archives have only small numbers of professional staff, all of whom may be involved in processing, including describing, deposits. Conversely, most archivists do other work as well as archival description. The uniqueness of archival materials means that they are invariably described in-house: the metadata cannot be acquired from external sources. There is thus somewhat less need for adherence to cross-institutional standards, though there are of course recognized principles of best practice, and standards are becoming more relevant as finding aids are moved online.

Because access to physical archival resources is usually restricted, it is particularly important that archival description is accurate and thorough. However, it is also important that backlogs of materials waiting for processing are addressed. Similar debates to those in librarianship have thus ensued, balancing quality and quantity (Gorzalski, 2008).

Museum documentation

Museum resource description, or *documentation*, whether primarily for curatorial purposes or for patrons, is usually produced by museum staff who are, first and foremost, subject experts, although a museum's online site may be managed by a metadata specialist. Visiting a virtual museum may not be quite the same as a physical visit, but it is a genuine learning experience, and the importance of providing high-quality metadata to support such a visit is increasingly recognized, with metadata standards in the museum and art domains now established.

Records management

The difference between the jobs of records managers and archivists could be viewed as a matter of emphasis, with the former responsible for records of a less historical and more current nature. As a result, records managers are also more likely to be dealing with electronic records and computerized database systems (in particular, electronic document and records management systems). Nevertheless, the ways in which records managers organize and describe their resources are quite similar to those of archivists. As with archival description, accuracy and thoroughness is very important: lost records can cause significant economic damage, particularly if the organization is legally obliged to keep them. Like archivists, records managers operate in a wide range of organizational settings (though there are considerably more records managers than archivists in the corporate world).

Information architecture

Many of the documents produced by the staff of organizations need to be shared, either with other staff via an intranet, or with the general public via a website. The organization of information on intranets and websites has become a distinct field of expertise, known as *information architecture*. Just like other kinds of resource, online resources can be arranged in structures that facilitate retrieval. They can also be linked with labels that use appropriate terminology, while these labels can themselves be arranged in helpful ways (Barrick et al., 2005). As well as menus and site maps, larger sites may also benefit from a search engine, which might index metadata (e.g. manually assigned keywords) as well as content.

Most websites and intranets are not subject to continuous redevelopment, which would probably confuse users more than it would help them. Thus, information architecture tends to be carried out as a project, which may also look at other aspects of a site's usability, such as its graphic design. This means that information architects often work as consultants and may refer to their field in broader terms, such as 'web design' or 'user experience'. Larger organizations may also employ a permanent *web manager*, who ensures that the information architecture holds together over time, as content is revised.

Firms of information architects were first established during the 'dot-com' boom of the late 1990s, but many struggled when the bubble burst, and some are struggling again in the aftermath of the global financial crisis (along with many other companies). Although an effective website is now seen as critical to the success of many businesses and most organizations, there are still relatively few full-time information architects. When companies look to cut costs, the website redesign may well be postponed, or done without the help of a specialist. Nevertheless, the demand for skilled information architects remains amongst those with the funds to hire them. For those without such funds, various checklists and guides expounding the basic principles of information architecture are readily available. Organizations would do well to note that it has been estimated that as much as 10% of a company's salary costs are spent on ineffective searches for information (Brodkin, 2007).

End-users

In the past, end-users rarely contributed metadata to information retrieval systems. Some published reviews of books, movies, albums and so on, in journals, newspapers and magazines, but these were rarely included in retrieval tools. However, in the digital environment, it is much easier to link reviews to records; indeed, in the Web 2.0 environment, end-users can enter metadata directly into retrieval systems. Nor is this metadata limited to reviews and ratings. Index terms may also be contributed so as to help fellow end-users find, as well as select, resources. In some systems, end-users have provided enormous amounts of metadata and, in so doing, have revolutionized the practice of information organization.

End-users have been adding reviews and ratings to records on sites such as Amazon for over a decade. These records contain basic metadata supplied by commercial publishers. However, many online resources are quite dependent on end-user description, since they are published by end-users. Often, the content will also have been created by end-users. Sites such as Flickr and YouTube now host millions of resources (images and videos respectively) uploaded, together with their tags, by millions of members of the general public. The tags are critical to the retrieval of these resources, especially given the lack of textual content to search on; these collections are simply too big for professional indexing to be a viable option.

The tags assigned by contributors to these publicly built collections are often supplemented, however, by tags added by the users of the resources. By allowing anyone to tag resources, indexing becomes a communal activity and much more 'democratic' ('anarchic' might be a more accurate descriptor, though, as tags are usually not put to the vote). Hence, this phenomenon is often referred to as *social tagging*. A wide range of digital collections are not only being built by the online public, they are also being organized by them.

There are even collections of links (to all kinds of online resource) hosted by sites such as Delicious (http://delicious.com) and Diigo (www.diigo.com) and organized by communities of interest.

In fact, social tagging is not even restricted to digital resources. LibraryThing (www.librarything.com), for example, provides a platform for people to catalogue their personal libraries of printed books and other resources and to share these catalogues and tags with others. Tagging can likewise be shared at the level of the individual resource. End-users are able to annotate and index pages of e-books and so forth on a collaborative basis, giving rise to a modern form of *marginalia*.

Indexing by non-professionals has implications, however. There are issues of quality and coverage to consider. End-users are generally not paid to tag, and they may not necessarily be interested in doing it (Hunter, 2009). While it has been claimed that library catalogues, for instance, could be greatly enhanced by end-user indexing, participation rates amongst patrons have not been so encouraging. Without professionals to fill in the gaps, coverage may be patchy. Indeed, a vicious circle can occur: resources that are little tagged are more difficult to find, and thus less likely get tagged. One way to break this circle might be for user tagging to be pooled. For example, libraries in the ChiliFresh consortium (www.chilifresh.com/index.php) are sharing their tags in order to build up a critical mass of indexing.

When end-users do tag, they may not do it well. This might be because they are not so concerned about quality, or because they lack expertise. Further, they often tag for personal reasons, using terms of little or no value to other searchers (e.g. 'to read'), or of value only to searchers known to themselves, and they may be less interested in the effectiveness of their tags from a wider retrieval perspective. They also tend to employ terms that are relatively broad in scope (e.g. 'tree'), which may be less useful for a large collection (Guy and Tonkin, 2006).

In most cases, social tagging is *uncontrolled*, so that, for example, the tag 'football' could refer to several different kinds of sport (the value of controlled vocabularies is discussed in the next chapter). The indexing vocabularies generated by end-users have been dubbed *folksonomies*: taxonomies or classifications of the people. Although they may lack formal structure and consistency, they do have certain advantages. Their terms are more likely to be the terms users would naturally search on, while the lack of control allows for multiple perspectives, reflecting the different ways in which a resource could be used.

The comparative effectiveness of controlled vocabularies and folksonomies remains unclear. Smith (2007) has suggested that user tagging, which often generates more synonyms, tends to result in greater recall but less precision. Yet even if social tagging is not always as effective as professional indexing, it can still be useful. Moreover, it is *scalable*, to an extent that professional indexing is plainly not. It should also be noted that end-users can be supported in various ways to improve their contributions. For instance, forms can be provided to control vocabulary, or suggestions can be automatically made for disambiguation. Folksonomic inconsistencies can also be ironed out, to some extent, through *post-hoc* analysis. The two approaches to knowledge organization – professional indexing and social tagging – are compared in Table 4.3. We shall consider them further in Chapter 9.

Table 4.3 *Comparison of two approaches to knowledge organization (source: Mai, 2011)*

	Authoritarian professional, expert-based	Collaborative democratic, every-one
Values	Transparency, consistency, interoperability, stability, professionalism	Inclusiveness, openness, conversation, collaboration, interpretation
Success factors	Understand and match users' information needs, ability to reflect the domain's structure, ability to modify system accordingly to changes in domain	Involvement of users in meaning making, ability to facilitate collaboration among users, ability to accommodate diverse interpretations
Challenges	Analysing the domain and understanding it and its users' information needs	Getting people involved in sharing interpretations and collaborating on a shared goal
Naming	Information objects are named centrally by professionals	Information objects are named locally by users
Authority	Established through reference to external sources	Established through autopoietic warrant

Computers

Certain attributes of digital information resources can be described very readily by computers, that is, those aspects pertaining to the computer files carrying the information. However, the information content itself is something computers still struggle with. Search engines can process 'bags' of words according to various algorithms and provide useful rankings of documents, but these are not descriptions. The best that 'expert systems' (such as the Web2MARC Generator) can do is produce 'skeletal' bibliographic records by identifying possible metadata from certain locations within web resources.

Automatic indexing is nevertheless a well-established field of research, although it has been partly superseded by efforts in content-based information retrieval. In automatic indexing, the computer's task is to provide terms that best represent the subject of a given resource. These terms may be derived directly from the content, or they may be based on a particular indexing language. In modern retrieval systems, however, index terms derived automatically from a text need not be presented to the user to select. Instead, the user typically enters terms in a search box and the system immediately returns the records, or resources, linked to those terms.

The automatic application of indexing languages remains of interest to a number of researchers, due to the inherent merits of controlled vocabularies (as discussed in the next chapter). Unfortunately, even with a predetermined vocabulary, and even when the resource is textual, computers still find it hard to identify the most appropriate terms to represent a resource's subject. Each document remains a bag of words, rather than something that is understood by the computer.

A field closely related to automatic indexing is that of *automatic classification*, in which a particular place in a classification scheme is chosen for each resource. Computers using a predefined classification scheme are typically 'supervised', which means that they start off with a set of 'training' documents, applying various machine-learning techniques. There is no doubt that computers are getting better at classifying documents, particularly in relatively narrow domains, but even in the best cases, they are still judged to be not quite as good as humans (Wang, 2009). Whether they are good *enough* really depends on the context.

Computers can also create their own classifications, usually based on *clustering algorithms*. The results are often interesting, but not necessarily intuitive or logical. They are usually flat (i.e. lacking hierarchical structure) and liable to change as new documents are added (Golub, 2006). Automatic clustering may work better as a post-search process, when result sets are presented to users for exploration. A result set clustered by the Yippy (formerly Vivisimo) search engine is shown in Figure 4.1.

Knowledge structures can also be automatically generated from collections of manually built controlled vocabularies. An example is the SKOSsy

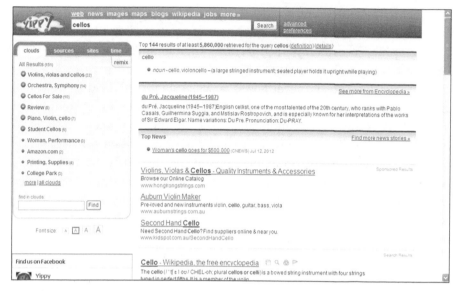

Figure 4.1 *Search results clustered (on the left) by Yippy (source: http://yippy.com)*

software, which derives vocabularies in English and German from the Semantic Web database DBPedia. The results are not always perfect, but can be edited by metadata specialists into useful products.

If computers have a hard time determining subject terms and creating structures, they have an even harder time producing coherent summaries comparable to abstracts written by humans. The best that computer applications can do, at the present time, is to identify and synthesize key sentences, or select a representative extract. Automatic *summarization* tends to be more effective with smaller documents, or less complex ones, or those without a strong narrative. There is even more work to be done before computers will be able to reliably present summaries of non-textual resources, such as cinematic or musical works.

We shall revisit the case for information retrieval by computer, as well as via social tagging, in Chapter 9. Irrespective of its source, however, the value of metadata can be assessed in certain basic ways, which we shall discuss in the next chapter.

References

Banush, D. and LeBlanc, J. (2007) Utility, Library Priorities, and Cataloging Policies,

Library Collections, Acquisitions, & Technical Services, **31** (2), 96–109.

Barrick, J. et al. (2005) Influencing Web-browsing Behavior with Intriguing and Informative Hyperlink Wording, *Journal of Information Science,* **31** (5), 433–45.

Bell, H. K. (2008) *From Flock Beds to Professionalism: a history of index-makers,* Oak Knoll.

Betts, L. and Hartley, J. (2008) Revising and Polishing a Structured Abstract: is it worth the time and effort? *Journal of the American Society for Information Science and Technology,* **59** (12), 1870–7.

Boydston, J. M. K. (2005) Supply and Demand for Cataloguers: present and future, *Library Resources & Technical Services,* **49** (4), 250–65.

Brodkin, J. (2007) *The Cost of Ineffective Search,* Network World, www.networkworld.com/news/2007/012307-wasted-searches.html.

Browne, G. and Jermey, J. (2007) *The Indexing Companion,* Cambridge University Press.

Golub, K. (2006) Automated Subject Classification of Textual Web Documents, *Journal of Documentation,* **62** (3), 350–71.

Gorzalski, M. (2008) Minimal Processing: its context and influence in the archival community, *Journal of Archival Organization,* **63** (3), 186–200.

Guy, M. and Tonkin, E. (2006) Folksonomies: tidying up tags? *D-Lib Magazine,* **12,** www.dlib.org/dlib/january06/guy/01guy.html.

Han, M.-J. and Hswe, P. (2010) The Evolving Role of the Metadata Librarian: competencies found in job descriptions, *Library Resources & Technical Services,* **54** (3), 129–41.

Hunter, J. (2009) Collaborative Semantic Tagging and Annotation Systems, *Annual Review of Information Science and Technology,* **43** (1), 1–84.

Janes, J. W. (1991) Relevance Judgements and the Incremental Presentation of Document Representations, *Information Processing & Management,* **27** (6), 629–46.

Lu, C., Marion, L. and Park, J. (2009) Cataloging Professionals in the Digital Environment: a content analysis of job descriptions, *Journal of the American Society for Information Science and Technology,* **60** (4), 844–57.

Mai, J.-E. (2011) Folksonomies and the New Order: authority in the digital order, *Knowledge Organization,* **38** (2), 114–22.

Primary Research Group (2011) *Academic Library Cataloging Practices Benchmarks.*

Schnittman, E. (2008) Discoverability and Access in Book Publishing: longtail marketing and content access models explored, *Publishing Research Quarterly,* **24** (2), 139–42.

Smith, T. (2007) Cataloging and You: measuring the efficacy of a folksonomy for subject analysis. In Lussky, J. (ed.), *Proceedings 18th Workshop of the American*

Society for Information Science and Technology Special Interest Group in Classification Research, ASIST.

Wang, J. (2009) An Extensive Study on Automated Dewey Decimal Classification, *Journal of the American Society for Information Science and Technology,* **60** (11), 2269–86.

Wellisch, H. H. (1994) Book and Periodical Indexing, *Journal of the American Society for Information Science,* **45** (8), 620–7.

Yee, M. M. (2009) Wholly Visionary: the American Library Association, the Library of Congress, and the card distribution program, *Library Resources & Technical Services,* **53** (2), 68–78.

5

Metadata quality

Introduction

We have talked previously about the purpose of different elements of resource description. In this chapter, we discuss what makes for *effective* metadata, as not all metadata fulfils its purpose equally well. There are several aspects to metadata quality, all of which the metadata specialist, in particular, needs to bear in mind. We shall also look at mechanisms for improving the quality of metadata, such as vocabulary control, and for assuring quality, and end our discussion by considering the costs that effective metadata incurs.

We should note first that the quality of metadata is dependent on both the elements represented and the values of these elements. We shall start by revisiting our earlier discussions about how some elements may be more *functional* than others in addressing users' information needs. We shall also consider the importance of *comprehensiveness*, whereby fuller descriptions, with more elements, address users' needs more thoroughly. Moving on to values, we shall discuss how their *accuracy* and *clarity* affect quality, and then spend some time on an aspect of great importance at both element and value levels, namely, *consistency*.

Functionality

Numerous metadata elements could be recorded in the description of an information resource. Some, however, are likely to be more useful than others. As we have already noted, their utility depends on the information context: users' needs, users' behaviour, the retrieval system and so on. Since it is not feasible to include all possible elements in a description, those that are included should be the most supportive of functional requirements. Determining exactly which ones these are is no easy task, and inevitably involves a degree of guesswork (we cannot be sure of future use), but careful study of the information context usually provides the metadata specialist with plenty of pointers.

Some aspects of the information context may be easier to study than others. Metadata specialists should generally be able to ascertain how their retrieval systems work, at least in basic terms. This may cover indexing rules, indicating which elements are indexed for certain searches, and which ones are not. If a particular record element is not indexed, this makes it of no use for the purposes of *finding* resources. Systems knowledge may also extend to display rules. If an element is not displayed, this makes it of no use for *selection* purposes. Ideally, metadata specialists should have a say in what is displayed and indexed.

Perhaps the most difficult aspect of the information context to study is the user. Not only are there likely to be many different users, but their information needs are often difficult to pinpoint (even for the users themselves). Nevertheless, user studies are routinely conducted in some subfields of information organization, such as information architecture, and are becoming more common in others.

Comprehensiveness

The comprehensiveness of resource description is not quite the same thing as the *amount* of metadata, which depends on the extent of each value, as well as the number of elements, recorded. However, there is clearly a trade-off between comprehensiveness and cost, with fuller descriptions generally taking longer to create. Metadata creators are thus often faced with a choice: describe more resources in less detail, or fewer resources in more detail. The level of detail may be based on the nature of the material and/or the nature of the user. Internet resources, for example, may be described in less detail, to support discovery but not selection, as they can be inspected directly (Harcourt, Wacker and Wolley, 2007; Liu, 2004). Users of university libraries may be provided with fuller descriptions than, say, users of school libraries. Library cataloguers often talk in terms of 'minimum' records and 'full' records, and of levels in between. Most libraries end up with a mixture of record levels represented in their catalogues.

Accuracy

The accuracy of metadata is, of course, often critical. Resources are usually found, identified, selected or obtained on the basis of small pieces of information, so a small error can make all the difference. Inaccuracies can occur in either the observation of the attribute (e.g. a misinterpretation of the subject) or the recording of the value (e.g. a typographical error). Even metadata specialists can make mistakes, particularly if they are unfamiliar with the content or nature of the resource. Further, their mistakes may have a more detrimental effect because of the high level of trust attached to their descriptions.

Fortunately, modern computer systems allow metadata to be edited much more readily than was the case in the past. Their greater accessibility also makes it more likely for errors to be spotted and amended. In the Web 2.0 environment, editorial capacity may even extend to members of the general public, as well as to fellow information professionals. Some types of inaccuracy, such as mis-spelling, can also be identified, or at least suggested, by the computer systems themselves.

A special case of inaccurate metadata is when the value for an attribute of an information resource *changes*, but is not correspondingly changed in the description. Whether an attribute of an information resource *can* change depends on how the information resource, as well as the attribute, is defined, although all resources can change at the item level (e.g. its physical condition might deteriorate). A whole category of resources, including serials and websites, are defined by library cataloguers as *continuing*, that is, resources that continue to develop over time. Consequently, as new issues of a serial are published, their details are added to its record. Likewise, when a website is revamped, this needs to be reflected in its record. Of course, there is a cost involved in updating descriptions to match constantly changing resources, and metadata specialists may need to consider whether a change is significant enough to warrant attention.

Clarity

Accurate metadata is of little use if it is unintelligible. An obvious example of this is where elements are recorded in a language unknown to users. Even if the language is known, users may be unfamiliar with terms or abbreviations employed by metadata creators. Indeed, library cataloguers have often been criticized for using jargon and abbreviations known only to themselves.

Thus, they commonly refer to the main title as the 'title proper', a subtitle as 'other title information', and the same title in a different language as a 'parallel title'. They may not even use words, but instead assume that users are, or become, familiar with particular punctuation. International Standard Bibliographic Description (ISBD) signifies a subtitle by a preceding colon, a parallel title by an equals sign, dimensions by a semi-colon and so on. The good news is that metadata specialists are increasingly aware of the need to translate their jargon into less technical language so that a wider audience can understand it.

Even when common language is used, there are still choices to be made. Some terms may be clearer than others. When the metadata is restricted to a small number of terms, as in the case of a website menu, the terms need to be selected with particular care. As well as being somewhat ambiguous, language changes over time. Terms familiar to people a century ago may not be so now. Thus, values may need to be revised not only because resources change, but because they themselves change.

Metadata is sometimes disambiguated through the addition of clarifying terms. This most often occurs when a word, called a *homonym*, has completely different meanings. For example, the subject term 'Banks' could be clarified with the qualifier '(Oceanography)' to indicate that it has nothing to do with finance. One of the aims of controlled vocabularies (discussed later in this chapter) is to ensure that homonyms are used for only one of their meanings.

Although metadata needs to be clear, it also needs to be reasonably brief. That is, it should be *succinct*. There are two reasons for this. First, it enables more information to be presented to the user: more elements and more descriptions. Second, it may improve the precision of search results, as the more terms used, the more danger there is of irrelevant, or less relevant, hits. However, brevity was probably more important in the days of card catalogues and non-digital metadata, when space constraints and printing costs were major issues.

Consistency

Using the same elements across descriptions, and the same values for particular meanings, greatly enhances retrieval. It allows for semantic interoperability within and across systems. A subject search may 'miss' resources if some records do not include a subject element. Likewise, resources may be missed if some indexers use subject terms not used by the searcher. Consistency also helps users to read and interpret descriptions, by allowing them to become familiar with structures and terminology. Thus consistency can help with all functions of metadata (finding, identifying, selecting, obtaining and navigating).

Lancaster (2003, 71) lists seven factors affecting the level of indexing consistency:

> number of terms assigned
> controlled vocabulary versus free text indexing
> size and specificity of vocabulary
> characteristics of subject matter and its terminology
> indexer factors
> tools available to indexer
> length of item to be indexed.

Information organization has traditionally investigated these factors with the aim of increasing consistency, particularly *between* indexers. It has, however, been pointed out that consistent indexing could be consistently bad. Thus, most indexing studies assume that agreement amongst indexers is more likely to be based on accurate insights than inaccurate ones. While this may be true, it still does not necessarily follow that consistent indexing is reflective of consistency amongst searchers. As Mai (2011, 116) argues, 'in large and heterogeneous settings where there are no unified contexts, goals, or objectives against which the objects can be named and ordered, professionals cannot, in a meaningful way, answer the question: "What is it?"' For instance, some members of a community might consider a documentary to be about terrorism, whereas for others it might be about freedom fighters. In such cases, indexing variations may be a virtue, covering a broader range of views as to what a document is about.

Nevertheless, consistency between indexer and searcher (if not between indexers) is a good thing. Indexers can increase this kind of consistency by learning more about the searcher and by teaching the searcher more about the indexing practice. A chief way of achieving consistency is through *standardization*. We have already noted how information resource description is often conventionalized, and how these conventions sometimes become standards. There are two basic reasons for applying standards: they ensure 'best practice' and they ensure consistency. The importance of consistency in information organization makes the application of standards a major concern for most metadata specialists. There are standards for elements, values, formats and transmission. We shall look more closely at a whole host of standards for information resource description in Chapters 7 and 8.

Vocabulary and authority control

Achieving consistency of metadata values can be particularly challenging, but can also greatly improve the effectiveness of an information retrieval system. The values used by the searcher may not be consistent with the values used by the indexer unless both searcher and indexer share a common (i.e. standardized) language, known as a *controlled vocabulary*, in which all values are controlled so that each has a single, specific meaning, and so that no concept can be expressed using more than one value.

Vocabulary control has been a key process in information organization practice for many decades, especially in relation to subject indexing. To explain how it works, let us take a concrete example. Suppose a database provides access to articles on health topics. Some indexers might decide to use the term 'influenza' to describe the subject of some of the articles; other indexers might use the term 'flu' instead. In fact, some indexers might use the term 'influenza' on some occasions, but 'flu' on others. There is clearly a lack of consistency here, as the two words mean the same thing, that is, they are *synonyms*. To retrieve all the relevant articles, users would need to search on both 'influenza' and 'flu'. Unfortunately, they might not think to do this. (They might not even think of the two words.) To relieve users of this cognitive load, a controlled vocabulary can be applied, so that indexers are directed to always use one of the terms (say, 'influenza') and never the other term (say, 'flu'), for the disease. If users search under 'flu', they are referred to the other, *preferred* term ('influenza'), or the system automatically retrieves the records with the preferred term.

Controlled vocabularies indicate their preferred terms through *cross-references*. They are conventionally set out in this sort of way:

Flu
   use **Influenza**

The cross-reference advises indexers and, if necessary, searchers to use 'influenza' and not 'flu'. Cross-references may also be employed to deal with different word forms, such as alternative spellings, e.g.

Organisations
> *use* **Organizations**

They may also be used to conflate near-synonyms, when it is thought that the meanings would not be sufficiently distinctive in the searcher's mind, e.g.

Images
> *use* **Pictures**

Similarly, antonyms might sometimes be treated as two sides of the same coin, e.g.

Sickness
> *use* **Health**

Compilers of controlled vocabularies rarely attempt to cover every term that might be expressed in natural language. They may, however, try to cover all the *concepts* that an indexer might want to use a term for, in a given context. Thus a medical vocabulary might cover most diseases, though it might not include a reference from, say, 'chin cough', an old name for whooping cough. Controlled vocabularies are mostly limited to a particular subject area, and often to a particular (natural) language. Synonyms for concepts to be covered may be cross-referenced, and homonyms disambiguated. The resulting set of preferred terms, each representing a particular concept, are the *only* terms that can be used by the indexer when applying the controlled vocabulary.

Indexing (including subject indexing) does not have to be controlled, of course, and many retrieval systems function reasonably well without a controlled vocabulary. However, vocabulary control can, at least in some contexts, lead to a greater correspondence between what is searched for and what is retrieved. Furthermore, it can also provide a logical *structure* for the indexing/search language, which may improve the *accuracy* of both indexing and searches. This entails making a different kind of cross-reference, indicating a certain relationship between the concepts of two preferred terms. Instead of 'use' or 'see', the cross-reference may advise to 'see also'. For example, the following cross-reference indicates that there is an *associative* relationship between the concepts represented by the two terms 'trees' and 'shrubs':

Trees
  see also **Shrubs**

That is, the two terms stand for slightly different, but related, things. An indexer or searcher looking up 'trees' in the controlled vocabulary is thereby alerted to another term, which might be a more accurate term to use, or which might be used in addition. More specific types of relationship might also be indicated, such as 'broader' terms (i.e. for broader concepts) and 'narrower' terms (i.e. for narrower concepts). Chapter 8 looks further at the ways in which controlled vocabularies are structured through these (assigned) relationships.

We have already seen how terms can be disambiguated through the use of qualifiers, as in 'Banks (Oceanography)'. Controlled vocabularies quite often make use of such qualifiers, but may also elaborate on the meaning of a term by adding a more detailed *scope note*, indicating the scope of the term's intended use. For example, a note might advise:

  Use **Trees** *for tall woody plants, but use* **Shrubs** *for shorter woody plants with multiple stems.*

Thus, scope notes provide definitions for, and demarcations between, index terms.

Values can be controlled for all sorts of other metadata elements apart from subject. In library cataloguing, the names of people and organizations (referred to as 'corporate bodies') are also commonly controlled. This is necessary because people and organizations sometimes change their names, or use different forms of a name, as well as sometimes sharing the same name. Cataloguers often refer to the compilation of controlled terms and names as *authority control*. Hence they create 'name authority files' and 'subject authority files' by establishing *authorized* (i.e. preferred) name headings and subject headings. Authority files are routinely consulted when catalogue records are created.

Names are cross-referenced in authority files in ways similar to those for subject terms. Thus, the authorized name for a person is referenced from other names they might be known by, e.g.

  Munro, H. H.
    see **Saki**

When people are considered to have different 'bibliographic identities' through their use of different names for different kinds of resource (e.g. fiction versus mathematical treatise), they may be represented in the catalogue by more than one authorized heading. The two names would be linked, both ways, through cross-references of the form:

Carroll, Lewis
see also **Dodgson, Charles**

Library cataloguers also encounter different authors with the same name. There have been thousands of people called 'John Smith', for instance, including many associated with various information resources. The cataloguer may attempt to disambiguate by inserting a middle name or initial. For instance, they might use 'John Andrew Smith' for one author, and 'John Kevin Smith' for another. If the cataloguer has the misfortune to be confronted with two people with *exactly* the same name, they might look to distinguish between them in some other way. This is why we sometimes see years of birth in library catalogues. For example,

Smith, John Francis, 1932–
Smith, John Francis, 1957–

Of course, the user may not know when the John Francis Smith that they are interested in was born. Nevertheless, the cataloguer has saved the user some work by separating out two quite distinct sets of resources: those associated with the John Francis Smith born in 1932 and those associated with the John Francis Smith born in 1957. After a brief perusal of the records under each heading, the user is likely to be able to identify the set of resources relevant to their search.

Library cataloguing deals with names of organizations in similar fashion, although changes of name are often considered to constitute a change of organization, in which case both names are authorized. For example,

Amoco
see also **BP**

Organizations also sometimes have more than one form of name, in which case *see* references may be made, e.g.

British Petroleum
  see **BP**

Different organizations with the same name are also disambiguated, e.g.

Holy Cross Church (Bearsted, England)
Holy Cross Church (Warsaw, Poland)

More advanced authority control work covers other elements such as titles and series names. By increasing consistency, authority control supports bibliographic control. In a fully controlled catalogue, all the headings in the bibliographic records are linked to corresponding authority records in authority files. The authority records provide not only the authorized headings, but also cross-references and notes.

Unfortunately, authority control work entails a great deal of time and effort on the part of the cataloguer, which is why many libraries do not maintain their own authority files. Nevertheless, their catalogues can still be supported by externally maintained files, such as those of the Library of Congress, which can be downloaded on a regular basis. In any case, most library management systems give cataloguers the option of creating and editing 'local' authority records.

Principles of best practice

We have touched on several important aspects of metadata quality, which represent criteria that might be used to evaluate information resource description. Clearly, it is not the case that all metadata is equal, although it may be difficult to ascertain how much better some resource descriptions are than others. Ultimately, what makes for good metadata is its potential to support effective information retrieval. Its adherence to certain standards may indicate that professionals were involved in its creation, but this does not in itself make it good metadata. The standards being applied have to fit the information context. The mark of a good metadata specialist, in fact, is one who knows when to deviate from the standards, when to bend the rules. It could, for instance, be very helpful to add a certain element, despite its absence from a template. Although blind obedience to standards might save information professionals some time, with fewer decisions needing to be made, it may also result in less relevant resources for end-users and cost users more time.

Metadata creation is therefore not simply a matter of following rules and guidelines. It is also very much about exercising judgement, and developing knowledge and skills that will lead to better metadata. Metadata specialists need to know their users, their collections and resources, and the retrieval systems they are working with. They also need to develop an eye for detail, a very clear, succinct form of expression and a systematic and thorough approach. Faced with choices about what and how to describe, they need to apply principles, as well as standards.

Quality assurance

If the quality of metadata can make a significant difference to information retrieval, it makes sense for information agencies to monitor and evaluate resource description and, if necessary, take steps to improve it. The professionalization of metadata creation and management goes *some* way towards assuring quality. In the last chapter, we discussed various kinds of metadata specialist, many of whom will normally possess professional qualifications. However, these qualifications mostly pertain to a broader information field, such as librarianship or archival studies, and certainly do not guarantee the capacity to create high-quality metadata. Instead, they represent the first step on a developmental journey. Further steps can be supported by various forms of continuing professional development. Information agencies can also do much to assure quality by adopting various best-practice standards, although again, this does not confirm quality. Standards may not always be fully adhered to, nor, as we have just mentioned, are they always applied in the most effective way.

Ultimately, the product itself – the metadata – has to be examined and assessed. Many information agencies establish *quality control* (QC) processes in which metadata is checked when entered into the retrieval system. For example, a supervisor might monitor the records created by an inexperienced library cataloguer, or staff might check records downloaded from an external database. More independent evaluations, or *audits*, may also be carried out, as part of a *quality assurance* (QA) process, to check that the QC processes are themselves effective. Such audits often involve sets of quality *measures*, and *benchmarks* which the information agency aims to reach. QC and QA processes can be particularly important when most of the metadata is outsourced.

The evaluation of metadata can be based on all sorts of criteria, although one or more of those aspects of quality described earlier in this chapter is likely to be involved. Some evaluations can be assisted by computer programs (e.g. they may check for typographic, spelling, or formatting errors). However, deeper evaluations are usually conducted by human experts. Often information agencies devise their own *checklists* or *scorecards*, weighting the various criteria, according to their own information context. Checklists for indexing are discussed by Smith and Kells (2005), while a British Library cataloguing scorecard is described by Danskin (2006).

Even if metadata is deemed to be of excellent quality, it is of little value if the system in which it operates is ineffective. The evaluation of information retrieval systems has been carried out in both experimental and real-life settings for many years. The criteria that have been used include: the classic information retrieval measures of *recall* and *precision*; response time; usability; and user satisfaction. Metadata quality may be a factor in all of these, but never the only one.

Detailed discussion of the evaluation of information retrieval systems is outside the scope of this book, but we note the definitions of recall and precision, as metadata values can affect these measures very considerably.

$$\text{Recall} = \frac{\text{total relevant documents retrieved}}{\text{total relevant documents in system}}$$

$$\text{Precision} = \frac{\text{total relevant documents retrieved}}{\text{total documents retrieved}}$$

The two measures were first devised as part of the famous 'Cranfield' tests of the late 1950s and early 1960s (Sparck Jones, 1981a; 1981b), which indicated that there tends to be an inverse relationship between them: recall is increased at the expense of precision, and vice versa (Cleverdon, 1972). For instance, recall can be increased by indexing a document to a greater depth, so that more concepts are represented, but this is also likely to reduce precision, as the chance of 'false drops' likewise increases. We shall consider further the effect of indexing policy on retrieval in Chapter 8.

The measures of recall and precision have been criticized on a number of fronts. First, they are traditionally based on a binary distinction between relevant and irrelevant, when in reality relevance is a continuous variable. Second, they may not reflect what users actually look at, which may be just the first screen or two of search results. As Eastman (2002) points out, in the internet context, 300 hits may be better than 30,000 because it is the top few hits that matter. Third, the measures count similar documents in the same way as dissimilar ones, even though users may deem a document of little utility if they have already learnt the relevant information from other documents. It is also unclear whether the measures should be given equal weight in assessment, though certain formulae involving the two indices have been proposed (and used) to represent the 'optimal' trade-off. In addition, there are practical issues. For instance, recall can be difficult to measure when dealing with very large collection sets (the ultimate of which, of course, is the internet as a whole).

The overarching problem with these measures is that they are typically applied in experimental settings largely insulated from various real-world considerations. We have already noted how 'relevance' can include all sorts of criteria beyond topic, yet most information retrieval experiments dwell exclusively on this attribute. It is widely recognized that the effectiveness of a retrieval system is ultimately dependent on a range of factors, not just on how it performs in information retrieval experiments. No matter how high recall and/or precision, if users do not like using it, then the system cannot really be regarded as effective (Al-Maskari and Sanderson, 2010). As Mooer's Law states, 'an information retrieval system will tend not to be used whenever it is more painful and troublesome for a customer to have information than not to have it' (Chu, 2010, 10).

Cost-benefit analysis

High-quality metadata does not, as a rule, come cheap. It is typically produced by professionals entitled to a professional wage. The more detailed the description, the longer it takes to create, and the more expensive it becomes. Calhoun (2006) estimated that American research libraries spent a total of $239 million on technical services staff in 2004. Sometimes libraries and other information agencies may be fortunate enough to find metadata that they can use *gratis*, such as catalogue records downloadable from the Library of Congress website. This is unlikely to cover all of their needs, however. Most sources of high-quality metadata charge for it.

Metadata costs need to be weighed carefully against metadata benefits.

There are many competing claims on the finite resources of information agencies, as well as on the finite time of metadata specialists. An information agency is sometimes required to comply with a particular standard, but usually the choice to provide high-quality metadata is theirs. The general view is that the value of metadata has a 'long tail', with a handful of 'core' elements typically used a great deal and many 'minor' elements used only occasionally. Yet this still begs the question: at what point in the tail do costs outweigh value?

It is, unfortunately, rarely possible to answer this question very precisely. Although costs can usually be estimated in financial terms, putting a monetary value on metadata is a much more difficult exercise, and few attempts at it have been made (Hider, 2008). Those valuations that have been made have not drilled down to different levels of metadata quality. Moreover, they only suggest that metadata provides a certain value for money, not that it provides the *best* value for money.

Information agencies under budgetary pressures may be tempted to cut expenditure on metadata because of its relatively low profile: users may not notice its disappearance quite so much. However, low profile is not the same thing as low importance. Thus the challenge for metadata specialists is to demonstrate the high importance of resource description. It may be unrealistic to claim that all resources need very detailed metadata, but it may be possible to argue that some resources, at least, are important enough to warrant professional attention. The implementation of different 'levels' of resource description, even within a single retrieval system, is now very much the norm. Yet we end up asking the same question: what should these different levels be, and for which resources? Different information agencies will settle on different answers. It is a question we shall return to in Chapter 9.

Whatever the answer, professional description is more affordable if its cost can be shared across institutions. For a long time, information professionals have worked on ways of doing this; the next chapter looks at some of the fruits of their labours.

References

Al-Maskari, A. and Sanderson, M. (2010) A Review of Factors Influencing User Satisfaction in Information Retrieval, *Journal of the American Society for Information Science and Technology*, **61** (5), 859–68.

Calhoun, K. (2006) *The Changing Nature of the Catalog and its Integration with Other*

Discovery Tools: final report, Library of Congress, www.loc.gov/catdir/calhoun-report-final.pdf.

Chu, H. (2010) *Information Representation and Retrieval in the Digital Age*, 2nd edn, American Society for Information Science and Technology.

Cleverdon, C. W. (1972) On the Inverse Relationship of Recall and Precision, *Journal of Documentation*, **28**, 195–201.

Danskin, A. (2006) What Difference Does it Make? Measuring the quality of cataloguing and the catalogue, *Catalogue & Index*, **154**, 9–12.

Eastman, C. M. (2002) 30,000 Hits May Be Better than 300: precision anomalies in internet searches, *Journal of the American Society for Information Science*, **53** (11), 879–82.

Harcourt, K., Wacker, M. and Wolley, I. (2007) Automated Access Level Cataloging for Internet Resources at Columbia University Libraries, *Library Resources & Technical Services*, **51** (3), 212–25.

Hider, P. (2008) How Much Are Technical Services Worth? Using the contingent valuation method to estimate the added value of collection management and access, *Library Resources & Technical Services*, **52** (4), 254–62.

Lancaster, F. W. (2003) *Indexing and Abstracting in Theory and Practice*, 3rd edn, Facet Publishing.

Liu, Z. (2004) The Evolution of Documents and its Impacts, *Journal of Documentation*, **60** (3), 279–88.

Mai, J.-E. (2011) Folksonomies and the New Order: authority in the digital order, *Knowledge Organization*, **38** (2), 114–22.

Smith, S. and Kells, K. (2005) *Inside Indexing: the decision-making process*, Northwest Indexing Press.

Sparck Jones, K. (1981a) Retrieval System Tests 1958–1978. In Sparck Jones, K. (ed.), *Information Retrieval Experiment*, Butterworths.

Sparck Jones, K. (1981b) The Cranfield Tests. In Sparck Jones, K. (ed.), *Information Retrieval Experiment*, Butterworths.

6

Sharing metadata

Introduction

The standardization of metadata enables it to be used in different information retrieval systems, and thus in different institutions. The sharing of metadata offers several benefits to information agencies and other interested parties. Most importantly, it means that metadata only has to be created once, saving a great deal of time and expense. It likewise means that metadata creation can be centralized, and assigned to those most qualified to do it. In addition, quality may also be improved because of more people working with the same metadata: there is more chance of its being amended or enhanced.

Simply making metadata available to users is, of course, an act of sharing. However, this chapter focuses on the sharing of metadata amongst systems. In the online environment, this entails not only the standardization of the metadata itself, but also of its *transmission*. We shall discuss various transmission protocols, along with other standards, in Chapters 7 and 8. First, in this chapter, we shall look at some of the mechanisms and arrangements that enable systems to share metadata. These may involve a two-way *exchange* or a one-way *transfer* of resource description. Both the benefit and the cost of quality metadata have spurred many information agencies into collaborative action, with, as we shall see, some impressive results.

Library catalogue records

One of the most prevalent information retrieval systems prior to the arrival of computers was the library card catalogue. Librarians were quick to see the potential efficiency gains from having record cards copied and distributed for insertion into multiple catalogues. Not many libraries, however, were in a position to mass-produce their catalogue cards, and so sharing tended to be in one direction. The Library of Congress (LC) began its card distribution service in 1901 and has been a leading record supplier ever since (Yee, 2009). Other national libraries, such as the British Library (in the guise of the British National Bibliography), also came to assume a responsibility for providing catalogue copy to their library communities, while a few companies, such as H. H. Wilson in the USA, started supplying cards on a commercial basis. A small number of libraries sent copy to suppliers, such as LC, for editing and distribution.

The computer revolutionized not only the library catalogue, but also the sharing of its records. Indeed, machine-readable catalogue records were originally developed by LC in the mid-1960s to facilitate record distribution. Soon afterwards, libraries started to build the first automated library systems, at the heart of which were databases of bibliographic records. In the early days, these database systems tended to be shared by library consortia, since the costs involved were considerable. A notable example was a group of college and university libraries in Ohio, which in 1967 founded the Ohio College Library Center, later becoming the Online Computer Library Center, or OCLC (www.oclc.org). Its bibliographic database is now the world's largest repository of library catalogue records.

The shared databases were initially populated with machine-readable records from the main suppliers, such as LC. However, these records rarely accounted for all of a library's holdings and it was not long before constituent libraries started to contribute records of their own, which could thus be used by other libraries within their consortium. The exchange of library catalogue records had begun in earnest.

Bibliographic networks

In the 1970s and 1980s many more libraries acquired their own automated systems as they became more affordable, but this by no means spelt the end of shared databases. Instead, they became the hubs of *bibliographic networks*, in which libraries were, and still are, linked together through the central database. These networks offer both record copy and a platform for record exchange. They subscribe, on behalf of their member libraries, to the services of major record suppliers (also known as *bibliographic utilities*), whose files are uploaded to the central database for all members to access. In earlier times, records were downloaded into local systems via tape; nowadays, of course, they can be downloaded via the internet. When a record for a resource cannot be found, a cataloguer from one of the member libraries creates a record for it in the central database or, alternatively, creates a record in their local system, after which it is uploaded to the central database. The record can then be downloaded and used by any other member library that needs it. If member libraries ensure that all their holdings are represented in the central database, it also becomes, in effect, a *union catalogue*.

As library automation continued to expand through the 1980s and 1990s, many more libraries joined bibliographic networks, which often catered for particular types of library in particular geographic regions, that is, those with similar record supply needs. Some countries established national networks (e.g. the Australian Bibliographic Network, now Libraries Australia). University and research libraries in the UK formed the Consortium of University and Research Libraries (CURL); those in the USA had already established the Research Libraries Group (RLG). Some networks were affiliated to larger networks, such as OCLC. An example of a school library network is the Schools Catalogue Information Service (SCIS), which covers many of the school libraries in Australia and New Zealand.

As the networks grew in size, so did their databases. Figure 6.1 charts the growth of OCLC's database, now known as WorldCat. Other major bibliographic databases included: the Research Libraries Information Network (RLIN), the union catalogue of RLG; the University of Toronto Library Automated System (UTLAS); and the Washington (later Western)

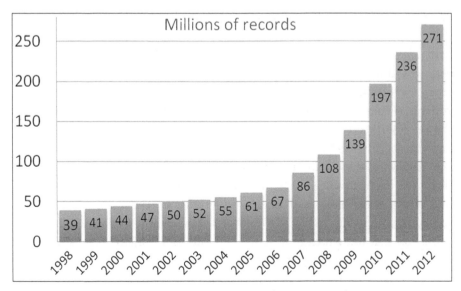

Figure 6.1 *OCLC WorldCat growth since 1998 (source: OCLC)*

Library Network (WLN). Many libraries, and not just the largest ones, contributed to the phenomenal growth of MARC records. The results are a great testament to library co-operation.

As libraries' internet connections became progressively faster and cheaper through the 1990s and 2000s, there became less of a need for bibliographic databases to be shared at a regional level. There has, therefore, been a trend towards consolidation, in which many smaller databases and networks have merged with larger ones. Some networks have survived by branching out into other areas of business, such as software development, document delivery and training. The majority of libraries in the English-speaking world are now serviced by just a handful of very large databases, with OCLC becoming the ever more dominant player (having acquired, amongst others, RLG, WLN and UTLAS). However, new companies, such as LibLime (www.liblime.com) and SkyRiver (http://theskyriver.com), have recently entered the market, promising easy-to-use services for considerably lower fees, so perhaps a tipping-point has been reached. At the time of writing, OCLC has, according to its website, over 25,000 institutional members, with over 70,000 libraries represented on WorldCat from across 170 countries and territories. Nowadays, the company provides many other services apart from record supply, yet WorldCat remains OCLC's primary asset. Its contents can be searched at www.worldcat.org.

While most bibliographic networks maintain a central database, modern computer architecture also allows libraries to download each other's records directly from each other's local systems. In this distributed model, the client software searches the servers of other catalogues for the required record and retrieves any matching records for downloading into its own system. However, although the model may seem straightforward and efficient, it can run into several problems (Cousins, 1999). Not all libraries are equipped with the necessary servers; when large numbers of systems are involved, traffic jams can occur; searches tend to be less precise; records do not benefit from the upgrading that occurs in a central database; and the cataloguing is less likely to benefit from centrally maintained authority files. For these reasons, and others, most bibliographic networks continue to use central databases, some of which are publicly available (such as the Copac catalogue, at http://copac.ac.uk, which represents the holdings of 'many major university, specialist, and national libraries in the UK and Ireland').

Nevertheless, a number of major libraries, including LC and the British Library, have made their records available for download directly from their catalogues over the internet. There is also the option of adopting a hybrid model of exchange, in which contributing libraries create metadata in their own systems, but also upload copies to a central database for searching Woodley (2005).

Whichever method is employed, the sharing of catalogue records requires libraries to agree on certain standards. This has always been the case: in earlier days, records were distributed on standard 3 by 5 inch cards to fit into catalogue drawers. Likewise, the format of machine-readable records had to be standardized so that different computers could store them. The record format developed by LC evolved into the Machine-Readable Cataloguing (MARC) standard used in countless automated library systems of today. The MARC format not only allows computer systems to import copies of catalogue records from other systems, it also indicates how the metadata in the records should be indexed and displayed, in other words, how the records should be processed, or 'read', by the computer system. We shall look at the MARC standard in more detail in the next chapter.

Agreeing to apply the MARC standard is only a first step when it comes to sharing library cataloguing, however. Most libraries want their catalogue records to contain particular elements recorded in particular ways. It is therefore very helpful if libraries agree to a minimum set of elements, to be based on certain *content* standards (some of which will be covered in Chapters 7 and 8).

As well as agreeing to adhere to format and content standards, libraries joining bibliographic networks sign up to a broader set of rights and obligations. They are usually charged various fees in return for access to the network's databases, and may be obliged to contribute records for resources not already represented in those databases. Typically, member libraries also have a responsibility to add holdings information to records they use, so as to maintain a union catalogue.

Adhering to a network's standards and policies does not prevent libraries from having cataloguing policies of their own. Many libraries, in fact, edit records in their local systems according to local policies that may be at odds with those of the network. This is not a problem, of course, as long as the changes are not also made to the 'master' record in the network's database. Increasingly, records are enhanced by the inclusion of tables of contents, dust jacket images and the like.

The sharing of catalogue records has enabled libraries to provide detailed catalogues that would otherwise probably not be viable. It has also enabled libraries to cast a wider net over the bibliographic universe. Although IFLA's programme of Universal Bibliographic Control (UBC) has now been superseded, its general aim remains: for the libraries around the world to co-ordinate their cataloguing so that all of the world's published knowledge is accounted for. The UBC system, in which national libraries take primary responsibility for publications emanating from their respective jurisdictions, likewise continues, supported by legal deposit laws.

Another notable arrangement amongst various major libraries, mostly but not exclusively in North America, is the Program for Cooperative Cataloging (PCC, www.loc.gov/aba/pcc), administered by LC. It comprises four components: the Name Authority Cooperative Program (NACO), the Subject Authority Cooperative Program (SACO), the Monographic Bibliographic Record Cooperative Program (BIBCO) and the Cooperative Online Serials Program (CONSER). The PCC website explains that: 'through these four programs, the PCC achieves several goals. The programs create and co-operatively maintain bibliographic records in the shared database OCLC and distribute authority records through the freely available LC/NACO and LC/SACO Authority Files. Bibliographic and authority records contributed by the diverse membership of the PCC assure access to rare, unique, or otherwise unknown resources.'

Metadata for search engines

As well as sharing their metadata with each other, libraries have now started supplying their records to internet search companies, in a bid to make their catalogues more accessible and visible across the web. For example, OCLC provides the contents of its WorldCat database for indexing on search engines such as Google, Yahoo! and Windows Live Search. The library community has spent enormous amounts of time and effort over the years producing detailed descriptions of its resources, and wants as many people as possible to benefit from this metadata.

Nor is it only libraries that want their resources to be easily found on the web. Other information agencies, such as museums and archives, are equally keen to promote their assets. Indeed, this may be the main reason for making their metadata sharable, since museums and archives generally have less cause to share metadata with each other, given the uniqueness of the items in their collections. Just as MARC records can be downloaded from library catalogues, other kinds of metadata can be harvested for reuse by various kinds of retrieval tool, including subject gateways and web search engines. To this end, the metadata is put up on servers that conform to a particular transmission protocol, such as that developed by the Open Archives Initiative (OAI, www.openarchives.org).

Similarly, universities and other research agencies are interested in raising the profile of the work carried out by their scholars and scientists. Many have built repositories for their staff's research publications and connected these to the web. The repositories can be searched through the metadata linked to each resource, but some institutions have taken the next step and offered this metadata for harvesting. In this way, valuable resources, such as NASA's technical reports, are now accessible through a wide range of websites, including those of Google Scholar and OAIster, OCLC's database of OAI metadata.

The development of freely accessible scholarly repositories, which form a key component of the 'open access' movement, is having a major impact on academic publishing. Commercial presses are revising their business models and using metadata to help promote their products, just as the not-for-profit information agencies are. They are also establishing partnerships and making deals with companies such as Google, supplying metadata and, in certain cases, partial access to the content itself. Some also provide metadata to libraries, known as *cataloguing in publication* (CIP) and used for provisional catalogue records.

Libraries, museums, archives, universities and publishers are all coming to realize that their websites are not necessarily the first port of call for information seekers. The reality is that, far more often, search engines such as Google are. Instead of battling against this reality, it may be better to adapt to the new information environment and work with these key players to uncover as much of the 'hidden web' as possible. OCLC and other agencies report that exposure via Google has resulted in marked increases in the use of both metadata and resources (Dawson and Hamilton, 2006).

Interoperability

The sharing of metadata between information retrieval systems works only through the co-operation of the parties involved. For metadata to be interoperable, that is, to work in different systems, then either it needs to be *standardized* or it needs to be *converted*. Where metadata is shared by a relatively homogenous community of practice, it may be possible for the agencies to agree on various standards, as has been the case in the library domain. However, if this is not possible, then metadata can still be shared if it is converted into a form that works in the host system. With information agencies increasingly working across domains, interest in this alternative path to interoperability has grown, to the extent that it is now quite common for retrieval systems to work with a mixture of standards and formats.

The conversion, or mapping, of metadata may be carried out at the level of format, element or value (as defined in Chapter 1). Often, it needs to take place at both format and element levels, and sometimes at all three. Applications based on generic mappings convert the incoming metadata into data that can be processed by the host system and that can provide for effective retrieval. The mappings of different sets of elements are sometimes called *crosswalks.* Unfortunately, mapping across metadata standards is rarely a straightforward, one-to-one exercise. Different element sets cover different attributes. Moreover, they often cover the same attributes in different ways, so that several elements may need to be mapped to a single element, and vice versa. As with the translation of natural languages, crosswalks can be a little rough around the edges, and different versions can be equally valid. In general, they work best when the standards involved have been developed within the same community of practice (Godby, Smith and Childress, 2003).

An example of a frequently applied crosswalk is that which converts MARC records into a simpler format called Dublin Core. (We shall examine both these standards more closely in the next chapter.) There are lots of fields in MARC that are simply not covered in Dublin Core. This may lead to significant data loss. Further, there are Dublin Core elements that may be covered by several MARC fields. For instance, the MARC format has different fields for the names of authors, co-authors, corporate authors and so on. They may all get mapped to the Creator element in Dublin Core. In this case the metadata is not completely lost, but some of its meaning is, so that its richness is reduced. Finally, there are MARC fields that partially map to a given Dublin Core element. For instance, the '700' field in MARC records can represent the name of a co-author, in which case it maps to the Creator element in Dublin Core, but it can also represent the names of other people associated with the resource, in which case the Creator element may not be appropriate. In such cases, the mapping becomes an approximation.

Metadata standards are still important even when crosswalks are used. If all of the imported metadata conforms closely to a particular standard, then a crosswalk may work reasonably well. However, if the metadata is not already standardized, then a great deal of manual editing may be required, which may not be practicable. Fortunately, there are now well-established metadata standards in many domains, not just librarianship, as we shall see in the following two chapters. These standards are being applied by increasing numbers of metadata creators, while crosswalks between many of them have also been established and are increasingly being implemented.

References

Cousins, S. (1999) Virtual OPACs versus Union Database: two models of union catalogue provision, *Electronic Library*, **17** (2), 9–103.

Dawson, A. and Hamilton, V. (2006) Optimising Metadata to Make High-value Content More Accessible to Google Users, *Journal of Documentation*, **62** (3), 307–27.

Godby, C. J., Smith, D. and Childress, E. (2003) Two paths to interoperable metadata. In *DC-2003: Proceedings of the International DCMI Metadata Conference and Workshop, September 28–October 2, 2003, Seattle, Washington USA*, http://library.oclc.org/cdm/singleitem/collection/p267701cdl27/id/354/rec/14.

Woodley, M. S. (2005) Crosswalks the Path to Universal Success? In Gill, T. et al. (eds), *Introduction to Metadata: pathways to digital information*, version 2.1, J. Paul Getty Trust, www.getty.edu/research/conducting_research/standards/intrometadata/metadata.html.

Yee, M. M. (2009) Wholly Visionary: the American Library Association, the Library of Congress, and the card distribution program, *Library Resources & Technical Services*, **53** (2), 68–78.

7

Metadata standards

Introduction

We have noted, in the preceding chapters, some of the benefits of applying various kinds of metadata standard. Their use can improve the consistency of resource description and facilitate the sharing of metadata; they can also assist with other aspects of metadata quality. A standard is more than a convention. It represents a practice that is *prescribed*, not simply what is normal. A standard may be aimed at staff inside a single organization (an *in-house standard*) or at a much broader community of practice, perhaps at national or international level. In order for it to be promulgated, a standard is set out in some form of document. Sometimes, this document may not explicitly claim the status of a standard, but is nevertheless followed by a large number of practitioners, making it a *de facto* standard. Many of the standards applied by metadata specialists fall into this category. Other standards, however, may be the product of an extensive consultation process and are formally approved by a professional body or standards agency. The International Organization for Standardization (ISO) defines, on its website, standards as 'documented agreements containing technical specifications or other precise criteria to be used consistently as rules, guidelines, or definitions of characteristics, to ensure that materials, products, processes and services are fit for their purpose'.

Standards have been developed for all aspects of metadata, including its values, elements, format and transmission. Many standards cover more than one of these aspects. However, we shall leave those that primarily relate to values, such as the controlled vocabularies we mentioned in Chapter 5, for the next chapter. In this chapter we shall look at key standards pertaining to elements, format and transmission.

Metadata standards sometimes consist of little more than a list (e.g. of elements), but often they are considerably more detailed. They may, for instance, include definitions, indicate relationships, specify circumstances of usage, advise how a resource should be analysed, or give options. The more detail, the greater the likelihood of consistency and quality metadata, although it also makes a standard more difficult and costly to apply.

There are, in fact, a wide range of factors that can influence the extent to which a metadata standard is adopted, including purpose, resource attributes, design, granularity, interoperability, support, growth, extensibility, reputation, ease of use and existing expertise (Kelly, 2006). Some standards are clearly more appropriate than others in a given context, and most are developed by and for a particular community of practice, such as those of librarians, archivists, curators and so on. Ultimately, there is a trade-off between the desire for consistency and best practice, on the one hand, and the desire to address local needs and economic realities, on the other.

We shall structure our discussion of metadata standards, in this chapter, around key information domains, and begin by examining some standards developed by a very large community indeed, namely, those who contribute to the world wide web.

Web publishing

Many of today's information resources and their associated metadata are intended for the web, where they can be accessed, potentially, by vast numbers of users. However, for this to happen, both resources and metadata need to be made available on, or through, web pages. In many cases, an information resource consists of web pages linked together to form websites and other kinds of web document. In other cases, the web page provides a link to another sort of file that can be run on an application designed for this purpose (for example, a WAV file, containing a video, can be opened up and run on the Windows Media Player). Similarly, metadata can be included in a web page, or the web page can point to another type of file, such as a MARC file, that contains the metadata. Either way, web pages need to be marked up in an encoding scheme recognized by the web browser.

HTML

The most widely used mark-up language for the web is the *Hypertext Markup Language* (HTML). HTML encodes pieces of text using tags that indicate their intended display attributes (e.g. font and size). Using HTML, metadata can be

```
<HEAD>
<TITLE>Stamp Collecting World</TITLE>
<META name="description" content="Everything you wanted to know
about stamps, from prices to history.">
<META name="keywords" content="stamps, stamp collecting,
stamp history, prices, stamps for sale">
</HEAD>
```

Figure 7.1 *Some HMTL-encoded metadata (source: Search Engine Watch,*
http://searchenginewatch.com)

encoded as part of a text, or it can be encoded specifically as metadata, if it refers to the text, by means of a 'meta' tag. Figure 7.1 shows some HTML tags for a web resource. The content of the title tag ('Stamp Collecting World') is displayed by the web browser. The content of the two meta tags, on the other hand, is not displayed to the user, but can be indexed by search engines. In this case, the tags are used to encode a 'description' of the resource, and some 'keywords' to be associated with it. All meta tags are optional; the title tag is required.

Although meta tags may seem like a good idea, they do not always feature prominently in search engine algorithms. As was noted previously, some websites include irrelevant meta tags in an attempt to obtain higher rankings amongst search results. Another problem is duplication: in many websites, multiple pages contain the same tags, despite representing slightly different content. Ardö (2010) concludes that meta tags cannot be readily trusted, although there are many that are both genuine and accurate, and which can be exploited if due care is taken. In any case, meta tags are recommended by most search engine optimization (SEO) experts.

Any metadata content of a textual nature can be encoded in HTML, since there are no rules about what can or cannot be included in its meta tag. The mark-up language supports the use of metadata on the web, without being a metadata standard per se. An application of the Standard Generalized Markup Language (SGML), it was developed in the early 1990s specifically to support the world wide web. Various versions and extensions of HTML have been developed since that time, including XHTML, which is intended to replace HTML in due course. XHTML is a marriage of HTML and another mark-up language, namely, the Extensible Markup Language (XML).

XML and RDF

Extensible Markup Language (XML) is one of the standards intended to underpin the 'Semantic Web', which is discussed further in Chapter 9. The mark-up language provides a more flexible and powerful alternative to SGML/HTML, and many of the more recently established metadata standards have been developed specifically for expression in XML. Like HTML, XML is not a metadata standard as such, but an encoding scheme that can be applied to all sorts of data. It has a simple but strict structure that tags data in a consistent way. The XML tags define their content, and are themselves defined by means of what is known as a *namespace*. This references an external document, elsewhere on the web, that sets out a particular *schema* or element set. Figure 7.2 shows XML-tagged metadata that is defined in terms of the Dublin Core (DC) schema. The computer can look up, i.e. link to, this schema at http://purl.org/dc/elements/1.1, as

```
<?xml version="1.0"?>
<metadata
xmlns="http://example.org/myapp/"
xmlns:xsi="http://www.w3.org/2001/XMLSchema-instance"
xsi:schemaLocation="http://example.org/myapp/
http://example.org/myapp/schema.xsd"
xmlns:dc="http://purl.org/dc/elements/1.1/">
<dc:title>
UKOLN
</dc:title>
<dc:description>
UKOLN is a national focus of expertise in digital information
management. It provides policy, research and awareness services
to the UK library, information and cultural heritage communities.
UKOLN is based at the University of Bath.
</dc:description>
<dc:publisher>
UKOLN, University of Bath
</dc:publisher>
<dc:identifier>
http://www.ukoln.ac.uk/
</dc:identifier>
</metadata>
```

Figure 7.2 *Some XML-encoded metadata (source: Guidelines for Implementing Dublin Core in XML, http://dublincore.org/documents/dc-xml-guidelines)*

indicated, and, by doing so, it can 'make sense' of the metadata in a way that it cannot when simply presented with a tag for, say, 'title'. This referencing process is, in essence, the basis of the Semantic Web, a web in which computers, as well as humans, derive 'meaning'. The goal is to create *linked* data.

XML is a very effective way of encoding metadata, as well as other kinds of data, for the web. However, it does not specify the structure of resource description itself. By analogy, we might consider a natural language such as English. It has established certain syntactic structures, but the same concept can still be expressed in different ways. For example, 'Tom chased Jerry' has the same meaning as 'Jerry was chased by Tom'. This may not be a problem for humans, who know the meaning of words in isolation, but computers require data to be structured in a standard way, if they are to interpret it successfully.

To standardize the way in which resources are described in XML, the *Resource Description Framework* (RDF, www.w3.org/RDF) was established by the World Wide Web Consortium (W3C). RDF specifies a structure based on what is known as a *triple*, consisting of a *subject*, followed by a *predicate*, and then by an *object*. In RDF, the subject is a resource, the object is a particular value, and the predicate is the relationship between subject and object, in other words, the metadata element. For example, the resource description, 'this book is about the Semantic Web', would, in RDF, be structured: this book / is about / the Semantic Web. The property (or attribute) 'is about' could be represented by the term 'subject' or 'topic', or any other term. Whichever is used, however, it should be derived from a documented schema referenced in a namespace. Similarly, the term used for the object (in this case, 'the Semantic Web') should, ideally at least, be derived from a referenced vocabulary, which can be set out in RDF according to the *Simple Knowledge Organization System* (SKOS, www.w3.org/2004/02/skos). In the example, the Library of Congress Subject Heading (LCSH) 'Semantic Web' could be used, since the vocabulary has been puboished as a SKOS. This would enable computers to explore ways in which the book's subject related to other subjects, and thus other resources. We shall return to LCSH in the next chapter.

The Dublin Core document referenced in the RDF/XML example in Figure 7.2 is also set out in a particular way, as an XML Schema. Another earlier standard for this was the Document Type Definition (DTD). Many element sets, including DC, have been published both as DTDs and XML schemas.

Another advantage of XML is that it allows for multiple schemas to be referenced within the same resource description: different namespaces can reference different schemas. This makes for richer metadata, though it also makes interoperability more of a challenge, and the construction of crosswalks between the various schemas all the more critical.

One other standard should be mentioned in connection with XML, namely, UNICODE, the universal character set. UNICODE allows for all sorts of non-roman characters, so that schemas and vocabularies can be based on just about any written language (Aliprand, 2000). It is another of the fundamental standards underpinning the development of the Semantic Web, along with XML, RDF and the Universal Resource Identifier (URI), used for linking together the data and resources. These standards provide the basis for further layers of standards, including ontologies, covered in the next chapter.

HTML, XHTML and XML are all maintained and developed by the W3C, the nearest thing that the web has to a governing agency. Particular 'dialects' of these languages have been developed for various types of information. For example, MusicXML can be used to mark up musical notation, and MathML for mathematical notation.

We shall now move on to standards developed specifically for information resource description. Most of these standards emanate from particular information professions and traditions, although it is worth noting that many computer scientists involved in Semantic Web technologies also have a keen interest in such standards and, in some cases, have developed their own. Examples include the Bibliographic Ontology (http://bibliontology.com), designed to express bibliographic references in RDF/XML, and the feed aggregator standards, such as RSS and Atom, which accommodate certain metadata elements relating to the content pushed to the user.

Libraries

Librarians started publishing guidelines for the construction of library catalogues in the second half of the 19th century. Earlier, some catalogues had been published together with details of the rules used in their construction, although these rules were provided more by way of explanation than as guidance for the creation of other catalogues. Some of these early catalogues and rules did, nevertheless, serve as a model for other catalogues, including, most notably, the '91 rules' for the (never completed) catalogue of the British Museum's Department of Printed Books (later the British Library), set out in its first volume, published in 1841. These rules, devised by Sir Anthony Panizzi, influenced Charles Cutter's *Rules for a Printed Dictionary Catalog* (1876), which, in turn, became the basis for the first cataloguing rules published by the American Library Association in 1878. Shortly afterwards, in 1881, the Library Association in the UK issued its first set of rules. The codification of library cataloguing had begun.

These early cataloguing rules covered the headings, as well as the rest of the record, known as the 'description'. They also covered cross-references. The cataloguer was told what to put and how to put it. Cutter's rules dealt with the construction of subject headings as well as headings for authors and titles (in his *Dictionary Catalog* (Cutter, 1876), the three types of heading were interfiled), but subject access was generally not covered in later cataloguing rules. Instead, lists of subject headings were developed and published separately, with one particular set, the Library of Congress Subject Headings (LCSH), becoming widely adopted, eventually, across the English-speaking library world. (We shall look at subject headings in the next chapter.)

In the introduction to his *Rules*, Cutter (1904) outlined his objectives for the library catalogue thus:

(1) To enable a person to find a book of which:
  • the author;
  • the title; or
  • the subject is known.
(2) To show what the library has:
  • by a given author;
  • on a given subject; or
  • in a given kind of literature.
(3) To assist in the choice of a book;
  • as to its edition (bibliographically); or
  • as to its character (literal or topical).

By the late 19th century, major library collections comprised tens, or even hundreds, of thousands of books, and the importance of an effective catalogue was reflected in Cutter's objectives, placing the user at the centre of library cataloguing. Ultimately, cataloguing was not about following bibliographic conventions, but about providing access to a collection of resources.

The initial cataloguing rules issued by the American and British Library Associations were replaced in 1908 by a new set, or *code*, for author and title entries (there were separate American and British editions; Library Association and American Library Association, 1908). Although fairly widely adopted in North America and Britain (particularly by those libraries wishing to share catalogue cards), these rules were by no means the final word in library cataloguing. As libraries continued to catalogue, the more cases there were of the rules proving inadequate or unsatisfactory. This gave rise to the creation of many additional rules, and caveats to existing rules, and, ultimately, a revised and very much expanded edition of the rules (from 88 to 408 pages), published by the ALA in 1941.

Some librarians, however, questioned whether so many rules were really necessary, including Seymour Lubetzky, who was given the job of reviewing the rules used at the Library of Congress. He argued that the proliferation of rules could be avoided if a set of guiding principles was applied to the construction (or elimination) of each rule (Lubetzky, 1953). The result was a more streamlined code, published by the Library of Congress in 1949. It did not, however, cover headings, only the description underneath them; another set of rules for the selection and construction of author and title headings was published by ALA in the same year (1949). In 1960, Lubetzky produced a draft revision of the ALA's rules for headings, again working from a set of guiding principles. These principles became the basis for the so-called 'Paris Principles', which emanated from an international cataloguing conference held in 1961 in Paris (Anderson and Chaplin, 1963).

AACR and ISBD

Lubetzky's work ultimately led to the new cataloguing code of 1967, *Anglo-American Cataloguing Rules* (AACR), which covered both headings and description, and also non-book materials. It was published by both the American and British Library Associations, again in American and British versions, and adopted, most importantly, by the Library of Congress. Thereafter, AACR replaced the earlier codes in libraries across the English-speaking world.

AACR was, however, less frequently adopted in non-English speaking countries (although it has been translated into over 20 languages). For one thing, there was less economic incentive to do so, as there was less scope for record sharing, given the limited extent to which collections overlapped with those in Anglo-American libraries. Moreover, other library communities had developed their own cataloguing codes, written in their own languages and based on local publishing and bibliographic conventions. Although these conventions were not entirely different from those of the Anglo-American tradition, significant differences did exist. For instance, as we noted in an earlier chapter, the Anglo-American tradition recognizes certain kinds of 'corporate authorship', in which groups of people, or 'corporate bodies', are considered responsible, as a whole, for the content of a particular resource; however, this concept is somewhat foreign to other European traditions. An example of a cataloguing code developed outside of Anglo-American practice was the *Instruktionen für die Alphabetischen Kataloge der Preußischen Bibliotheken* (often referred to as the 'Prussian Instructions'), first published in 1899, which were eventually replaced by the *Regeln für Alphabetische Katalogisierung* (RAK), in the 1970s.

Nevertheless, the Paris Principles demonstrated that common ground could be found amongst the world's librarians, and in 1971 the International Federation of Library Associations (IFLA) published the first *International Standard Bibliographic Description* (ISBD), specifically for monographs (i.e. books). ISBDs for other materials followed, as did ISBD(G), for library materials in general. The ISBD standard prescribes the elements for cataloguers to include in their description of library resources and how this description is to be presented. An example of the ISBD format is given in Figure 7.3. The various elements are organized in a set order, with particular punctuation marks used to demarcate them (more economical than using words, as well as being language neutral). It should be borne in mind that ISBD was first developed in the days of the card catalogue, although the latest, consolidated edition of ISBD was published in 2011 (IFLA, 2011b).

The Anglo-American library community was keen for AACR to align with ISBD, and also wished to see a unification of the American and British texts.

Text (visual) : unmediated

Canadian migration patterns from Britain and North America / edited by Barbara J. Messamore. – Ottawa : University of Ottawa Press, cop. 2004.

viii, 294 p. : ill., maps ; 23 cm. – (International Canadian studies series = Collection internationale d'études canadiennes)
Includes bibliographical references. – ISBN 0-7766-0543-7

Figure 7.3 *ISBD example (source: www.ifla.org/files/cataloguing/isbd/isbd-examples_2011.pdf)*

A Joint Steering Committee (JSC) was established in 1974 to work towards a new edition of AACR that would incorporate rule revisions made since 1967, and also represent a comprehensive review of the code in light of ISBD and other developments. The JSC included representatives from the British Library and the Canadian Library Association, as well as the Library of Congress and the American and British Library Associations. The result of JSC's labours was the second edition of AACR, commonly referred to as AACR2, published jointly by the American and British Library Associations in 1978. Shortly afterwards, AACR2 was adopted by the Library of Congress, the British Library, the National Library of Canada, the National Library of Australia and most other libraries in the English-speaking world.

Revised versions of AACR2 were published in 1988, 1998 and 2002. The code is still very much in use, although the intention is for the new RDA standard (see below) to replace it. AACR2 contains a lot of rules, but it also provides for different levels of description, and many rules are not applicable at the first, or minimum, level. There are also a number of 'optional' rules. In any case, its rules are not always followed to the letter: they may be modified or even ignored, to suit local needs and policy. Many libraries, particularly in North America, follow the *Library of Congress Rule Interpretations* (LCRI; LC, 2010), which are essentially the Library of Congress's own policy guidelines concerning the application of AACR2.

AACR2 is organized into two parts, as shown in the table of contents (Figure 7.4). The first part deals with description and the second part covers headings. Chapter 1 is particularly important, as it contains more general rules: how and what to describe, irrespective of the kind of resource. The next 11 chapters provide rules for 'classes of material'. Chapter 12 was revised in 2002 so that it covers not only serials, but also other types of 'continuing' resource, including so-called 'integrating' resources, such as websites. The last chapter in Part 1 deals with 'analytics', that is, the ways in which components of a resource can be described. The second part of AACR2 covers the selection of headings (Chapter 21) and their construction (Chapters 22 to 25), and the construction of cross-references to and from these headings (Chapter 26).

AACR2 runs to some 750 pages in its 2005 revision. Chapters are broken down into sections, sub-sections and individual rules within sub-sections. The rules are referenced with the number of the chapter and section, the letter of the sub-section and a number for the rule within the sub-section. For example, rule 8.5D6 is about recording the dimensions of technical drawings

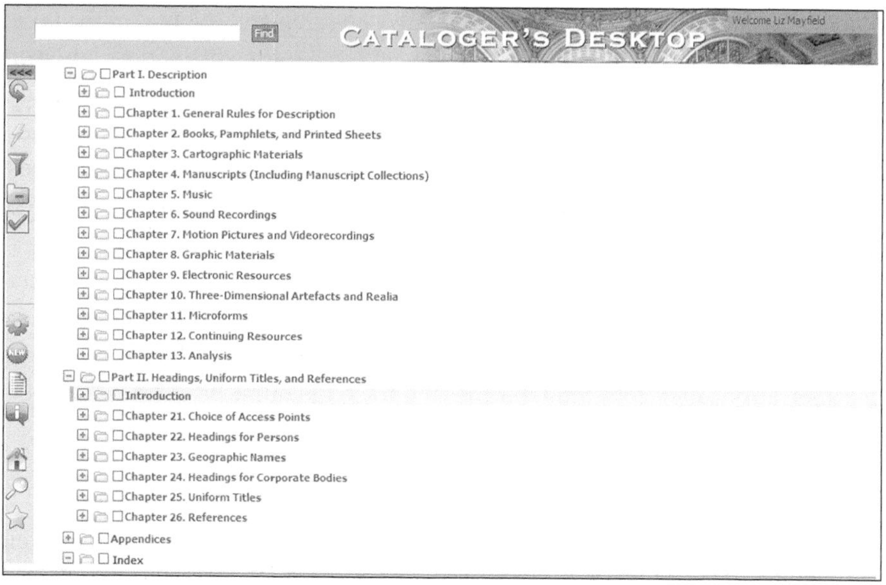

Figure 7.4 *Contents of AACR2 (2005)*

and wall charts: it is located in Chapter 8 for graphic materials, section 5 for physical description, sub-section D for dimensions, and rule 6 for technical drawings and wall charts. The actual rule instructs the cataloguer thus:

> Give the height × width when extended and (when appropriate) folded, separating the dimensions by a comma.

Some rules even have referenced sub-rules. AACR2 is not a standard to be memorized overnight. (A *Concise AACR2*, edited by Michael Gorman (Gorman, 2004), is available for those looking for a simplification of the full code.)

As mentioned earlier, AACR2 allows for three levels of description (under 1.0D). The first level represents the minimum elements to be included in the description; the second, an intermediate set; and the third, all elements covered by the rules. Most library cataloguing applies the second level, or an approximation of it. This still represents the application, or potential application, of a large number of the rules in Part 1.

Many of the rules in Part 2 of AACR2 are applied only occasionally, for several reasons. In most cases, the selection of headings for catalogue records is quite straightforward. In the case of a book with one author, for example, the name of the author is used for the main entry heading and the title of the book is used for an added entry heading. In any case, the distinction between headings for main and added entries is less important in online catalogues, where as much of the record can be displayed as the user wishes. Furthermore, headings for people and corporate bodies can just be copied over if they already exist in the catalogue or in an authority file. Even when they do need to be constructed, the basic rule may suffice: use the form of the name as it appears on the chief source of information, such as the title page (although the form is usually inverted, so that surnames come first). However, for those cataloguers who undertake authority control work, many of the rules in Part 2 will be applicable from time to time (the trick, of course, is to know when).

RDA and FRBR/FRAD

AACR2 was initially developed when card catalogues were still the norm, well before the advent of the web. Even in its later revisions, the code talks about 'headings' and 'main entries', terms and concepts that have much less relevance in the online environment. Although AACR2 covers resources such as websites, it has had difficulty keeping up with the evolution of digital technologies. Some of the examples it uses might be considered more appropriate for 20th, rather than 21st, century libraries. This issue has been exacerbated by AACR's emphasis on different classes of material, so that there is a continual need to update the rules as new kinds of resources are added to library collections.

AACR2's alignment with ISBD was an advantage in the 1970s, increasing the standard's compatibility with cataloguing codes used in non-English-speaking countries, but it had become something of a liability by the 2000s. In fact, modern online catalogues, when displaying records, break up the ISBD format, adding labels and dropping punctuation to make descriptions more intelligible. Furthermore, although ISBD and AACR2 identify various elements within eight 'areas of description', they are not systematically defined, nor are they very refined. This lack of precision makes for resource descriptions that may be rich, but also less conducive to computer processing.

Ultimately it was decided by the Joint Steering Committee of AACR that, instead of another edition of AACR covering more of the emerging information resources, what was needed was a complete overhaul of the standard. The aim was to create a cataloguing code that would give rise to resource descriptions which were computer as well as people friendly. The new standard, *Resource Description and Access* (RDA), was released in 2010 (Joint Steering Committee for

Development of RDA, 2010). Unlike AACR, RDA does not prescribe the ISBD format; in fact, it does not prescribe any format. Instead, RDA focuses on content, i.e. the elements and their values. (The code does cover certain 'format' decisions pertaining to specific elements and values, such as name inversion and capitalization, but the rules allow for digitally derived data to be left as is).

RDA accommodates ISBD-based descriptions, but it also accommodates other formats that may be more useful in the online environment. Importantly, it enables resource descriptions to be expressed schematically, making them compatible with standards such as RDF/XML. The RDA schema covers more elements than AACR does, for several reasons. First, RDA defines elements more narrowly. For example, RDA distinguishes between a 'title proper' that is derived from the resource and a 'title proper' that is constructed by the cataloguer (when there is no title presented on the resource), treating them as different elements. Second, RDA does not limit resource description to the ISBD elements. In an attempt to make itself more relevant to information agencies and metadata specialists outside of the library domain, the code covers elements not ordinarily considered by librarians (e.g. provenance, an important element, as we previously noted, in archival description). Third, RDA aims to cover all the elements that might be usefully included in authority records as well as in bibliographic records, whereas AACR2 covers only the headings and cross-references in authority records, although IFLA's *Guidelines for Authority Records and References* is also available (IFLA, 2001). These elements include various attributes of the persons, corporate bodies and other entities, apart from their names, that authority records represent, as well as notes about the headings themselves.

In total, RDA identifies 463 elements and sub-elements for bibliographic records and 59 for authority records, according to the Open Metadata Registry. Of course, for any given information resource, only some of these elements will be applicable. Furthermore, most of the elements are not required: only a relatively small subset of elements is defined by RDA as 'core', i.e. those that must be recorded, if applicable.

Although RDA goes beyond AACR2 in coverage and scope, the new code has retained many of AACR2's rules, albeit sometimes in a modified form. After all, AACR2 has produced some very workable catalogues. Nevertheless, a large number of rules for specific materials have been replaced with more generic ones. There has also been an attempt to reach out to the international community by making the standard more linguistically neutral. For instance, AACR2 sometimes requires the cataloguer to select the English form of a name, whereas RDA prescribes that the most appropriate form is chosen, depending on the language of the catalogue's users. This move, however, has also resulted in the dropping of certain Latin terms (e.g. 'et al.' for 'and others') that, it has been argued, are understood across linguistic communities, thereby actually *hindering* the international exchange of cataloguing, as vernacular terms may need to be edited.

For RDA to be built from the ground up, rather than simply extending AACR2, it needed to be based on a model of how an effective catalogue functions. (We might recall how Cutter had stated, more than a century before, the functions of the catalogue that his rules aimed to support.) Fortunately for the developers of RDA, an IFLA study group had recently published the *Functional Requirements for Bibliographic Records* (IFLA, 1998), which provides an entity-relationship model, introduced in Chapter 2 and as outlined in Figure 7.5. This kind of model is commonly employed in database design. In FRBR, the various entities and their interrelationships are described, we will recall, in terms of the elements required by users to accomplish four key

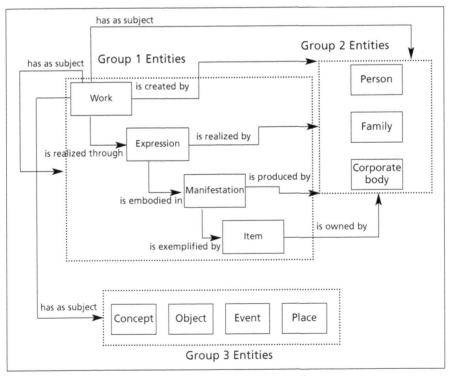

Figure 7.5 *FRBR group 1, 2 and 3 entities, and their relationships (source: www.frbr.org/files/entity-relationships.png)*

retrieval tasks at the library catalogue (finding, identifying, selecting and obtaining a resource), making them the elements to be included in bibliographic records.

A more detailed snapshot of the FRBR model in operation is provided in Figure 7.6, using standard entity-relationship diagramming. Each FRBR entity (depicted as a rectangle) has a relationship (depicted as a diamond) with one or more other entities. Both entities and relationships can have attributes (ovals), although, in FRBR, relationship attributes are lumped in with the entity attributes.

FRBR defines three sets, or groups, of entities. The first group comprises the different 'levels' of information resource, i.e. works, expressions, manifestations and items. The second group consists of the different kinds of agent that can have a relationship with information resources, i.e. persons, families (added later) and corporate bodies. The third group represents the different things that can have a 'subject' relationship with information

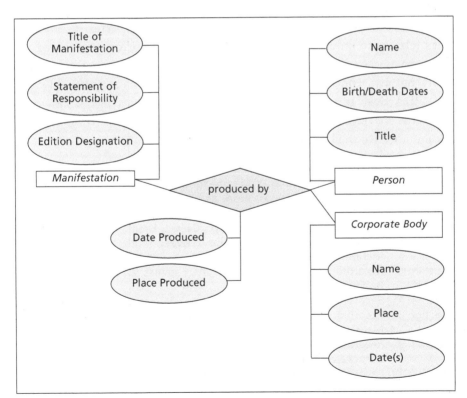

Figure 7.6 *Some entities, relationships and attributes from FRBR (source: Maxwell, 2008, 9)*

resources, i.e. concepts, objects, events and places. Relationships occur between entities in the same group, as well as between those in different groups. Indeed, relationships occur between different instances of the same entity (e.g. one work might be 'based' on another work). FRBR might be seen as the culmination of earlier work on 'bibliographic relationships' and 'bibliographic families' (Leazer and Smiraglia, 1999); a pioneer in this field of study was Tillett (1991), who identified a taxonomy of relationships between library resources: equivalence, derivative, descriptive, whole–part, accompanying, sequential and shared-characteristic.

FRBR had already become quite influential in library cataloguing circles when it was adopted for RDA. Just as ISBD influenced the organization of AACR2, so FRBR provides the basis for RDA's organization, which is outlined in Figure 7.7. RDA consists of 38 chapters altogether (numbered 0–37), grouped into 10 sections.

The first four sections contain the rules for describing the various attributes of the various entities. The first two deal with the group 1 entities, and the third covers the group 2 entities. The fourth section is reserved for rules relating to group 3 entities, but the only rules currently provided are those for places (in RDA, places may be related to any group 1 or group 2 entity, not just works), and so section 4 mostly serves as a 'placeholder'. In fact, RDA does not really need to cover these entities per se, as other standards are customarily used for subject description, including many of the vocabularies we shall meet in the next chapter.

Section 1: Recording Attributes of Manifestation and Item
Section 2: Recording Attributes of Work and Expression
Section 3: Recording Attributes of Person, Family, and Corporate Body
Section 4: Recording Attributes of Concept, Object, Event, and Place
Section 5: Recording Primary Relationships between Work, Expression, Manifestation, and Item
Section 6: Recording Relationships to Persons, Families, and Corporate Bodies
Section 7: Recording Relationships to Concepts, Objects, Events, and Places
Section 8: Recording Relationships between Works, Expressions, Manifestations, and Items
Section 9: Recording Relationships between Persons, Families, and Corporate Bodies
Section 10: Recording Relationships between Concepts, Objects, Events, and Places

---

Figure 7.7 *Contents of RDA (2010)*

The last six sections of RDA focus on the relationships between entities. Section 5 covers the so-called 'primary' relationships, i.e. the relationships between the group 1 entities for the same resource. For example, there are rules about how to describe the nature of the expression of a work. Section 6 deals with relationships between group 1 entities and group 2 entities. For example, how a person is related to a work. Section 7 is intended to cover relationships between group 1 entities and group 3 entities, but has not yet been developed. Section 8 deals with relationships amongst group 1 entities (for different resources) and amongst instances of those entities. For example, how one work is related to another work. Similarly, section 9 deals with relationships amongst group 2 entities and their instances, such as the relationship between two corporate bodies. Finally, section 10 is intended to cover relationships amongst group 3 entities, but is currently another placeholder.

The 10 sections are divided into chapters in different ways, but mainly according to particular entity types. Within each chapter (or at least those chapters that have been developed), the rules are grouped together according to the specific element they cover. We may recall that in AACR2 the rule dealing with the dimensions of technical drawing and wall charts is at 8.5D6. In RDA, a similar rule appears at 3.5.1.4.11, for 'sheets' (note the more generic nature of this rule). This reference can be broken down thus:

Chapter 3 Describing Carriers
    .5 Dimensions
        .1 Basic Instructions
            .4 Dimensions of Carrier (as opposed to containers, etc.)
            .11 Sheets

This may look like a somewhat more complicated arrangement than in AACR2, and it probably is, but it should be noted that RDA has been designed as an online cataloguing tool and contains many hyperlinks that improve navigation. In any case, RDA (like AACR2) is clearly aimed at the metadata specialist.

Shortly after FRBR was first published, IFLA established a working group to look at the elements needed for authority records. Its final report, *Functional Requirements for Authority Data* (FRAD), was published by IFLA in 2009 (IFLA, 2009a). FRAD is based on the FRBR model, but focuses on the group 2 entities. Its analysis is also based on a slightly different set of user tasks, since authority records function differently from bibliographic records. The tasks are: to find an entity associated with a resource; identify that entity; contextualize the entity amongst similar entities; and justify the preferred name for the entity. The last of these tasks is carried out primarily by cataloguers, rather than end-users. RDA identifies those attributes and relationships of the group 2 entities which support these tasks. In other words, it identifies the elements required for authority control work.

Another IFLA report, the *Functional Requirements for Subject Authority Data* (FRSAD), covers the group 3 entities in a similar way to FRAD. However, the report (IFLA, 2011a) was approved only in 2010, and so was too late to be adopted for RDA.

RDA not only identifies sets of elements, it also offers *vocabularies*, or sets of values, for some of its elements. The possible values for the RDA element of 'content type', for example, are as follows:

cartographic dataset
cartographic image
cartographic moving image
cartographic tactile image
cartographic tactile three-dimensional form
cartographic three-dimensional form
computer dataset
computer program
notated movement
notated music
performed music
sounds
spoken word
still image
tactile image
tactile notated music
tactile notated movement
tactile text
tactile three-dimensional form
text
three-dimensional form
three-dimensional moving image
two-dimensional moving image

other

unspecified

Thus, RDA *controls* the vocabulary for the description of this element. RDA's vocabularies are considered to be a valuable supplement to the RDA element sets, as they can likewise be utilized by Semantic Web technologies. We shall look at them again in the next chapter.

RDA also declares allegiance to the new *Statement of International Cataloguing Principles*, published by IFLA in 2009 (IFLA, 2009b). The statement is the product of a series of meetings amongst cataloguing experts from around the world, including representatives from the Anglo-American library community. Its aim is to serve as the basis for the development of all cataloguing codes, so that these codes result in more 'international sharing of bibliographic and authority data.' Whereas the Paris Principles of 1961 covered only the choice and form of headings, the 2009 Principles are intended to cover all aspects of cataloguing. The most general Principles are: convenience of the user; common usage; representation; accuracy; sufficiency and necessity; significance; economy; consistency and standardization; and integration.

The development of RDA was a somewhat protracted process. Many cataloguers and other information professionals provided input, although the wide range of views on the various drafts meant that the code was, and still is, subject to a fair amount of controversy. Ultimately, RDA was published about a decade after work began on it. This is, in fact, comparable with the germination of earlier codes (e.g. the time between the Lubetzky drafts and the publication of AACR). However, in today's world a decade can be a very long time.

Unfortunately, RDA's publication did not result in immediate adoption. The Library of Congress, together with the (US) National Library of Medicine (NLM) and the (US) National Agricultural Library (NAL), decided to conduct extensive 'tests' with the new code, which focused on its usability (US RDA Test Coordinating Committee, 2011). The upshot of these tests was a further delay as text was rewritten to make it more cataloguer friendly. The need for clear, simple language should not be underestimated. Osborn (1941) famously warned that the complexity of the doomed 1941 rules would lead to greater backlogs. Today, efficient processing of library materials is even more of an imperative. The ideas expressed in RDA are not simple, however, and there will always be a tension between the needs for logical consistency and for convenience.

LC, NLM and NAL have announced that they will adopt the code in 2013, paving the way for the rest of the library community, including the national libraries of the UK, Canada and Australia, to do the same. The jury remains out on RDA, however, until it finally is implemented. At a certain level, the code can be applied without radical change. Indeed, it has entailed only relatively minor amendments to the existing MARC record format. The creation of records for works and expressions, as well as for manifestations, that RDA enables may not materialize, due to economic and practical constraints. This may reassure some cataloguers, but it will beg the question of whether RDA was worth all the time and effort.

On the other hand, RDA has the potential to revolutionize library cataloguing. Whether it does so or not, and whether that revolution will lead to improved access, is hard to predict. A growing number of commentators have expressed the view that no revolution can take place until cataloguers drop the MARC format, along with AACR2. Yet even if MARC is replaced, the resources that a full implementation of RDA would require still need to be justified.

MARC

We encountered the *Machine-Readable Cataloguing* (MARC) standard in the previous chapter. MARC is a record exchange format used by automated library systems to share and process cataloguing data. Many millions of MARC records have been created and exchanged since it was first developed in the 1960s, making it one of the most successful library standards of all time. MARC is not a set of cataloguing rules, like RDA or AACR. It does not tell the cataloguer what metadata to record. Rather, it tells the cataloguer how to *encode* the metadata so that it can be 'read' by a computer.

Although several other computer record formats have been developed for cataloguing over the years, there are relatively few library automated systems in the world that do not use MARC. It complies with the international standard, ISO 2709:2008 (*Format for Information Exchange*), which 'specifies the requirements for generalized exchange format which will hold records describing all forms of material capable of bibliographic description as well as other types of records'. The MARC standard is, in fact, a 'family' of formats and versions, the lineage of which can be traced back to the initial automation projects at LC. The original 'LCMARC' led to the establishment of USMARC in the 1970s, a standard aimed primarily, as the name suggests, at American libraries. By the 1980s, many countries had developed their own MARC variants, such as CAN/MARC, UKMARC and AUSMARC. The USMARC format even had its own variants for different categories of library resource (books, serials, maps, etc.). Different formats were also developed for other types of record in addition to the bibliographic record, such as the authority record.

As library cataloguing became an increasingly international activity, with more and more records being shared amongst libraries from different countries, national MARC standards made less and less sense. Gradually, countries dropped their own variants in favour of USMARC, the standard on which the largest pool of MARC records, as well as many of the commercially available library automation systems, was based. In 1999, USMARC and CAN/MARC merged to become MARC21 (a MARC standard for the 21st century, it was claimed). Shortly afterwards, libraries in the UK decided to switch from UKMARC to MARC21 (Danskin, 2002). Although IFLA's UNIMARC (www.unimarc.net) might have a greater claim to be the official international standard, MARC21 (www.loc.gov/marc) has established itself as the predominant MARC variant. It is maintained by the Library of Congress and comprises formats for five different kinds of data: bibliographic, authority, holdings, classification and community. The bibliographic and authority record formats are the most widely used.

The *MARC21 Format for Bibliographic Data* is outlined in Figure 7.8. It is split up into various fields, numbered 001 to, potentially, 999, into which the data is inserted. Although there are many fields that could be used, most records include only a small proportion of them. The first few fields, commonly known as the 'fixed fields', are intended for coded information. All the other fields (010 onwards) can be of variable length, depending on the data (for instance, some titles are longer than others). Each field contains

---

00X: Control Fields
01X–09X: Numbers and Code Fields
1XX: Main Entry Fields
20X–24X: Title and Title-Related Fields
25X–28X: Edition, Imprint, Etc. Fields
3XX: Physical Description, Etc. Fields
4XX: Series Statement Fields
5XX: Note Fields
6XX: Subject Access Fields
70X–75X: Added Entry Fields
76X–78X: Linking Entry Fields
80X–83X: Series Added Entry Fields
841–88X: Holdings, Location, Alternate Graphics, Etc. Fields

Figure 7.8 *Summary of MARC21 fields*

particular data elements. For example, 245 is used for titles and statements of responsibility (for the resource), while 260 is used for publication details. Some fields (e.g. 245) are almost always used in records, others very rarely. The 9XX fields are reserved for 'locally defined' data elements, so the kind of data they represent varies from catalogue to catalogue.

The field numbers encode the data following them, performing a similar function to the meta tags in the mark-up languages that we have already looked at. Indeed, they are likewise referred to as tags. When a computer system conversant with the standard is fed a MARC21 record, and a field delimiter sign (indicating the end of one field and the beginning of another) is followed by, say, the '260' tag, it 'knows' that coming up next are the publication details.

MARC21 fields are divided into subfields, which are also defined by a particular code, consisting of a single letter or numeral. In the 245 field, for example, subfield *a* stands for the title proper (main title), while subfield *c* stands for the statement(s) of responsibility. In other fields, the same subfield codes have other meanings. For instance, in field 260, for publication details, subfield *a* stands for the place of publication and subfield *c* for the date. Subfields, like fields, may or may not be used: it depends on the data available and what the cataloguer wants to record. A field may contain just one subfield or it may contain several. Some fields and subfields are repeatable, others are not. Fields also include two character spaces known as *indicator positions*, sometimes used to further define the field.

Figure 7.9 shows the content of a typical MARC21 record. This is what the cataloguer might see when they are creating or editing a record, but not, of course, what is usually presented to end-users, who are seldom interested in the MARC codes. Guidelines for displaying bibliographic data to end-users have been developed by IFLA (*Guidelines for Online Public Access Catalogue (OPAC) Displays*, 2005).

We can see from Figures 7.8 and 7.9 that MARC21 structures bibliographic data in a way that reflects its close ties with AACR2 and ISBD. For instance, each of the eight areas of ISBD is designated its own MARC21 field (245 for the title and statement of responsibility area; 250 for the edition area; 260 for the publication details area; and so on). On the other hand, the MARC21 format also includes a large number of fields and subfields for elements not specifically covered by AACR2/ISBD. Conversely, a resource description based on AACR2/ISBD does not have to be encoded using MARC21, although there may be few alternatives.

We have already noted how RDA provides greater scope for cataloguers to

```
001       <control number>
003       <control number identifier>
005       19920331092212.7
007       ta
008       820305s1991####nyu###########001#0#eng##
020       ##$a0845348116 :$c$29.95 (£19.50 U.K.)
020       ##$a0845348205 (pbk.)
040       ##$a[organization code]$c[organization code]
050       14$aPN1992.8.S4$bT47 1991
082       04$a791.45/75/0973$219
100       1#$aTerrace, Vincent,$d1948-
245       10$aFifty years of television :$ba guide to series and pilots, 1937–1988
          /$cVincent Terrace.
246       1#$a50 years of television
260       ##$aNew York :$bCornwall Books,$cc1991.
300       ##$a864 p. ;$c24 cm.
500       ##$aIncludes index.
650       #0$aTelevision pilot programs$zUnited States$vCatalogs.
650       #0$aTelevision serials$zUnited States$vCatalogs.
```

Figure 7.9 *A MARC21 record*

apply other format standards, apart from ISBD. Likewise, it can operate independently of MARC. Other standards are now available for librarians looking to make their bibliographic data more interoperable. It may be, however, that the MARC standard will continue to underpin many library management systems for a while yet. It may not suit computers so much, but library users are accustomed to the 'thick description' that the MARC record offers (minus the codes). Moreover, libraries cannot afford to recatalogue their collections, and any conversion of their existing MARC databases to another format would inevitably result in considerable data loss. This loss has to be weighed against the potential benefits of creating records in a format that affords greater interoperability.

Nevertheless, as cataloguers switch from AACR2 to RDA, a tipping-point may soon be reached. The Library of Congress's recently announced Bibliographic Framework Transition Initiative, in which the MARC standard is to be reviewed, could result in what some would say is long overdue.

Z39.50

Modern online catalogues offer the user a wide range of options for searching on MARC records. However, users, including cataloguers, may sometimes prefer to let the computer do the searching, particularly when they want to cover several catalogues or when a large number of searches need to be carried out. Many library management systems have applications designed for this purpose, applying a *client–server protocol* known as Z39.50.

The American standards agencies ANSI and NISO first established the Z39.50 Information Retrieval Protocol in 1988; the most recent version was issued in 2003. It became an international standard (ISO 23950) in 1998. In order for a search application (the client) to successfully engage with a bibliographic database (the server), client and server need to speak the same language, i.e. protocol. If the protocol is standardized, clients can use the same protocol to engage with multiple servers, and vice versa.

The Z39.50 standard (www.loc.gov/z3950/agency) is maintained by the Library of Congress. The 2003 version allows for the retrieval of holdings data as well as bibliographic data. Like MARC, the standard is aimed at computers, and end-users may not even be aware of its implementation. However, people (preferably metadata specialists) have to configure both client and server to optimize retrieval through the protocol, since there are different ways in which bibliographic databases can be searched and different ways in which the catalogue records can be indexed. For instance, a title keyword search could aim to find words in titles listed in, say, a contents field, but it might not. Similarly, a database could index these words as part of a title keyword index, but it might not. To assist in the configuration process, a standard search profile may be adopted. Commonly, the Bath Profile, established by the international library community in 2000, is applied (The Bath Group, 2004).

SRU and CQL

Although Z39.50 works well with MARC, it also shares some of MARC's problems and is not readily applicable to systems based on newer formats and structures. Recently, a more adaptable retrieval protocol has been developed. *Search/Retrieve by URL* (SRU, www.loc.gov/standards/sru) enables search applications to communicate with systems outside of the library domain, such as search engines, as well as with online catalogues. It is also maintained by the Library of Congress and may end up superseding Z39.50. The protocol is 'XML focused' and utilizes *Contextual Query Language* (CQL), a standard syntax for representing search queries. SRU-based clients visit SRU-based servers at URLs that incorporate CQL. Further details are available on the SRU website.

Digital libraries

MARC was originally developed well before the advent of the internet, let alone the web. Since the late 1990s, there has been considerable debate around the standard's suitability for the contemporary computing environment. The format accommodates rich description, but elements that are not very clearly defined, nor coded in a way that is readily intelligible to most computer programmers. This might not be a problem if librarians were content with stand-alone OPACs with traditional interfaces, but many are not. Instead, they want a catalogue that has the look and feel of the Google interface, and one that is interoperable with other retrieval systems provided as part of a modern digital library, in which resources, as well as metadata, are accessible online. As a result, some librarians have advocated that MARC be replaced by a more contemporary standard, developed specifically for the web environment, such as Dublin Core (DC). We have already seen how DC can be used in tandem with RDF/XML. We shall now look at the standard in more detail.

Dublin Core

DC has its own ISO standard (15836:2003, *The Dublin Core Metadata Element Set*), and its own governing body, the Dublin Core Metadata Initiative (DCMI, http://dublincore.org), which works closely with W3C. The DC Metadata Element Set (DCMES) comprises a set of 15 elements, established in the late 1990s through a series of workshops involving metadata experts from several domains, including librarianship. The element set, or schema, was considered to represent a 'core' description applicable across these domains. Later, qualifiers, now called *refinements*, were added so that certain elements can, optionally, be defined more narrowly, in terms of various sub-elements. For example, the 'Date' element has several refinements, including 'Date Copyrighted'. Table 7.1 lists the DC elements and their refinements. In addition, DC allows for certain elements to be defined in terms of a particular set of values (i.e. vocabulary), called an 'encoding scheme' (but not in the sense that MARC and XML are encoding schemes). An example of an encoding scheme for the DC 'Subject' element is Library of Congress Subject Headings (LCSH).

Whereas MARC subfields are intended to be strung together in a particular arrangement, the DC elements and refinements are not *syntactically* dependent on each other. That is, they may be formatted in any order or arrangement. Instead, their interrelationships are of a *semantic* nature, with refinements being explicitly defined in relation to particular elements. As such, DC is a *logically structured* schema. In MARC, logical relationships between fields and subfields are far less clear.

DC certainly does not encompass the rich metadata found in MARC records, but it was never meant to. Instead, its element set constitutes a minimum, to be extended as required. The standard's main advantage is that, as a schema, its metadata can be more clearly 'understood' by computers. For example, in MARC21 the year given in field 260, subfield *c*, might be the year of publication or the year the resource was copyrighted. People may be able to infer the latter by noting a 'c' for copyright in front of the year, but computers are not necessarily so knowledgeable. In DC, however, the Date element can be refined to indicate what kind of date it is. Although, conversely, there are many elements and sub-elements not covered by DC that are covered by MARC, the point is that MARC has not been developed as a schema and cannot be readily extended to iron out ambiguities. DC, on the other hand, was designed to be extended, according to the context in which it is used.

Like RDA, DC does not prescribe any particular encoding system. It

Table 7.1 *Summary of DC elements, refinements and schemes (source: http://dublincore.org)*

DCMES element	Element refinement(s)
Title	Alternative
Creator	–
Subject	–
Description	Table Of Contents
	Abstract
Publisher	–
Contributor	–
Date	Created
	Valid
	Available
	Issued
	Modified
	Date Accepted
	Date Copyrighted
	Date Submitted
Type	–
Format	–
	Extent
	Medium
Identifier	–
	Bibliographic Citation
Source	–
Language	–
Relation	Is Version Of
	Has Version
	Is Replaced By
	Replaces
	Is Required By
	Requires
	Is Part Of
	Has Part
	Is Referenced By
	References
	Is Format Of
	Has Format
	Conforms To
Coverage	Spatial
	Temporal
Rights	Access Rights
	License
Audience	Mediator
	Education Level

Table 7.1 (continued)	
DCMES element	Element refinement(s)
Provenance	–
Rights Holder	–
Instructional Method	–
Accrual Method	–
Accrual Periodicity	–
Accrual Policy	–

is, however, commonly applied with XML or HTML. A large number of other schemas have been developed over the past decade or so, but DC has probably the broadest application. It is aimed at the general audience and is applicable across media types. DC is the most popular schema for web pages, although it is used, according to Ardö (2010), for only around 1.6% of them (the vast majority of web pages utilize no metadata schema, unfortunately).

DC and extensions of DC (some of which we shall encounter below) are also popular amongst librarians and other information professionals looking for a schema to apply to the description of resources in their digital collections, particularly when they are not represented in the main catalogue. In some cases, these records are excluded from the OPAC in order to avoid 'crowding out' the records for the physical collection, and this affords the opportunity to select different standards. In other cases, the digital resources are acquired together with pre-existing metadata, which may be based on standards such as DC. In any case, librarians may decide that traditional standards such as MARC do not adequately support the desired resource description, particularly if the resources are quite different from traditional library materials.

The RDA schemas for bibliographic and authority data have already been established as standard extensions of DC, which are known as *application profiles*. Cataloguers can, if they wish, describe their resources using these profiles in conjunction with RDF/XML, instead of MARC. It remains to be seen whether or not they do so, but if they do, library cataloguing is more likely to become an integral part of larger information retrieval systems and, ultimately, the Semantic Web.

MODS and METS

Another option for those looking for some middle ground between the complexity of MARC (or, for that matter, RDA) and the simplicity of DC is the *Metadata Object Description Schema* (MODS, www.loc.gov/standards/mods), established by the Library of Congress in 2002. It is based on a subset of the elements found in MARC but is structured in the same sort of logical way as

DC and designed to be encoded in XML, instead of in MARC. It also has an authority data counterpart called MADS (www.loc.gov/standards/mads). The schema has been adopted by a considerable number of digital library projects in recent years. Its 'top level' elements are listed below.

> titleInfo
> name
> typeOfResource
> genre
> originInfo
> language
> physicalDescription
> abstract
> tableOfContents
> note
> subject
> classification
> relatedItem
> identifier
> location
> accessCondition
> extension
> recordInfo

Yet another standard developed by the Library of Congress is the *Metadata Encoding and Transmission Standard* (METS, www.loc.gov/standards/mets). This is an XML schema that accommodates both discovery and administrative metadata. It is compatible with MODS, DC and MARCXML (i.e. MARC wrapped up in XML).

OAI-PMH

The DC equivalent of Z39.50 is the *Open Archives Initiative Protocol for Metadata Harvesting* (OAI-PMH). In the Open Archives Initiative, there are data providers and service providers. Data providers offer DC-based metadata of their (digital) resources; this metadata is harvested by service providers, via the protocol; the service providers upload the metadata into their own retrieval systems; metadata retrieved on these systems can link back to the data provider's resource.

Prominent examples of gateways to archives created through OAI harvesting include the Access2Archives project in the UK and the Online Archive of California in the USA. The standard is by no means restricted to archives, however, and has been utilized by a wide range of agencies, including libraries. Indeed, it could be used by any agency with DC-based metadata or that wishes to build a 'virtual collection' of publicly accessible resources (Hunter, 2009). Metadata is sometimes converted to or from DC before or after the protocol's application (e.g. DC records are harvested, then converted to MARC21 for uploading into a library catalogue).

OpenURL

A different type of protocol that has also been widely adopted in many digital libraries is *OpenURL* (ANSI/NISO Z39.88), a standard URL format that allows a search to be duplicated on other systems via a 'link resolver'. It is typically used to link together records for the same journal article available in the various databases that a library subscribes to and is particularly useful when trying to find a record linked to the full text.

Archives

In the past, archives had less need to share their metadata with each other because of the uniqueness of their collections. Thus there has not been the same economic incentive to standardize metadata across the archives community as there has been amongst libraries. However, the internet has provided archives with sufficient incentive to establish certain standards that ensure the effectiveness of their finding aids, which, by moving into the online environment, have become far more accessible to end-users. The standardization of archival metadata also allows it to be harvested by 'third party' systems, as the Open Archives Initiative has demonstrated. This, in turn, facilitates cross-collection and cross-institution searching. Archives, like libraries, need to promote their collections as widely as possible if they are to thrive in an increasingly crowded information environment.

Although there were standards for archival description before the arrival of the internet, archivists were (and in some cases still are) more likely to consult a manual setting out principles of best practice than to adhere to a particular set of rules. In fact, the codes that did exist were predominantly devised and applied by librarians for the treatment of manuscripts and other archival materials housed in libraries. The first set of rules for describing manuscript materials that was aimed specifically at archivists, as well as manuscript librarians, was *Archives, Personal Papers, and Manuscripts: a cataloging manual for archival repositories, historical societies, and manuscript libraries* (APPM), initially published in 1983. Its second edition, edited by Steve Hensen, was issued and endorsed by the Society of American Archivists (SAA) in 1989. The Bureau of Canadian Archivists published its own code, *Rules for Archival Description* (RAD), the following year. Both APPM and RAD were heavily influenced by AACR2, which in the opinion of some British archivists made them less than ideal. Consequently, the *Manual of Archival Description* (MAD) was developed by Michael Cook at the University of Liverpool. It was first published in 1986; MAD2 was issued in 1990 and MAD3 in 2000. The Australian Society of Archivists published an Australasian code, based on the 'series system' developed at the National Archives of Australia, in 2007.

ISAD(G)

The push towards standardization in archival description had begun somewhat parochially, but it did not take too long for the archives community to develop an international code. The first edition of the *General International Standard Archival Description*, or ISAD(G), was published by the International Council on Archives (ICA) in 1994. A second edition followed in 2000. Just as ISBD(G) is intended to apply to all kinds of library resources, so ISAD(G) aims to cover all sorts of archival materials. It sets out the various elements in a format that quite closely mirrors that of ISBD, with seven (instead of eight) 'areas of description'. This is no coincidence, as the standard was developed with a view to making it as compatible with library cataloguing as possible, given the significant overlap that exists. Unlike ISBD(G), however, and more like AACR and RDA, ISAD(G) also provides some rules on how to record the elements. Figure 7.10 provides an outline of the standard's contents and indicates the similarity in organization to Part 1 of AACR2 (compare Figure 7.4).

One important difference between archival standards such as ISAD(G) and the library cataloguing standards is the former's emphasis on *hierarchical* descriptions. Although AACR2, for instance, allows for 'analytics' and multi-level description (in Chapter 13), library cataloguers tend to focus on the

0. GLOSSARY OF TERMS ASSOCIATED WITH THE GENERAL RULES

1. MULTILEVEL DESCRIPTION
1.1 INTRODUCTION

2. MULTILEVEL DESCRIPTION RULES
2.1 DESCRIPTION FROM THE GENERAL TO THE SPECIFIC
2.2 INFORMATION RELEVANT TO THE LEVEL OF DESCRIPTION
2.3 LINKING OF DESCRIPTIONS
2.4 NON-REPETITION OF INFORMATION

3. ELEMENTS OF DESCRIPTION
3.1 IDENTITY STATEMENT AREA
3.1.1 Reference code(s)
3.1.2 Title
3.1.3 Date(s)
3.1.4 Level of description
3.1.5 Extent and medium of the unit of description (quantity, bulk, or size)
3.2 CONTEXT AREA
3.2.1 Name of creator(s)
3.2.2 Administrative / Biographical history
3.2.3 Archival history
3.2.4 Immediate source of acquisition or transfer
3.3 CONTENT AND STRUCTURE AREA
3.3.1 Scope and content
3.3.2 Appraisal, destruction and scheduling information
3.3.3 Accruals
3.3.4 System of arrangement
3.4 CONDITIONS OF ACCESS AND USE AREA
3.4.1 Conditions governing access
3.4.2 Conditions governing reproduction
3.4.3 Language/scripts of material
3.4.4 Physical characteristics and technical requirements
3.4.5 Finding aids
3.5 ALLIED MATERIALS AREA
3.5.1 Existence and location of originals
3.5.2 Existence and location of copies
3.5.3 Related units of description
3.5.4 Publication note
3.6 NOTES AREA
3.6.1 Note
3.7 DESCRIPTION CONTROL AREA
3.7.1 Archivist's Note
3.7.2 Rules or Conventions
3.7.3 Date(s) of descriptions

Figure 7.10 *Contents of ISAD(G) (2000)*

acquisition level. That is, libraries acquire books, journals, DVDs and so on, and these are what they catalogue (though they also provide article-level access to journals, etc. by subscribing to external databases). Archives, on the other hand, typically acquire collections, or parts of a collection, the description of which may be too 'blunt' for the user's needs. In order to help users to drill down to the relevant records and documents, archivists thus often describe their resources at several levels, as was explained in Chapter 3. This is reflected in their standards, so that ISAD(G), for instance, covers different 'levels' of description in the sense of fonds, series, files, etc.

ISAD(G) is still a relatively new standard but it has already been adopted by a large number of archives around the world. In the United States, the SAA developed a new code, called *Describing Archives: a content standard* (DACS), based on the ISAD(G). DACS (Hensen, 2007) superseded APPM, and is now being used in many of the country's archives. Meanwhile, in Canada, RAD underwent a major overhaul, resulting in a second edition (Bureau of Canadian Archivists, 2008) that is also broadly in line with ISAD(G).

Given its generic nature, ISAD(G) may need to be supplemented by guidelines for specific forms of archival material. For instance, film archivists sometimes use *Archival Moving Image Materials* (AMIM), issued by the Library of Congress (2000). ISAD(G) can also be used in conjunction with the *International Standard Archival Authority Record for Corporate Bodies, Persons and Families*, or ISAAR(CPF), which covers similar ground to Part 2 of AACR2. The second edition of ISAAR(CPF), published by the ICA in 2004, goes further than name control, however, and allows for the context (i.e. provenance) of collections to be described in detail, making it more akin to FRAD and RDA (Cunningham, 2007).

EAD

One reason why archivists have embraced the ISAD(G) standard is that its second edition is broadly aligned with *Encoded Archival Description* (EAD, www.loc.gov/ead), an encoding scheme specifically designed so that archival description can be processed and exchanged by computers. Although MARC has sometimes been used for this purpose, the archives community wanted a standard that more closely fitted its own metadata practices. EAD has the additional advantage of having been developed during the modern computing era. Its first edition was based on SGML; its second edition, published in 2002, is based on XML. Maintained by the Library of Congress in association with the SAA, its schema, comprising 146 elements, has been mapped to and from various other element sets, including DC and MARC. A companion standard, Encoded Archival Context (EAC, http://eac. staatsbibliothek-berlin.de/index.php), covers ISAAR(CPF) and archival authority data (equivalent, in a way, to the MARC authority format). A sample of EAD/XML encoding is shown in Figure 7.11.

EAD has been used to support a wide range of online finding aids. Like ISAD(G), EAD is designed for multi-level description, whereas MARC is used mainly at the collection level (Gabriel, 2002). However, for *digital archives* (in which digital versions of the resources themselves can be accessed), other schemas designed for particular materials are sometimes applied. For example, for digitized photographic collections, archivists might adopt the SEPIA Data Element Set (SEPIADES, www.ica.org/7363/paag-resources/ sepiades-recommendations-for-cataloguing-photographic-collections.html), developed by the European Commission on Preservation and Access.

```
<corpname>New York University</corpname>
<address>
<addressline>
</addressline>
</address>
</repository>
<origination label="Creator" encodinganalog="100">
<persname>Butler, Charles, 1802-1897.  </persname>
</origination>
<physloc audience="internal" encodinganalog="852  $z">New York University Archives</physloc>
<abstract label="Abstract" encodinganalog="520  $a">Charles Butler was born in New York in
1802.  He was a lawyer whose endeavors included anti-Masonry, New York politics, western
state bond issues and speculation, canal, road and railroad construction, and philanthropy.
The papers of Charles Butler span the years 1817 to 1908, and  include correspondence,
business papers, legal documents, ledger books, pamphlets, and maps.</abstract>
</did>
<custodhist id="a16" encodinganalog="561  $a">
<head>Provenance</head>
<p>These papers were donated to the New York University Archives by Charles Butler's
daughter, Emily Ogden Butler, in 1925.</p>
</custodhist>
<accessrestrict id="a14" encodinganalog="506  $a">
<head>Access Restrictions</head>
<p>Open for research without restrictions.</p>
</accessrestrict>
<userestrict id="a15" encodinganalog="540  $a">
<head>Use Restrictions</head>
<p>Permission to publish materials must be obtained in writing from the:<lb/>
<address>
<addressline>New York University Archives<lb/>
</addressline>
<addressline>Elmer Holmes Bobst Library<lb/>
</addressline>
```

Figure 7.11 *Sample Encoded Archival Description in XML (source: www.nyu.edu/its/pubs/connect/spring05/cricco_stevens_xml.html).*

Museums

Many of the resources held in museums, like those in archives, are unique, or at least rare. Nevertheless, along with archivists, museum curators recognize the value of establishing metadata standards to ensure that their descriptions function effectively in the modern online environment. One problem, however, is the diversity of museum artefacts. Different museums focus on very different things, from postage stamps or motor cars to natural history or space. Even within a museum collection, a wide range of media can be represented.

A museum may decide to use a generic standard, such as Dublin Core, and extend it to suit specific needs and practices. Indeed, many *digital museums* are based on in-house extensions and customizations of DC. However, some metadata standards have been designed specifically for (and by) the museum community. In the UK, the *Standard Procedures for Collections Recording Used in Museums* (SPECTRUM) was developed in the early 1990s by the Museum Documentation Association. Now in its third edition, SPECTRUM (McKenna and Patsatzi, 2005) provides guidelines on the process and content of museum resource documentation. Its schema, which was adopted by the international Consortium for Interchange of Museum Information (CIMI) in the early 2000s, has been applied by a considerable number of museums around the world.

Shortly after SPECTRUM first came out, the International Council of Museums (ICOM), through its International Committee for Documentation (CIDOC), published *International Guidelines for Museum Object Information: the CIDOC information categories* (Grant, Nieuwenhuis and Petersen, 1995). In a sense, this is the museum equivalent of ISAD and ISBD, but it is quite different in scope and content, covering attributes rarely described in library catalogues or archival finding aids. As we mentioned in Chapter 3, museum curators are particularly focused on managing their physical collections, as well as providing access to them, and this is reflected in their documentation standards. The 22 'information groups' into which the CIDOC categories (i.e. elements) have been organized are listed below.

Acquisition Information
Condition Information
Deaccession and Disposal Information
Description Information
Image Information

Institution Information

Location Information

Mark and Inscription Information

Material and Technique Information

Measurement Information

Object Association Information

Object Collection Information

Object Entry Information

Object Name Information

Object Number Information

Object Production Information

Object Title Information

Part and Component Information

Recorder Information

Reference Information

Reproduction Rights Information

Subject Depicted Information

More recently, CIDOC has developed a 'Conceptual Reference Model' (CRM, www.cidoc-crm.org), based on its *Guidelines*, the aim of which, more or less, is to do for museum documentation what FRBR has done for library cataloguing, and provide 'definitions and a formal structure for describing the implicit and explicit concepts and relations used in cultural heritage documentation.' (A new model, called FRBRoo, attempts to harmonize FRBR and CRM.) CRM identifies 137 properties required for the documentation of museum objects. The schema has been published in XML, and the model has been approved by the ISO (21127:2006, *A Reference Ontology for the Interchange of Cultural Heritage Information*) (ISO, 2006a).

Despite appearing somewhat detailed, the CIDOC *Guidelines* and CRM aim to cover museum documentation in general. More specific standards may be followed for the description of artefacts pertaining to particular fields, either in addition to or instead of the more general standards. These include the Canadian Heritage Information Network (CHIM, www.rcip-chin.gc.ca/index-eng.jsp) Data Dictionaries: there is one for the humanities and another for the natural sciences. In the visual arts, two schemas widely used are VRA Core (www.loc.gov/standards/vracore), issued by the Visual Resources Association (VRA), and *Categories for Descriptions of Works of Art* (CDWA) (Baca and Harpring, 2009), published by the Getty Research Institute. It is important to bear in mind that these schemas are designed to cover attributes both of the digital images of artworks and of the artworks themselves. Art curators may also use a set of guidelines such as the VRA's *Cataloguing Cultural Objects* (Baca et al., 2006), which advise how to record the elements.

Although most curators are keen to promote their collections online, it has been observed that the curatorial tradition is perhaps a little less predisposed to making resource description freely accessible. This is because curatorial description aims to explain and educate, not merely to provide access. As such, it entails a high level of scholarship and adds considerable value, thus representing, according to Roel (2005, 22), 'a class of capital with which [curators] can always potentially cost-recover or generate income. Within the culture of museums, staff have traditionally been disinclined to make their collections available in an unmediated manner.'

Book publishing

Conventions such as the title page have been established in book publishing for hundreds of years, yet before the arrival of digital technologies there were few external standards for publishers to follow. Instead, presses would develop in-house standards for the presentation of metadata on and in their publications. By the early 20th century, publishers of scholarly books and journals were starting to issue detailed guidelines to their authors, in order to create a standardized writing style that was acceptable to the academic community. Some of these guidelines developed into *style manuals* that were adopted by other publishers. Examples include: the *Chicago Manual of Style*, issued by the University of Chicago Press (2010); the *Publication Manual of the American Psychological Association* (2010); the *MLA Handbook for Writers of Research Papers*, issued by the Modern Language Association of America (2008); and *AMA Manual of Style*, published by the American Medical Association (Iverson et al., 2007). These manuals focus on considerations such as spelling and punctuation, but also cover bibliographic aspects such as references, headings and abstracts. Copy editors are often employed to ensure that texts adhere to the favoured style. Colleges and universities may also require their students to adhere to a particular style in their essays and dissertations. More formal standards for referencing include ISO 690:2010, *Guidelines for Bibliographic References and Citations to Information Resources* (ISO, 2010).

However, in the online environment the use of standards is not only a matter of style. Publishers of electronic texts need to adhere to various encoding standards so that their resources can be accessed by and displayed on computers (including e-readers). We have already looked at basic mark-up languages such as HTML, used for web pages. More sophisticated encoding schemes, specifically for texts, have also been developed. Perhaps most notably, a scheme for encoding scholarly texts from the humanities and social sciences was established by the Text Encoding Initiative (TEI, www.tei-c.org) in the 1990s. TEI files include a *header* in which particular metadata elements can be recorded. These elements are based on those found in library cataloguing; indeed, TEI recommends the use of AACR2 to record the metadata. The elements form a schema that can be expressed in both SGML and XML.

The TEI standard is employed in some major collections of digital texts, but not by many commercial publishers. Instead, librarians have been encouraging publishers to record metadata for both their e-books and printed books in another electronic format, called ONIX (www.editeur.org/8/ONIX), which has been developed specifically for the purpose by EDItEUR, an international group of book industry bodies. ONIX can make it easier for publishers and distributors to transfer their metadata to booksellers, and thereby help to promote their products (there are ONIX formats for other media, such as videos, as well as for books). Based on an e-commerce metadata model called 'indecs', ONIX maps quite neatly onto MARC (though it covers some additional elements such as 'announcement date' and weight), and so has the potential to also save library cataloguers a good deal of work. Although ONIX is not yet pervasive in the publishing world, it is supported by publishers' associations and its use is increasing.

Book indexing

Book publishers are less likely to issue guidelines to their indexers than they are to their authors. This is because there is seldom a great need for book indexes to be consistent with each other, although it is important that they are internally consistent. Book (and e-book) indexers develop their own practices and usually adopt different styles and arrangements for different kinds of publication. They may follow recommendations made in the professional literature that deal with particular issues, such as the treatment of certain concepts or word forms, but they are rarely required to do so. Nevertheless, their practices tend to broadly coincide with general standards such as ISO's *Guidelines for the Content, Organization, and Presentation of Indexes* (999:1996).

Database indexing

Indexers contributing to databases, on the other hand, usually need to provide standardized metadata. Typically, they use an in-house template that sets out the elements required; it may be accompanied by guidelines on how to record particular elements and analyse particular attributes. A general standard on how to analyse the subject of a document, and that might be of assistance, is *Methods for Examining Documents, Determining their Subjects, and Selecting Indexing Terms* (ISO 5963:1985). It includes the following list of questions for indexers to ask themselves:

1 Does the document deal with the object affected by the activity?
2 Does the subject contain an active concept?
3 Is the object affected by the activity defined?
4 Does the document deal with the agent of this action?
5 Does it refer to particular means for accomplishing the action?
6 Were these factors considered in the context of a particular location or environment?
7 Are any dependent or independent variables identified?
8 Was the subject considered from a special viewpoint not normally associated with that field of study?

Formal guidelines for abstract writers include ANSI/NISO Z39.14 (ANSI/NISO, 1997).

E-research

While many databases provided to the academic and research communities are proprietary, we have already noted a special category that is at the forefront of the 'open access' movement. Many universities have constructed repositories to disseminate their staff's research findings, as reported in their publications. The metadata associated with these publications is usually collected by means of a template. In this case, however, the template may be developed with reference to external standards, in order to optimize interoperability, since the aim is to make the research outputs as widely accessible as possible. Typically, a mainstream schema such as DC or MODS is adopted, or extended.

The open access movement is not, however, limited to researchers' findings; their data can also be usefully disseminated for the benefit of the research community at large. Given the incredible amounts of data stored on computers around the world, opportunities for its re-use abound. Universities and other research institutions are therefore starting to set up *data repositories* to facilitate this, such as the UK Data Archives and the Australian National Data Service.

Research data is used in quite different ways from other kinds of information, and its metadata is correspondingly different. The unit of description (i.e. the resource) in data repositories is the *dataset*. All sorts of standards for describing datasets have been and are being developed, according to the nature of the data. In the natural sciences, a prominent one is the Content Standard for Digital Geospatial Metadata (CSDGM, www.fgdc.gov/metadata/csdgm), developed by US Federal Geographic Data Committee. It consists of a schema for the description of geospatial datasets used in fields such as cartography and surveying. The schema comprises 340 elements, reflecting the multifaceted nature of scientific data. The Australasian equivalent of CSDGM is ANZLIC (www.anzlic.org.au); the ISO counterpart is 19115:2009, *Geographic Information: metadata* (ISO, 2009a). A notable schema for biological data is Darwin Core (DwC, http://rs.tdwg.org/dwc/index.htm), developed by the Taxonomic Databases Working Group. Standards for the social sciences include those developed by the Data Documentation Initiative (DDI, www.ddialliance.org). An example of a more generic standard is the DataCite Metadata Schema (http://schema.datacite.org), which consists of 17 mandatory 'properties', as listed in Table 7.2.

The power and capacity of today's computers make e-research an exciting area to work in. The demand for metadata, and metadata standards, to manage datasets is likely to increase dramatically in the years to come.

Education

The open access movement is also encouraging the free exchange of another type of information resource produced by academics, namely, their teaching materials. In fact, various repositories have been set up so that all sorts of (digital) learning resources, from school to postgraduate level, can be shared, for the benefit of both educators and students. Like any other repository, they require resources and their associated metadata to adhere to particular standards. Several metadata schemas have been developed specifically for learning objects. The Institute of Electrical and Electronics Engineers (IEEE) first published its Learning Object Metadata standard (IEEE-LOM,

ID	Property
	Table 7.2 *Mandatory properties of the DataCite Metadata Schema (source: http://schema.datacite.org)*
1	Identifier (with type attribute)
2	Creator (with name identifier attributes)
3	Title (with optional type attribute)
4	Publisher
5	PublicationYear
6	Subject (with schema attribute)
7	Contributor (with type and name identifier attributes)
8	Date (with type attribute)
9	Language
10	ResourceType (with description attribute)
11	AlternateIdentifier (with type attribute)
12	RelatedIdentifier (with type and relation type attributes)
13	Size
14	Format
15	Version
16	Rights
17	Description (with type attribute)

http://ltsc.ieee.org/wg12) in 2002. Meanwhile, the Dublin Core community established an Education Application Profile (http://dublincore.org/educationwiki/DC_2dEducation_20Application_20Profile). These standards have a large number of implementations and can work with XML. Other notable extensions of DC for educational materials include the schema established by the Gateway to Educational Materials (GEM, www.thegateway.org) project in the United States, and the standard issued by the Education Network Australia (EdNA, http://apps-new.edna.edu.au/edna_retired/edna/go.html). An example of an IEEE-LOM variant is CanCore, developed in Canada.

Audiovisual industries

Those who specialize in the production of audiovisual resources, such as photographers, musicians and film makers, have also developed particular standards so that their work can be readily shared. Digital images, audio and video are normally created in standard file formats, with certain metadata elements (e.g. date of recording and file size) automatically inserted. Supplementary metadata may be added to improve retrieval, either inserted into the file or appended to it. 'Low level' attributes, such as 'colour spaces' and 'audio spectrum spread', can be identified by computer, but higher-level description concerned with 'meaning' usually requires human input, and a considerable degree of judgement.

Common file formats for images include JPEG, TIFF and GIF. All three accommodate basic metadata in designated sections. For more detailed descriptions, a wide range of standards are available, covering different kinds of image. We have already mentioned VRA Core and CDWA, used for art works. News photos are commonly described using a schema known as IPTC Core (www.iptc.org/site/Photo-Metadata/IPTC_Core_&_Extension), derived from a file format developed by the International Press Telecommunications Council (IPTC). Another notable format is DIG35 (www.i3a.org/technologies/digitalimaging/metadata), from the International Imaging Industry Association (I3A).

Common audio file formats include WAV, AIFF and MP3, which accommodate metadata in the same way as image file formats do. More detailed metadata can be inserted into files by means of a supplementary standard, such as ID3, often used in conjunction with MP3 to describe music recordings. Frameworks for the description of music include the Music Ontology (http://musicontology.com), which separates out works from manifestations.

Most video file formats, of course, store both moving images and sound. Widely used formats include AVI, MP4 and IFF. Several encoding schemes catering specifically for metadata, used in conjunction with the video files to support retrieval systems, also exist, the most notable of which is MPEG-7 (http://mpeg.chiariglione.org/standards/mpeg-7/mpeg-7.htm), developed by the Moving Picture Experts Group. The standard, compatible with XML, specifies a set of 'descriptors', and 'description schemes' containing these descriptors, that can be used to describe various features of still images, three-dimensional models, audio, speech and video (Jörgensen, 2007). MPEG-7 has been successfully integrated into the Moving Image Collections portal, which provides bibliographic access to some 275,000 titles across 11 collecting sites (Agnew, Kniesner and Weber, 2007). Another notable standard is Public Broadcasting Core (PBCore, http://pbcore.org), a set of elements used to describe the output specifically of broadcast media.

Business

Many companies generate large numbers of documents, and information managers who work in these companies often develop and promote in-house standards for their description. As many of these documents are not intended for external consumption, there is less need to apply external standards, and records management systems such as Hewett Packard's TRIM allow each organization to define its own metadata elements and values. Nevertheless, companies may decide to follow what they believe to be best practice. They also need to ensure that their record-keeping complies with the law.

Several metadata schemas for record-keeping, in both the private and public sectors, have been published in recent years. A notable example is the Australian Recordkeeping Metadata Schema (McKemmish et al., 2000), which is an extension of DC. There are also vocabularies available for particular elements, some of which are listed in the RKMS Register. A more general standard is ISO 23081, *Records Management Processes: metadata for records* (ISO, 2006b, 2009b and 2011)

Government

Agencies of government generally have more cause than businesses to share their documents and records. Indeed, they are often legally bound to do so. They may also be directed to provide an appropriate level of access through the application of certain metadata standards. Most of these standards have been developed specifically for use in the online environment and may be viewed as part of the move towards e-government, providing citizens with greater access to information and more opportunity for participation.

In the USA, government agencies are mandated to provide a specific set of metadata elements for their public documents, as part of the Government Information Locator Service (GILS, www.archives.gov/records-mgmt/policy/gils.html). This schema is in fact a profile for the Z39.50 protocol (outlined earlier in this chapter), enabling web users to retrieve the documents via Z39.50 servers. It comprises a total of 88 elements that cover all sorts of 'informational' publications and has been adopted not only by government agencies but also by a number of community organizations. Its Z39.50 derivation means that it maps quite well to and from MARC and can be supported by library management systems.

In the UK, the e-Government Metadata Standard (e-GMS, www.esd.org.uk/standards/egms) is mandated for government agencies as part of the eGovernment Interoperability Framework (eGIF). Its schema is a fairly basic extension of DC, with six additional elements. The Australian Government Locator Service (AGLS, www.agls.gov.au) has established a similar schema, also based on DC, with four additional elements. It is maintained by the National Archives of Australia (www.agls.gov.au). Meanwhile, the Canadian government has set out another DC extension, with two extra elements.

Registries

We have cited just some of the metadata standards being applied by members of various communities of practice. Metadata specialists need to keep track of these standards as they develop and, it seems, multiply. They need to select the most appropriate standards for their information context; they may also need to know about standards they do not use, so that they can build crosswalks between them and those that they do apply. To assist with this, registries of standards (and also of crosswalks between standards) have been set up. They may cover both schemas and vocabularies, typically in XML format. Notable examples include the Open Metadata Registry (http://metadataregistry.org), the Dublin Core Metadata Registry (http://dcmi.kc.tsukuba.ac.jp/dcregistry), and Schemapedia (http://schemapedia.com). Their expansion mirrors the growing interest in the Semantic Web.

While standard schemas are needed to achieve a basic level of interoperability, the values in which these schemas are recorded also need to be standardized if metadata is to attain higher levels of quality. We shall turn our attention to various standard vocabularies that have been developed for this purpose in the next chapter.

References

Agnew, G., Kniesner, D. and Weber, M. B. (2007) Integrating MPEG-7 into the Moving Image Collections Portal, *Journal of the American Society for Information Science and Technology*, **58** (9), 1357–1363.

Aliprand, J. (2000) The Unicode Standard: its scope, design principles, and prospects for international cataloguing, *Library Resources & Technical Services*, **44** (3), 160–7.

American Library Association (1878) Condensed Rules for Cataloging, *Library Journal*, **3**, 12–19.

American Library Association (1941) *ALA Catalog Rules, Author and Title Entries*.

American Library Association (1949) *ALA Cataloging Rules for Author and Title Entries*, 2nd edn, American Library Association.

American Library Association (1967) *Anglo-American Cataloging Rules*, Library Association, 1967.

American Psychological Association (2010) *Publication Manual of the American Psychological Association*, 6th edn.

Anderson, D. and Chaplin, A. H. (eds) (1963) *International Conference on Cataloguing Principles, Paris, 9th–18th October 1961: report*, K.G. Saur.

ANSI/NISO (American National Standards Institute and National Information Standards Organization) (1997) *Guidelines for Abstracts* (Z39.14).

ANSI/NISO (2010) *The OpenURL Framework for Context-Sensitive Services* (Z39.88).

ANZLIC, www.anzlic.org.au.

Ardö, A. (2010) Can We Trust Web Page Metadata? *Journal of Library Metadata*, **10** (1), 58–74.

Australian Society of Archivists (2007) *Describing Archives in Context*.

Baca, M. and Harpring, P. (eds) (2009) *Categories for Descriptions of Works of Art*, www.getty.edu/research/publications/electronic_publications/cdwa/index.html.

Baca, M. et al. (2006) *Cataloguing Cultural Objects: a guide to describing cultural works and their images*, ALA Editions.

Bibliographic Ontology, http://bibliontology.com.

Bureau of Canadian Archivists (1990) *Rules for Archival Description*.

Bureau of Canadian Archivists (2008) *Rules for Archival Description*, 2nd edn.

Canadian Heritage Information Network, www.pro.rcip-chin.gc.ca.

CanCore, www.cancore.ca.

Cook, M. and Procter, M. (2000) *Manual of Archival Description*, 3rd edn, Gower.

Cunningham, A. (2007) Harnessing the Power of Provenance in Archival Description: an Australian perspective on the development of the Second Edition of ISAAR(CPF), *Journal of Archival Organization*, **5** (1/2), 15–31.

Cutter, C. A. (1876) *Rules for a Printed Dictionary Catalog*, Government Printing Office.

Cutter, C. A. (1904) *Rules for a Dictionary Catalog*, 4th edn, USGPO.

Danskin, A. (2002) Today MARC Harmonisation, Tomorrow the World Wide Web: UKMARC, MARC21, XML and ONIX, *Catalogue & Index*, **143**, 1–3.

Data Documentation Initiative, www.ddialliance.org.

DataCite, *DataCite Metadata Schema Repository*, http://schema.datacite.org.

Dublin Core Metadata Initiative, *DC-Education Application Profile*, http://dublincore.org/educationwiki/DC_2dEducation_20Application_20Profile.

Dublin Core Metadata Initiative, *The Dublin Core Metadata Registry*, http://dcmi.kc.tsukuba.ac.jp/dcregistry.

EDItEUR, *ONIX*, www.editeur.org/8/ONIX.

Education Network Australia, *Edna.edu.au*, http://apps-new.edna.edu.au/edna_retired/edna/go.html.

e-Government Metadata Standard, www.esd.org.uk/standards/egms.

Encoded Archival Context, http://eac.staatsbibliothek-berlin.de/index.php.

European Commission on Preservation and Access, *SEPIADES*, www.ica.org/7363/paag-resources/sepiades-recommendations-for-cataloguing-photographic-collections.html.

Gabriel, C. (2002) Subject Access to Archives and Manuscript Collections: an historical overview, *Journal of Archival Organization*, **1** (4), 53–63.

Gateway, www.thegateway.org.

Gorman, M. (2004) *The Concise AACR2*, 4th edn, American Library Association, Canadian Library Association, Chartered Institute of Library and Information Professionals.

Government Information Locator Service, · www.archives.gov/records-mgmt/policy/gils.html.

Grant, A., Nieuwenhuis, J. and Petersen, T. (eds) (1995) *International Guidelines for Museum Object Information: the CIDOC information categories*, International Committee for Documentation of the International Council of Museums.

Hensen, S. L. (1989) *Archives, Personal Papers, and Manuscripts: a cataloging manual for archival repositories, historical societies, and manuscript libraries*, 2nd edn, Society of American Archivists.

Hensen, S. L. (2007) *Describing Archives: a content standard*, Society of American Archivists.

Hunter, J. (2009) Collaborative Semantic Tagging and Annotation Systems, *Annual Review of Information Science and Technology*, **43** (1), 1–84.

International Council of Museums, International Committee for Documentation, *The CIDOC Conceptual Reference Model*, www.cidoc-crm.org.

International Council on Archives (2000) *ISAD(G): General International Standard Archival Description*, 2nd edn, www.icacds.org.uk/eng/ISAD%28G%29.pdf.

International Council on Archives (2004) *ISAAR (CPF): International Standard Archival Authority Record for Corporate Bodies, Persons and Families*, 2nd edn, www.icacds.org.uk/eng/ISAAR%28CPF%292ed.pdf.

International Federation of Library Associations (1971) *ISBD(M): International Standard Bibliographic Description for Monographic Publications*.

International Federation of Library Associations and Institutions (1998) *Functional Requirements for Bibliographic Records: final report*, K. G. Saur.

International Federation of Library Associations and Institutions (2001) *Guidelines for Authority Records and References*, 2nd edn, K. G. Saur, www.ifla.org/files/cataloguing/garr/garr.pdf.

International Federation of Library Associations and Institutions (2009a) *Functional Requirements for Authority Data: a conceptual model*, K. G. Saur.

International Federation of Library Associations and Institutions (2009b) *IFLA Cataloging Principles: the Statement of International Cataloguing Principles*, K. G. Saur.

International Federation of Library Associations and Institutions (2011a) *Functional Requirements for Subject Authority Data (FRSAD): a conceptual model*, K. G. Saur.

International Federation of Library Associations and Institutions (2011b) *ISBD: International Standard Bibliographic Description*, Consolidated edn, De Gruyter Saur.

International Federation of Library Associations and Institutions, *UNIMARC*, www.unimarc.net.

Institute of Electrical and Electronics Engineers, *Learning Object Metadata*, http://ltsc.ieee.org/wg12.

Instruktionen für die Alphabetischen Kataloge der Preußischen Bibliotheken (1899), Asher.

International Imaging Industry Association, *DIG35*, www.i3a.org/technologies/digitalimaging/metadata.

International Organization for Standardization (1985) *Methods for Examining Documents, Determining their Subjects, and Selecting Indexing Terms* (5963).

International Organization for Standardization (1996) *Guidelines for the Content, Organization and Presentation of Indexes* (999).

International Organization for Standardization (1998) *Information Retrieval (Z39.50): application service definition and protocol specification* (23950).

International Organization for Standardization (2003) *The Dublin Core Metadata Element Set* (15836).

International Organization for Standardization (2006a) *A Reference Ontology for the Interchange of Cultural Heritage Information* (21127).

International Organization for Standardization (2006b) *Records Management Processes: metadata for records. Part 1, Principles* (23081-1).

International Organization for Standardization (2008) *Format for Information Exchange* (2709).

International Organization for Standardization (2009a) *Geographic Information: metadata* (19115).

International Organization for Standardization (2009b) *Records Management Processes: metadata for records. Part 2, Conceptual and Implementation Issues* (23081-2).

International Organization for Standardization (2010) *Guidelines for Bibliographic References and Citations to Information Resources* (690).

International Organization for Standardization (2011) *Records Management Processes: metadata for records. Part 3, Self-Assessment Method* (23081-3).

International Press Telecommunications Council, *IPTC Core & Extension*, www.iptc.org/site/Photo_Metadata/IPTC_Core_&_Extension.

Iverson, C. et al. (2007) *AMA Manual of Style: a guide for authors and editors*, 10th edn,

Oxford University Press.

Joint Steering Committee for Development of RDA (2010) *RDA: Resource Description and Access*, American Library Association.

Joint Steering Committee for Revision of AACR (1978) *Anglo-American Cataloguing Rules*, 2nd edn, American Library Association.

Joint Steering Committee for Revision of AACR (2005) *Anglo-American Cataloguing Rules*, 2nd edn, 2002 revision, 2005 update, American Library Association.

Jörgensen, C. (2007) The MPEG-7 Standard: multimedia description in theory and application, *Journal of the American Society for Information Science and Technology*, **58** (9), 1323–8.

Kelly, B. (2006) *Choosing a Metadata Standard for Resource Discovery*, www.ukoln.ac.uk/qa-focus/documents/briefings/briefing-63/html.

Leazer, G. H. and Smiraglia, R. P. (1999) Derivative Bibliographic Relationships: the work relationship in a global bibliographic database, *Journal of the American Society for Information Science*, **50** (6), 493–504.

Library Association (1881) *Cataloguing Rules of the Library Association of the United Kingdom*.

Library Association and American Library Association (1908) *Cataloguing Rules: author and title entries*, Library Association.

Library of Congress (1949) *Rules for Descriptive Cataloging in the Library of Congress*.

Library of Congress (2000) *Archival Moving Image Materials: a cataloging manual*, 2nd edn.

Library of Congress (2010) *Library of Congress Rule Interpretations*.

Library of Congress, *Encoded Archival Description*, www.loc.gov/ead.

Library of Congress, *MARC21*, www.loc.gov/marc.

Library of Congress, *MARC21 Format for Bibliographic Data*, www.loc.gov/marc/bibliographic.

Library of Congress, *Metadata Authority Description Schema*, www.loc.gov/standards/mads.

Library of Congress, *Metadata Object Description Schema*, www.loc.gov/standards/mods.

Library of Congress, *Search/Retrieval by URL*, www.loc.gov/standards/sru.

Lubetzky, S. (1953) *Cataloging Rules and Principles: a critique of the A.L.A. rules for entry and a proposed design for their revision*, Library of Congress.

Maxwell, R. L. (2008) *FRBR: a guide for the perplexed*, ALA Editions.

McKemmish, S. et al. (2000) *Australian Recordkeeping Metadata Schema*, www.infotech.monash.edu.au/research/groups/rcrg/projects/spirit/deliverables/austrkms-schemes.html.

McKenna, G. and Patsatzi, E. (2005) *SPECTRUM: the UK museum documentation standard*, 3rd edn, MDA.

Modern Language Association of America (2008) *MLA Style Manual and Guide to Scholarly Publishing*, 3rd edn.

Moving Picture Experts Group, *MPEG-7*, http://mpeg.chiariglione.org/standards/mpeg-7/mpeg-7.htm.

Music Ontology, http://musicontology.com.

National Archives of Australia, *AGLS Metadata Standard*, www.agls.gov.au

Open Archives Initiative, *Protocol for Metadata Harvesting*, www.openarchives.org/OAI/openarchivesprotocol.html.

Open Metadata Registry, http://metadataregistry.org.

Osborn, A. (1941) The Crisis in Cataloging, *Library Quarterly*, **11** (4), 393–411.

Panizzi, A. (1841) Rules for the Compilation of the Catalogue. In *Catalogue of Printed Books in the British Museum*, vol. 1.

Regeln für Alphabetische Katalogisierung (1977), Reichert.

Roel, E. (2005) The MOSC Project: using the OAI-PMH to bridge metadata cultural differences across museums, archives, and libraries, *Information Technology and Libraries*, **24** (1), 22–24.

Schemapedia, http://schemapedia.com.

Taxonomic Databases Working Group, *Darwin Core*, http://rs.tdwg.org/dwc/index.htm.

The Bath Group (2004) *The Bath Profile: an international Z39.50 specification for library applications and resource discovery*, release 2.0, www.collectionscanada.gc.ca/bath/91/tp-bath2-e.pdf.

Tillett, B. B. (1991) A taxonomy of bibliographic relationships, *Library Resources & Technical Services*, **35** (2), 150–58.

University of Chicago Press (2010) *The Chicago Manual of Style*, 16th edn.

US Federal Geographic Data Committee, *Content Standard for Digital Geospatial Metadata*, www.fgdc.gov/metadata/csdgm.

US RDA Test Coordinating Committee (2011) *Report and Recommendations*, Library of Congress, http://www.loc.gov/bibliographic-future/rda/source/rdatesting-finalreport-20june2011.pdf.

Visual Resources Association. *VRA Core*, www.loc.gov/standards/vracore.

W3C. *Resource Description Framework*, www.w3.org/RDF.

8

Vocabularies

Introduction

In the previous chapter we looked at some important standards pertaining to the elements, format and transmission of metadata. This chapter looks at the standardization of metadata values. Prescribed sets of values are often referred to as vocabularies. They may be used for indexing, for display or both. Many vocabularies are designed to cover a particular knowledge domain, and to describe the *subject* of information resources. Sometimes, they are called *knowledge organization systems*. Zeng and Chan (2003, 377) define such systems as 'tools that present the organized interpretation of knowledge structures'. However, vocabularies have also been developed for other elements, apart from subject.

The values used to describe a resource are always relative, that is, they allow resources to be compared and contrasted with each other. *Controlled* vocabularies enable resources to be organized systematically into groups. Other value systems are *quantitative* in nature, applying some form of measurement. There are also systems that prescribe a unique value to each resource for the purposes of *identification* rather than selection. We shall take another look at systems of identification towards the end of the chapter. First, however, we shall discuss the various types of controlled vocabulary that have been developed to describe and organize information resources.

Controlled subject vocabularies

An information resource's subject can, of course, be described in uncontrolled, natural language. We have already observed, however, that the standardization of vocabulary (beyond simply specifying that it should be in a particular natural language, such as English) can improve retrieval, especially if both indexer and searcher use the same controlled vocabulary. The aim is for each concept to be represented by one, and only one, particular term, and for each term to mean only one particular concept.

The application of controlled vocabularies, especially subject vocabularies, is not necessarily so straightforward. This is partly because of the limitations of any given vocabulary and partly because of the nature of what is being described. The 'subject' of a resource is not always something that can be easily identified, and is ultimately a matter of judgement: it will be viewed differently by different people. This is true no matter how much guidance is given on how to analyse a resource's subject, although detailed guidelines may result in more consistency. Furthermore, there are different ways in which subject analysis can be translated into the terms of a controlled vocabulary. For example, a resource may cover multiple topics, but usually only some of them will be represented. Translation, as well as subject analysis, is ultimately dependent on how 'subject' is defined. Before we discuss particular vocabularies, we shall first consider some of the basic questions that metadata specialists need to address when applying them.

Coverage is one of the key issues of subject description. Sometimes, the whole of a resource covers a certain subject; for example, a book could be said to be 'all about dogs'. Many resources, though, are not all about one particular thing. A book might be about volcanoes *and* earthquakes, for instance. Indexers would usually still want to enter terms for these topics, if both were given a fair amount of coverage in the resource. As a minimum, then, the 'main' topics are described, which together represent the subject of the resource *as a whole*. This is sometimes referred to as *summary level* indexing.

However, a book about volcanoes and earthquakes is also likely to be about lots of sub-topics too. Sections of the book might be about a particular volcano or about lava flows or about quake-proof buildings and so on. How many, if any, of these sub-topics should be represented in the subject description? To use the technical term, how *exhaustive* should the indexing be? There is no right or wrong answer to these questions, but it is likely to affect retrieval in certain ways. Some subject vocabularies are accompanied by guidelines on the indexing of sub-topics.

Another key issue of application is that of *specificity*. Generally, indexers follow the principle that the meaning of the index term (descriptor) should be *coextensive* with the topic. For example, a book on dogs is indexed using a term such as 'dogs' ('canines' might be an alternative), rather than, say, 'pets' or 'animals'. Obviously this cannot be done if the vocabulary does not incorporate that level of specificity; it is also a principle that needs to be applied with care, for it can lead to overly specific interpretations of subjects. For instance, a picture of a particular dog could be indexed with the term 'golden retriever', when the picture might be mostly used as an example of a dog, rather than a particular breed. In such cases, it might in fact be best to enter both the narrower and broader terms.

There has been much discussion over the years about the appropriate *depth* of indexing, which can refer to the level of specificity available in the vocabulary, or to the degree of exhaustivity in the indexer's analysis. In both respects, as we noted earlier, deeper indexing tends to lead to greater recall, but less precision. A rough measure of 'depth' is indexing *density*, that is, the number of descriptors per words of text.

The nature of language means that some more specific concepts require multiple terms to fully represent them. Examples of so-called *compound* concepts abound: 'Australian birds', 'fruit tree maintenance', 'looking after pet dogs', 'American society during the 1930s', 'microorganisms in water' and so forth. The question here is how, and when, to *co-ordinate* the terms representing the sub-concepts. One option is for them to be brought together in the indexing vocabulary itself, as phrases or as *strings* of terms. Thus the phrase 'Australian birds' could be authorized as a subject heading, or alternatively:

Birds – Australia

This kind of co-ordination of terms is known as *pre-coordination*, since the terms are co-ordinated prior to indexing and searching. However, another option is for terms not to be brought together in the indexing vocabulary, but to stand on their own and then be combined in the indexing and searching stages. Thus the vocabulary might instead include the two separate headings:

Australia
Birds

The indexer would enter both headings in a record to describe the subject of the resource. Similarly, the searcher would enter both headings in their search query. This approach is known as *post-coordination*.

Before the advent of computers, most subject indexing languages were essentially pre-coordinated, as there was no easy way of combining different index entries. However, modern database systems have changed all this and many end-users are now familiar with 'Boolean' search techniques, in which different terms are combined in a single query, through the 'AND', 'OR' and 'NOT' operators of Boolean logic. Post-coordinated indexing tends to be less restrictive and therefore richer, as well as requiring less expertise on the part of both indexer and searcher. Nevertheless, pre-coordination still has its merits, since it can lead to greater precision. This is because the way in which terms are combined in pre-coordinated vocabularies tends to express something about the nature of the interrelationship of their concepts. Thus, pre-coordinated strings describe compound concepts more fully and reduce the likelihood of false associations between different terms. Conversely, when pre-coordinated vocabularies are 'factorized' so that string elements are separated out, the result may be an increased level of usability, but also a loss of meaning.

Whatever the kind of vocabulary, and however it is applied, quality subject description requires careful analysis of a resource's content. Expertise in the subject field may also help, but perhaps most important is knowledge of users' information needs. Subject indexing has sometimes been considered from an 'objectivist' perspective, assuming that the content of a document has an intrinsic meaning that the indexer is tasked to represent. The reality, of course, is that meaning is always interpreted. Even if we can be sure of what a resource is intended to be about, this may not necessarily reflect what the prospective user makes of the resource. Since different users are likely to have different interpretations of and uses for a resource, there is often more than one 'right' solution to subject description, though some solutions may be more or less effective than others, in different contexts. A controlled vocabulary may reduce the number of solutions, but does not eliminate alternatives.

Subject headings

The development of controlled subject vocabularies for information resource description began in 19th-century libraries, alongside the development of the 'descriptive cataloguing' codes outlined in the previous chapter. Librarians such as Charles Cutter recognized that their patrons did not always know which book they wanted; sometimes they just knew that they wanted information about a certain topic. Library cataloguers did not have the time, or expertise necessarily, to describe subjects in any detail, but they were able to summarize them in a few words, which could be used as headings for patrons to look up in the card catalogue. Underneath each subject heading would be records for relevant, or potentially relevant, items. The benefits of using a particular set of headings were soon recognized, to deal with synonyms and the other issues discussed in Chapter 5. Initially librarians constructed headings according to their own preferences but, once the Library of Congress started distributing its record cards, the application of a common vocabulary made a good deal of economic sense.

LCSH

Controlled subject vocabularies are often developed for resources in particular fields or of a particular form. However, a few are applied to resources across more or less the whole gamut of recorded knowledge. Most notably, the *Library of Congress Subject Headings* (LCSH) are used to index the content of most public and academic library collections in the English-speaking world. The list of headings was begun at LC over 100 years ago and has grown steadily in size and sophistication ever since. The latest (33rd) edition comprises over 300,000 'base' headings (Library of Congress, 2011).

LCSH are no longer printed on catalogue cards, of course, but are entered into bibliographic databases and online catalogues as *access points*. They are what catalogue users are typically searching on when they carry out a subject search on the OPAC. Naturally, LCSH reflect the holdings of the Library of Congress; fortunately, the LC collections are amongst the largest and broadest in the world.

Many LCSH consist of a string of *subdivisions*, combined to represent a particular compound concept. Often, a subdivision is added to a base heading to extend a string. For example, a geographical subdivision such as 'Australia' could be added to the base heading 'Birds – Conservation' to make 'Birds – Conservation – Australia'. Thus LCSH provides for a large amount of pre-coordination. However, this has its limits and a single string cannot always be constructed to incorporate all of the concepts of a topic, so that sometimes two or even three headings are needed. For instance, the topic 'knitting socks' would be represented by 'Knitting' and 'Socks'.

Importantly, the *order* of the subdivisions in each string is fixed (i.e. controlled), at least for any given concept. For example, the heading 'Birds

– Conservation – Law and legislation' would be used for resources about law and legislation relating to the conservation of birds (the meaning can usually be ascertained by reading backwards). If the subdivisions in the string were rearranged it would either become invalid (as LCSH) or represent a different concept.

In the modern online catalogue, there is less need for terms to be pre-coordinated than there was in the days of the card catalogue, as the OPAC user is able to combine words from different headings to represent their desired topic. Strings can sometimes still be helpful for browsing purposes, when users are navigating a collection, provided that the system arranges the strings correctly. However, they take a considerable amount of time and expertise to construct and can also be difficult for computers to process. Attempts have been made, therefore, to break up LCSH strings, the most notable being Faceted Application of Subject Terminology (FAST), which separates out the different types of subdivision into topical, geographical, chronological and form facets (Chan and O'Neill, 2010). The FAST vocabulary does not, however, break down strings of multiple topics (let alone phrases).

LCSH incorporates cross-references so that the indexer, and end-user, can navigate their way through its knowledge organization system. An extract from a recent edition is shown in Figure 8.1. LCSH has adopted the standard kinds of reference, i.e.

UF (use for)
BT (broader term)
NT (narrower term)
RT (related term)

For instance, the heading 'Birds' is given as a BT of a number of headings, including 'Parrots', of which 'Cockatoos' is an NT. These hierarchical relationships can be of different types. For example, 'Apples' and 'Oranges' are both *kinds* of 'Fruit', whereas the 'Ear' and 'Nose' are both *parts* of the 'Head', and 'Phar Lap' and 'Red Rum' are both *instances* of 'Race horses'. Headings conceptually related in non-hierarchical ways are denoted by means of RT references. For example, 'Birds' is an RT of 'Ornithology'. References are made in both directions, so that 'Ornithology' is also an RT of 'Birds', and 'Parrots' is a BT of 'Cockatoos'. Many synonyms and near-synonyms are also covered by LCSH (though by no means all). Thus 'Tiger' is *used for* (UF) 'Panthera tigris'.

Birds *(May Subd Geog)*
   QL671-QL699 (Zooloogy)
  UF Aves
       Avian fauna
       Avifauna
  BT Amniotes
       Vertebrates
  RT Ornithology
  NT Anseriformes
       Beneficial birds
       Bird pests
       Birds of prey
       Cage birds
       Caprimulgiformes
       Captive wild birds
       Casuariiformes
       Cavity-nesting birds
       Charadriiformes
       Ciconiiformes
       Coliiformes
       Colonial birds
       Columbiformes
       Cuculiformes
       Dangerous birds
       Divers (birds)
       Exotic birds
       Extinct birds
       Falconiformes
       Flightless birds
       Forest birds
       Galliformes
       Grebes
       Gruiformes
       Introduced birds
       Kiwis
       Loons
       Nocturnal birds
       Ornamental birds
       Ostriches
       Owls
       Parasitic birds
       Parrots
       Passeriformes
       Pelecaniformes
       Penguins
       Photography of birds
       Piciformes
       Piscivorous birds
       Procellariiformes

       Provincial birds
       Rare birds
       Rarites
       Rheiformes
       Softbills
       State birds
       Talking birds
       Tinamiformes
       Trogoniformes
       Vultures
       Water birds
—**Anatomy**
    QL697 (Zoology)
    SF767. B57 (Veterinary anatomy)
  UF Avian anatomy
       Bird anatomy
  NT Bill (anatomy)
       Feather tracts
       Feathers
       Gizzard
       Salt gland
       Syrinx (bird anatomy)
       Tarsometatarsus
       Tibiotarsus
—Attracting
  USE Bird attracting
—Banding
  USE Bird banding
—**Behavior** *(May Subd Geog)*
—**Breeding** *(May Subd Geog)*
  BT Aviculture
—**Collection and preservation**
  (May Subd Geog)
  QL677.7
  NT Bird trapping
—Collisions with aircraft
  USE Aircraft bird strikes
—**Conservation** *(May Subd Geog)*
  QL676.5-QL676.57 (Zoolology)
  UF Birds, protection of
      (former heading)
— —**Law and legislation**
  (May Subd Geog)
  BT Game laws
— —**Societies, etc**
  NT Audubon Societies
—Control
  USE Bird pests—Control

Figure 8.1 *Extract from LCSH (2007)*

Some LCSH can describe *form* (e.g. through the 'form' subdivisions), as opposed to subject. That is, the vocabulary includes terms to represent not only what a resource is about, but what it *is*. Thus there are terms for maps, periodicals, pictures and so on; there are also terms for fiction, poetry and so forth. Some of these terms, however, are now being separated out into an accompanying *Library of Congress Genre/Form Terms for Library and Archival Materials* (LCGFT). LCSH also allows for the names of specific persons, organizations and works, if they are the subject of a resource, even though they are not listed in the vocabulary (instead, headings from the LC name authority files are used).

LCSH is updated on a weekly basis, with new headings added as and when resources on new subjects are acquired by LC and other libraries that participate in its Subject Authority Cooperative (SACO) program. The database is accompanied by a *Subject Headings Manual,* issued by LC (2008–), which details how LCSH should be applied. For example, it stipulates that a topic should be the subject of at least 20% of a resource in order to be assigned a heading. It also prescribes which terms can be added to different strings. Although the manual increases the extent to which the vocabulary is controlled, it requires a high level of commitment on the part of the cataloguer, and not all libraries follow it very closely.

LCSH has received a fair amount of criticism over the years, despite its widespread use. Its structure is not only largely pre-coordinated, it is also, at times, inconsistent. The terms themselves can be somewhat antiquated and there is a natural bias toward American language and culture (e.g. 'Football' means American football). It has also been criticized for its 'establishment' predisposition (most notably by Sanford Berman). LC has responded by making incremental improvements, rather than with wholesale replacement. No other existing vocabulary has the coverage of LCSH, however, and building a new vocabulary from scratch would be a very costly exercise. Moreover, LCSH is used in millions of catalogue records; introducing a new vocabulary would inevitably lead to uneven retrieval across the catalogue. The sheer pervasiveness of LCSH led to the British Library re-adopting it in 1995, after many years spent developing and applying its home-grown vocabularies of first, PRECIS and then, COMPASS (MacEwan, 1996). Heiner-Freiling (2000) reports that LCSH is used in a total of 24 national libraries, while translated or modified versions of it are employed in another 12.

Other subject heading lists

There are, nevertheless, other lists of subject headings applied by significant numbers of libraries. *Sears List of Subject Headings* was designed, from the 1920s onwards, for use in smaller library collections and for less 'academic' audiences. Now in its twentieth edition (2010), it continues to be used in many school library catalogues, particularly in North America. Another prominent list is the *Medical Subject Headings* (MeSH, www.nlm.nih.gov/mesh), issued by the National Library of Medicine in the USA. It is used in many health libraries, as well as in the popular MEDLINE database. In the publishing industry, the subject headings list developed by the Book Industry Standards and Communications (BISAC, www.bisg.org/what-we-do-20-73-bisac-subject-headings-2011-edition.php) is often applied, including by the Google Books search engine.

Outside of the English-speaking world, *Répertoire d'autorité matière encyclopédique et alphabétique unifié* (RAMEAU, http://rameau.bnf.fr) is provided by the Bibliothèque nationale for libraries in France, while *Répertoire de vedettes-matières* (RVM, https://rvmweb.bibl.ulaval.ca) is applied mostly in Canada. RAMEAU is, in fact, based on RVM, which itself is based on LCSH (Bélair, Bourdon and Mingam, 2005). *Regeln für den Schlagwortkatalog* (RSWK, 2010) forms the basis of many subject heading lists in Germany and other German-speaking countries. Lists have also been compiled in other major languages.

Subject thesauri

Another form of subject vocabulary often employed by library cataloguers and database indexers is the subject thesaurus. This is usually designed for automated retrieval rather than for the card index, and so comprises terms referred to as 'descriptors' instead of 'headings'. Subject thesauri are also more than just lists; they represent *structures* based on systematic cross-referencing. Although LCSH and other subject heading lists include a good many cross-references, they are essentially *compilations* of terms. In contrast, subject thesauri are constructed, from the outset, as systems of interrelated concepts. Their terms are normally post-coordinated, rather than strung together.

In ordinary language, a thesaurus provides synonyms and other words that are conceptually related to its entry words. A subject thesaurus serves a similar function, but is more selective in the vocabulary it covers, usually focusing on a particular field and on terms likely to be used to describe the subject of information resources. This likelihood is sometimes referred to as *warrant*, which is used to 'justify and subsequently verify decisions about what classes/concepts should appear [in the controlled vocabulary]' (Kwaśnik, 2010). There are two types of warrant: literary warrant, which involves the examination of the information resources ('literature'), and user warrant, which considers the terms and concepts users are searching for information on. There tends to be considerable overlap between the two types, but some resources may use relatively obscure terminology, rarely employed by the general population, while some end-users may describe various concepts colloquially, in terms not commonly employed in the published literature. Most controlled vocabularies are based on some sort of combination of literary and user warrant, although subject thesauri may emphasize user warrant more, and literary warrant less, than may subject heading lists.

Subject thesauri are thus constructed by studying how a particular field of knowledge is conceptually structured and terminologically labelled. A recommended methodology for doing this is known as *facet analysis*, through which the various facets of a subject are identified. Typically, a sample of topics from across the subject area are examined and organized into appropriate categories (facets). For example, in the case of cookery, the topics 'baking', 'boiling' and 'grilling' might be grouped together, as might 'chocolate', 'flour' and 'eggs'. The first group might be labelled 'techniques', and the second group 'ingredients'. Techniques and ingredients would thus be two facets of cookery. Often, facets are themselves organized into sub-facets, and the conceptual structure may incorporate several levels. For example, grilling might itself be deemed a 'facet' of techniques. Various kinds of grilling, such as char-grilling, might then be represented in the sub-facet. The result of facet analysis is a *faceted thesaurus*, often complemented by a faceted classification scheme (see the next section).

The conceptual structure of subject thesauri is established through cross-references. By convention, in English-based vocabularies the abbreviations BT, NT and RT are used, together with UF and USE to cover non-preferred terms. Scope notes may also be included under some descriptors, to clarify meaning. The size of subject thesauri varies considerably, according to the breadth and depth of the subject. Some are published for the benefit of other libraries and information agencies with collections of resources on the same (or similar) subject. Critically, they are made available to end-users so that the same terms (for the same concepts) are used, in theory at least, by both indexers and searchers. Nowadays, many thesauri are integrated into the online retrieval system itself.

Subject thesauri take a lot of time and effort to build and maintain, so this is usually done only when there is no existing thesaurus available to do the job. Fortunately, there are a large number of thesauri available, covering all kinds of subject areas. Prominent examples include the Education Resources Information Center's *ERIC Thesaurus* (www.eric.ed.gov/ERICWebPortal/ thesaurus/thesaurus.jsp) for education, the *Inspec Thesaurus* (Institution of Electrical Engineers, 2007) for science and engineering, *AGROVOC* (http://aims. fao.org/standards/agrovoc/about) for agriculture, the J. Paul Getty Trust's *Art and Architecture Thesaurus* (AAT, www.getty.edu/research/tools/vocabularies/ aat) for the visual arts, the *Thesaurus of Graphic Materials* (I and II) compiled by the Library of Congress (www.loc.gov/rr/print/tgm1 and www.loc.gov/ rr/print/tgm2), also for the visual arts, and the *Getty Thesaurus of Geographic Names* (TGN, www.getty.edu/research/tools/vocabularies/tgn); while the *UNESCO Thesaurus* (http://databases.unesco.org/thesaurus) covers a broad range of subject matter, in English, French, Spanish and Russian. The term 'Secondary schools' from the *UNESCO Thesaurus* is presented in Figure 8.2.

Most commonly, subject thesauri are used to index articles in periodical databases, but they are also used in library cataloguing and other forms of resource description. For instance, some museums in the UK use the *British Museum Materials Thesaurus*, and some archives, such as the AIM25 consortium (Archives in London and the M25 Area, www.aim25.ac.uk), are starting to use controlled vocabularies to facilitate cross-collection access via

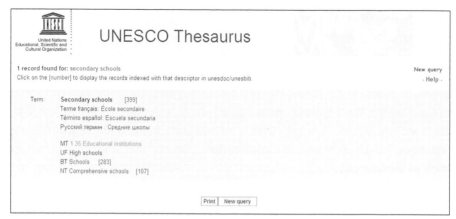

Figure 8.2 *Term from the UNESCO Thesaurus (source: http://databases.unesco.org/thesaurus)*

the web (Gabriel, 2002; Escrig-Giminéz and Giminéz-Chornet, 2011). Also in the UK, the *Integrated Public Services Vocabulary* (IPSV, http://doc.esd. org.uk/IPSV) has been developed so that the subjects of documents produced by different government agencies can be described using the same language.

Overarching standards representing best practice in the construction of subject thesauri include the revised British standard, BS 8723-1/2:2005 (British Standards Institution, 2005a and 2005b), the IFLA *Guidelines for Multilingual Thesauri* (2009), and the new ISO standard for thesauri, *Thesauri and Interoperability with Other Vocabularies*, ISO 25964-1:2011. Software is also available to assist in the systematic development of thesauri.

Subject classification schemes

So far, we have dealt with vocabularies based on a natural language, such as English. However, we noted in Chapter 3 that an *artificial* notation is sometimes employed to arrange materials (or links to them) in a particular order. While a subject headings list or thesaurus enables resources to be grouped together, or collocated, through the assignment of a particular term, the resulting group or *class* of resources still needs to be positioned amongst other groups if the collection as a whole is to be effectively presented to users. Arranging thesaurus descriptors alphabetically is not going to produce a very logical sequence of resources. Instead, a notation may be devised, so that when this notation is ordered alphabetically or numerically, similar classes end up near to each other. This is more effective as users are more likely to be interested in similar topics than in dissimilar ones. The result is a subject classification scheme.

There are, of course, many possible ways to 'logically' arrange topics: the conceptual proximity of topics is a subjective matter. There are, therefore, many possible classification schemes, even for the same set of topics and sub-topics. However, a classification scheme, just like a thesaurus, takes a lot of time and effort to construct and maintain. Accordingly, librarians and other metadata specialists usually prefer to apply an existing scheme rather than reinvent the wheel. A local scheme would also prevent them from using notations based on standard classification schemes that they might find in records downloaded from external databases. We shall look at some of the standard schemes shortly.

Most subject classification schemes, just like most other subject vocabularies, are built on principles such as literary and user warrant. They can also be constructed through facet analysis, just as subject thesauri can. In fact, the structure of a faceted thesaurus is a classification scheme, and many subject thesauri assign notation to each of their descriptors so that resources can be arranged in this structure. In this way, subject thesauri can double as classification schemes and provide two vocabularies: one for indexing and one for arrangement. Such thesauri/schemes are sometimes called *thesaurofacets*.

Generally, multiple descriptors are used to index a resource, whereas only one notation is used to 'classify' it (although in online classifications, links to digital objects can be placed in multiple classes). If different facets of a subject are to be co-ordinated, this is done as part of the scheme, that is, the facets are pre-coordinated. Unfortunately, this does not circumvent the problem of *scatter* if a resource is assigned only one place in the scheme: resources that are similar with respect to a particular facet still end up being scattered across the scheme if that facet is represented towards the end of the notation.

Library classification schemes are primarily used to arrange physical items on shelves, although many OPACs can also display shelf lists, i.e. records in shelf order. The two leading general classification schemes employed in the English-speaking library world are Dewey Decimal Classification (DDC) and Library of Congress Classification (LCC). Both originated in the 19th century as libraries moved from closed to open stacks.

DDC

The *Dewey Decimal Classification* (DDC, www.oclc.org/dewey) was first published by Melvil Dewey in 1876; it is now in its 23rd edition (2011). There is also an abridged version of the scheme, now in its 15th edition, often used in school and other smaller libraries. Table 8.1 shows how DDC has grown as library collections and recorded human knowledge have expanded.

DDC is based, in the first instance, on disciplines, as we can see from Figure 8.3,

Table 8.1 *Dewey Decimal Classification (full) editions*

Edition	Year of publication	Volume(s)
1	1876	1 vol
2	1885	1 vol
3	1888	1 vol
4	1891	1 vol
5	1894	1 vol
6	1899	1 vol
7	1911	1 vol
8	1913	1 vol
9	1915	1 vol
10	1919	1 vol
11	1922	1 vol
12	1927	1 vol
13	1932	1 vol
14	1942	1 vol
15	1951	1 vol
15 (Rev)	1952	1 vol
16	1958	2 vols
17	1965–67	2 vols
18	1971	3 vols
19	1979	3 vols
20	1989	4 vols
21	1996	4 vols
22	2003	4 vols
23	2011	4 vols

000	Computer science, knowledge & systems
010	Bibliographies
020	Library & information sciences
030	Encyclopedias & books of facts
040	[Unassigned]
050	Magazines, journals & serials
060	Associations, organizations & museums
070	News media, journalism & publishing
080	Quotations
090	Manuscripts & rare books
100	Philosophy
110	Metaphysics
120	Epistemology
130	Parapsychology & occultism
140	Philosophical schools of thought
150	Psychology
160	Logic
170	Ethics
180	Ancient, medieval & eastern philosophy
190	Modern western philosophy
200	Religion
210	Philosophy & theory of religion
220	The Bible
230	Christianity & Christian theology
240	Christian practice & observance
250	Christian pastoral practice & religious orders
260	Christian organization, social work & worship
270	History of Christianity
280	Christian denominations
290	Other religions
300	Social sciences, sociology & anthropology
310	Statistics
320	Political science
330	Economics
340	Law
350	Public administration & military science
360	Social problems & social services
370	Education
380	Commerce, communications & transportation
390	Customs, etiquette & folklore
400	Language
410	Linguistics
420	English & Old English languages
430	German & related languages
440	French & related languages
450	Italian, Romanian & related languages
460	Spanish & Portuguese languages
470	Latin & Italic languages
480	Classical & modern Greek languages
490	Other languages
500	Science
510	Mathematics
520	Astronomy
530	Physics
540	Chemistry
550	Earth sciences & geology
560	Fossils & prehistoric life
570	Life sciences; biology
580	Plants (Botany)
590	Animals (Zoology)
600	Technology
610	Medicine & health
620	Engineering
630	Agriculture
640	Home & family management
650	Management & public relations
660	Chemical engineering
670	Manufacturing
680	Manufacture for specific uses
690	Building & construction
700	Arts
710	Landscaping & area planning
720	Architecture
730	Sculpture, ceramics & metalwork
740	Drawing & decorative arts
750	Painting
760	Graphic arts
770	Photography & computer art
780	Music
790	Sports, games & entertainment
800	Literature, rhetoric & criticism
810	American literature in English
820	English & Old English literatures
830	German & related literatures
840	French & related literatures
850	Italian, Romanian & related literatures
860	Spanish & Portuguese literatures
870	Latin & Italic literatures
880	Classical & modern Greek literatures
890	Other literatures
900	History
910	Geography & travel
920	Biography & genealogy
930	History of ancient world (to ca. 499)
940	History of Europe
950	History of Asia
960	History of Africa
970	History of North America

Figure 8.3 *The hundred divisions of Dewey Decimal Classification (2011)*

which provides an outline of the scheme.

There are, of course, many sub-classes below the broad, three-digit classes and these are represented in the notation by means of a decimal point. An example of the way in which decimal numbers express conceptual hierarchy is given in Figure 8.4. In general, a sub-class is expressed through another decimal place; the more levels of hierarchy, the greater the number of decimal places.

```
600 Technology
630 Agriculture and related technologies
636 Animal husbandry
636.7 Dogs
636.72   Nonsporting dogs
636.728 Poodles
636.8 Cats
```

Figure 8.4 *Example of conceptual hierarchy expressed through DDC notation (source: DDC, 2011)*

The 'base' DDC numbers (including decimal numbers) are set out in the Schedules, from 001 to 999. However, these are by no means the only numbers that comprise the scheme. In addition, there are various ways in which numbers for more specific topics can be *built*, similar to the ways in which subject headings, such as LCSH, can be extended by means of generic subdivisions. A base number found in the Schedules can be extended by following instructions, where they occur, underneath the base number. This might involve tacking on bits of numbers from elsewhere in the Schedules, or adding numbers from one or more of six Tables provided for outside of Schedules. Sometimes, numbers are built using a combination of numbers from several sources. However, no other numbers apart from those in the Schedules and Tables can be used. The Tables are listed below; they cover various facets that frequently feature in compound topics.

T1   Standard Subdivisions

T2   Geographic Areas, Historical Periods, Biography

T3   Subdivisions for the Arts, for Individual Literatures, for Specific Literary Forms

T4   Subdivisions of Individual Languages and Language Families

T5   Ethnic and National Groups

T6   Languages

An example of a built DDC number would be 338.3720946, for the Spanish fishing industry: 338.372 is the base number for fishing, 09 has been added from Table 1, for geographical treatment, and 46 from Table 2, for Spain.

To the extent that the Dewey scheme allows for number building, it is said to be *synthetic*. Conversely, to the extent that DDC nevertheless stipulates a list of base numbers on which to build, it is *enumerative*. Another important aspect of a scheme such as DDC is its *hospitality*. This refers to the degree to which a scheme's notational structure accommodates new notations to represent new topics. Accordingly, many DDC numbers are left 'unassigned', while for new sub-topics there is usually the option of adding another decimal place.

The online version of DDC, namely WebDewey (www.oclc.org/dewey/versions/webdewey), is continuously updated, whereas the printed edition is revised about every seven years. There is also a relative index, which facilitates subject (as opposed to disciplinary) access. The scheme is published by OCLC and enjoys broad and international institutional support. It is applied by most public libraries in North America, the UK and Australasia, and by many other kinds of libraries and in many other countries, too. According to its website, DDC serves over 20,000 libraries across the world and has been translated into more than 30 languages.

LCC

The *Library of Congress Classification* (LCC, www.loc.gov/catdir/cpso/lcc.html) was created and adopted by the Library of Congress in 1897. It was based, in part, on the Cutter Expansive Classification, a scheme which did not survive the test of time, but whose system of 'Cutter numbers' has been used by many libraries, including LC, to create a specific position for each item within a class number (see below). LCC was published in piecemeal fashion in the early part of the 20th century and revisions for different sections continue to be published from time to time. Unlike DDC, it has been developed in tandem with a set of subject headings, namely LCSH.

The scheme is based on disciplines and uses a system of notation that expresses conceptual hierarchy, though to a lesser extent than DDC numbers do. In contrast to DDC, LCC notation uses both letters and numbers, beginning with one or more letters followed by a number, which may include a decimal point. Following this, are one or more 'Cutter numbers', which begin, in fact, with a letter, e.g. 'D64'. If there are two, the first represents a facet of the subject (e.g. 'Dogs'); the Cutter at the end always represents a 'bibliographic' aspect of the item (usually the surname of the first author) and is unique to that particular class, providing the item with an exact (relative) place on the shelf (i.e. its shelf mark). An example of an LCC 'number' would be QE537.2.J3, for earthquakes in Japan: QE537.2 is for general works on earthquakes and J3 a Cutter for Japan. In the Library of Congress catalogue, this is followed by 'N5713', a Cutter for the author (Takeshi Nishimura). Figure 8.5 provides an overview of the scheme.

LCC also allows for some number building, by means of 'auxiliary tables' and so forth, but there is less scope for synthesis than there is in DDC. This is generally considered a disadvantage, as enumerative schemes tend to be shallower. It also makes the LCC schedules much more voluminous (there are 41 volumes, in fact).

With its letters and Cutters, LCC is quite hospitable to new topics, but its revision programme is less systematic than DDC's, mainly because the scheme is maintained by a single institution, namely, LC. Most academic libraries in North America use LCC, but it is less popular amongst other libraries, even though they are likely to use LCSH. The online version, Classification Web, is continuously updated. There is, no analytical index to the schedules as a whole, although LCSH serves this function to some extent.

A	General Works
B	Philosophy, Psychology, Religion
C	Auxiliary Sciences of History
D	History – General & Europe, Asia, Africa
E/F	History – United States, Canada, and Latin America
G	Geography, Anthropology, Recreation
H	Social Sciences
J	Political Science
K	Law
L	Education
M	Music
N	Fine Arts
P	Language and Literature
Q	Science
R	Medicine
S	Agriculture
T	Technology
U	Military Science
V	Naval Science
Z	History of Books; Library Science; Bibliography

Figure 8.5 *Summary of Library of Congress Classification*

UDC

Another general classification scheme used by significant numbers of libraries, including a large number in the non-English speaking world, is *Universal Decimal Classification* (UDC). The scheme was developed at the turn of the 20th century and based on the 5th edition of DDC (1894); it was first published in 1904–7, in French. The brainchild of two Belgian bibliographers, Paul Otlet and Henri La Fontaine, UDC was a product of the 'documentation' movement, which was interested in organizing not only library materials but all kinds of information resource, at an international level. The scheme's origins are reflected in its strength in science and technology fields. It is likewise less biased than are DDC and LCC towards Anglo-American culture and language.

UDC is also relatively synthetic, and as a result accommodates a greater degree of specificity. There are 10 auxiliary tables, which can be used in combination to create very many numbers. Its notation uses decimals, but also incorporates (optionally) various punctuation marks to indicate the ways in which concepts are co-ordinated. For example, 311:[622+669](485) stands for statistics (311) of mining (622) and metallurgy (669) in Sweden (485).

The scheme is managed by the UDC Consortium (www.udcc.org). Its official languages are French, German and English. Like DDC, it has been translated into many other languages. Although UDC has its theoretical merits, it remains far less used than DDC and LCC, particularly in the English-speaking world (the full English edition was not, in fact, completed until 1980). Unfortunately, this represents something of a vicious circle: with fewer libraries using the scheme, there is less institutional support to maintain it and UDC revisions are comparatively protracted, which does little to encourage adoption. Its use in fewer libraries also means less record copy with UDC numbers, which likewise does little to help its cause. It is also worth bearing in mind the extensive amount of work involved in reclassifying large library collections, which can make the *status quo* an attractive option, regardless of the scheme in use. Nevertheless, UDC is applied by libraries in over 100 countries (Slavic, 2008), most notably in Europe and, to a lesser extent, Africa.

Specialized classification schemes

While schemes such as DDC, LCC and UDC have proved effective for organizing library collections covering a broad range of subjects, they may lack sufficient depth for more specialized collections (Eerola and Vakkari, 2008). As a result, a considerable number of schemes have been developed over the years for so-called 'special' libraries, to cater for particular fields. Some of these schemes represent an expansion of an existing general scheme. For instance, *National Library of Medicine Classification* (NLM, www.nlm. nih.gov/class) utilizes the QS–QZ and W–WZ parts of LCC; it is employed in many medical libraries. Similarly, *Moys Classification* (Moys, 2001) can be used instead of the K class of LCC; it is widely used in British law libraries. Other schemes are more idiosyncratic, such as the *Pettee* scheme for theology (Pettee, 1967) or the *British Catalogue of Music Classification* (Coates, 1960). Examples of schemes for particular kinds of material are the *International Patent Classification* (www.wipo.int/classifications/ipc/en), and the *Boggs and Lewis* scheme for maps (Boggs and Lewis, 1945).

Many of the specialized schemes developed in the past four decades are, to a greater or lesser extent, of the thesaurofacet variety mentioned earlier (the original being developed by Aitchison, Gomersall and Ireland in 1969 for engineering). The principles of faceted classification were first set out by members of the Classification Research Group, formed in the 1950s, who, in turn, were influenced by several earlier schemes, including *Colon Classification* (CC), invented by the Indian library pioneer S. R. Ranganathan (2006), and *Bliss Classification* (BC, www.blissclassification.org.uk), developed by Henry Bliss. Although these two schemes are used in very few contemporary libraries, their theoretical legacy is significant (Satija, 1997).

In a completely faceted classification scheme, notation for any facet of a subject can be combined with notation for any other facet. The key is that they be combined in a consistent way. In Figure 8.6 concepts represented in a hypothetical classification scheme are arranged into three facets (language, form and period). Within each facet, the *array* of concepts is ordered according to the notation assigned them: how they are ordered depends on their nature. In the example, two of the three arrays are ordered alphabetically, the other chronologically.

To express compound topics, notation from the relevant facets is joined

Language	Form	Period
E = English	1 Drama	a 19th century
F = French	2 Fiction	b 20th century
G = German	3 Poetry	

Figure 8.6 *Facets and arrays for a literary classification scheme*

together. For example, if one wanted to express the topic 'French poetry in the 19th century' using the notation in Figure 8.6, the notations F (for French), 3 (for Poetry) and a (for 19th century) would be combined, e.g. F3a. The order in which notation is combined is referred to as the *citation order*. As long as all classifiers follow this order, they will end up with the same class number for any given topic. Theoretically, citation order should be the reverse of the *filing order*, that is, the order in which the notation for the concepts would be filed individually. We also see this *principle of inversion* at work in general schemes such as DDC, when earlier numbers are added to later ones.

Faceted classification allows for more flexibility and hospitality, and can be processed more readily by computers. Editors of older classifications, such as DDC, are interested in making their schemes more faceted, mirroring recent attempts to factorize subject headings such as LCSH.

Call numbers

While library classification schemes are designed to support browsing and can be used as an alternative way to find resources on the catalogue, they also serve as the basis of *call numbers*, which are used to locate physical items (otherwise known as their 'mark and park' function.) Usually, a call number indicates its resource's location relative to other resources in a collection, rather than fixing the resource's physical position. Call numbers generally consist of the notation from a classification scheme (the class number), followed by an item number, such as a Cutter number. Librarians often try to ensure that no two resources are assigned the same call number.

Taxonomies and ontologies

Library classification schemes have sometimes been used to arrange resources, or at least links to resources, in online directories (e.g. both the CyberDewey hotlist of internet sites and the Centre for Digital Library Research at the University of Strathclyde's BUBL catalogue of internet resources are, or were, arranged by DDC). However, they may not always be the most appropriate means of arranging digital collections, for several reasons. For one thing, the content of digital collections often differs significantly from that of physical library collections. Also, online resources tend to be more diverse in nature, more granular and more current.

Managers of newly established digital collections are usually free to arrange their resources as they see fit. Schemes designed for more general online collections include that of the Open Directory Project (Figure 8.7). Most digital collections, however, focus on a particular subject area and are organized according to similarly focused schemes, developed in house.

At the level of the website or intranet, pages and their links likewise benefit from logical arrangement. In the field of information architecture, the resulting schemes are commonly referred to as *taxonomies*. There has been some debate over the difference (or lack of it) between a taxonomy and a classification scheme, but for our purposes the main difference is that a library classification scheme employs artificial notation to maintain a particular order, whereas a taxonomy does not need to because of its independence from the resources it represents (Gilchrist, 2003). Whereas books are taken off shelves to be read, links on a site can be used but still

Figure 8.7 *Top level of the Open Directory Project (source: www.dmoz.org)*

remain in position. Taxonomies have, of course, been developed for purposes other than information organization, the classification system used in natural history being a case in point.

Information architects develop taxonomies in order that networked environments may be navigated effectively. A taxonomy's *labels* (i.e. vocabulary) may also be used for indexing and 'search' purposes. Some taxonomies are, in fact, quite similar in nature to the faceted subject thesauri-cum-classification schemes we talked about earlier and can be constructed and maintained using thesaurus management software. When building their taxonomies, information architects often spend a good deal of time and effort researching the way in which end-users (whether customers or staff) think of and talk about a certain subject area or *knowledge domain*. In other words, particularly close attention is paid to user warrant.

Most taxonomies are developed in a quite specific organizational context, and although components may be used for other sites, few taxonomies attain the status of an external 'standard'. Moreover, taxonomies tend to be works in progress, due to the 'integrating' nature of many of their sites. Also in contrast to library classification schemes, taxonomic schemes designed by information architects are sometimes *polyhierarchical*, allowing for more than one citation order, as Figure 8.8 illustrates. This addresses the problem of scatter, allowing for multiple access to particular content, but also introduces an element of ambiguity, and possible confusion.

A distinction is also sometimes made between taxonomies and *ontologies* (Gilchrist, 2003). An ontology is a knowledge structure as conceived (and labelled) by people. Such a structure may not be limited to taxonomic

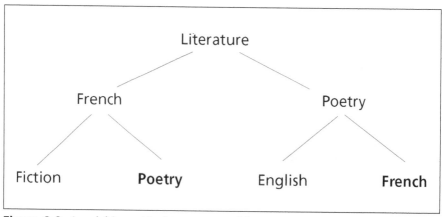

Figure 8.8 *A polyhierarchical taxonomy with two locations for French poetry*

relationships, of the 'x is a kind of y' type. All sorts of other relationships might be specified. For example, x might *produce* y, so that 'chefs' would be related to 'dishes'. A considerable amount of work has been done, particularly in the field of artificial intelligence, on developing fuller ontologies, in which various types of relationship are formally expressed, through different systems of logic (Gruninger et al., 2008).

Perhaps the most concrete outcome of these efforts for the field of information organization has been the application, in some more advanced retrieval systems, of ontologies known as *topic maps*. Figure 8.9 shows a topic map for a fragment of Australian literature, in which the exact nature of the relationship between different concepts is specified. The increase in precision that this affords has been demonstrated to improve information retrieval (Yi, 2008). Another advantage that topic maps have over taxonomies and subject thesauri is their open-endedness, which allows them to be more readily revised and expanded (Yi, 2008). Topic maps are beyond the scope of the Resource Description Framework, and have their own framework instead, namely, ISO/IEC 13250:2003.

Nevertheless, the greater sophistication of ontologies such as topic maps comes with its problems. Critically, they are much more difficult to construct and use. While information scientists continue to work on advanced ontologies needed to power their Semantic Web technologies, doubts remain as to whether their ambitions will be

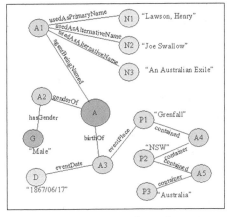

Figure 8.9 *Topic map for a fragment of Australian literature (source: Fitch, 2002)*

realized. (We shall discuss the Semantic Web's prospects in the next chapter.)

Ultimately, the distinction between 'taxonomies' and 'ontologies' can be represented by a continuum of vocabularies, running from the library thesauri and classification schemes through to the products of computer science. It is important to note that even the less sophisticated vocabularies can form part of a Semantic Web, since they all describe relationships between values (Hjørland, 2007). Indeed, several traditional systems, including LCSH and DDC, have been published in RDF/XML, applying the W3C's SKOS model for this very purpose. To express more sophisticated

vocabularies in RDF/XML, W3C's *Web Ontology Language* (OWL, www.w3.
org/TR/owl-ref) can be used.

Non-subject vocabularies

As any concept could, potentially, be the subject of an information resource,
all vocabularies could, theoretically, be used to describe subjects. This does
not, of course, preclude controlled vocabularies being developed for other
kinds of resource attribute. Nor does it preclude vocabularies being
developed to cover several attributes; indeed, many of them do, including, for
example, LCSH and DDC.

Table 8.2 outlines the three basic types of taxonomy found on websites and
intranets: subject, organizational and functional. Organizational taxonomies
describe the business unit to which a document pertains (e.g. the 'Marketing
Department'); functional taxonomies describe the purpose of a document
(e.g. 'accounts'). The general attributes of content, provenance and use are
reflected in this typology. Blackburn (2006) concludes that a *hybrid* of the
three types often makes for the most appropriate taxonomy.

More extensive vocabularies have also been developed specifically for
function. For instance, the National Archives of Australia's *Australian
Government Interactive Functions Thesaurus* (AGIFT, www.naa.gov.au/records-
management/publications/agift) can be used to record the 'function' element
in the AGLS schema mentioned in the previous chapter. Such vocabularies
are particularly dependent on user warrant; indeed, as Connelly (2007, 41)

Table 8.2 *Taxonomy types (source: Blackburn, 2006)*

Taxonomy type	Pros	Cons
Subject	• Common approach recognizable by most users (library, Yellow Pages, internet sites) • Many sources of existing and reusable schemes	• Requires understanding of terminology or supporting thesaurus
Business-unit based	• Familiar to users (mimics most existing paper filing systems)	• Organizational changes require maintenance of the taxonomy • Shared documents are difficult to classify
Functional	• Endures organizational changes	• Difficult to address case files

argues, 'user involvement is quite simply the most critical aspect of functional classification system design'.

Another set of values that may be controlled, particularly in library cataloguing, is that used for authorship. We looked at name authority files in Chapter 5. The most widely used are those maintained by the Library of Congress and those libraries that are members of its Name Authority Cooperative (NACO) programme. According to LC's website, the LC/NACO files comprise some 8.2 million records: 6 million for personal names, 1.4 million for corporate names, 180,000 for conference names, 120,000 for geographic names, and 0.5 million for (work) titles. A number of other national libraries also maintain extensive name authority files, some of which are linked to the NACO files through the *Virtual International Authority File* (VIAF, http://viaf.org) system. Another important database for artists' names is the J. Paul Getty Trust's *Union List of Artist Names* (ULAN, www.getty.edu/research/tools/vocabularies/ulan/index.html), used by museums and galleries, as well as libraries.

More vocabularies have recently been developed as part of the new library cataloguing code, RDA (Joint Steering Committee for Development of RDA, 2010). As well as lists of terms for the broad 'content' and 'carrier' categories, controlled vocabularies have been registered for the following elements: aspect ratio, form of musical notation, form of notated music, layout of cartographic images, mode of issuance, other distinguishing characteristic of the expression of a legal work, production method for tactile resource, reduction ratio, scale, sound content and status of identification. Some commentators claim that these vocabularies are just as important to cataloguing's future as are the RDA element sets.

Vocabulary mapping

We noted in Chapter 6 how the interoperability of information retrieval systems is supported by mapping different sets of elements and values. Most vocabularies, however, are much more extensive and complicated than schemas, and are especially difficult to map. Not only do terms have to be translated, they also have to be fitted into different conceptual structures. Most mappings forfeit some meaning, particularly across different natural languages. Nevertheless, if the Semantic Web is to have a future, ontologies need not only to be formalized, they also need to be linked, so that they can be applied to other contexts. For instance, e-learning resources are usually viewed through the prism of a particular curriculum context, and are thus best described using a local ontology. However, if these resources are to be used outside of this context, the ontology needs to be mapped to vocabularies employed by external repositories (Gašević and Hatala, 2006).

Various approaches have been tried to 'join up' vocabularies. In some instances, a *macrothesaurus* has been developed, particularly where the vocabularies represent different domains or languages. Landry (2004) reports how the Multilingual Access to Subjects (MACS) project has integrated subject headings from three different lists: LCSH (in English), RAMEAU (in French) and the *Schlagwortnormdatei* (SWD, based on RSWK, in German). The European Heritage Network (HEREIN) project also offers a trilingual thesaurus. In other cases, a 'hubs and spokes' approach is adopted. For example, in the High-Level Thesaurus Project (HILT), each local vocabulary was mapped to DDC, established as the *switching language* (Will, 2002; Dunsire and Nicholson, 2010).

Most vocabulary mapping carried out thus far has been done manually. A partially automated approach used catalogue records in the OCLC WorldCat database to map LCSH and DDC. Fully automated approaches have not achieved that much success to date; Zeng and Chan (2003) are of the view that both manual and machine mapping efforts will continue into the foreseeable future.

Identification systems

Finally, we come to a special type of 'vocabulary' that is also controlled, but is used solely to identify particular resources, rather than to 'describe' them. The attribute to which these identifiers pertain is thus the assignation itself. Identification systems, such as the International Standard Book Number (ISBN) and the Universal Resource Identifier (URI), aim to establish (and maintain) a one-to-one relationship between identifier and resource. This can assist both humans and computers. Indeed, as we noted earlier, URIs are a key component of the Semantic Web, which depends on unambiguous links rather than on the statistical probability of search engines. While some subject vocabularies may be losing ground in today's online environment, identification systems are increasing in importance.

Usually, identification systems are maintained by a particular agency or group of agencies charged with the responsibility of assigning new identifiers to new resources. We cited several systems in Chapter 2, operating at the different FRBR levels. They can also be used to control values for information resource attributes such as authorship. For example, the *International Standard Name Identifier* (ISNI) has recently been established as an ISO standard (27729:2012) (ISO, 2012) to cover people and organizations 'that participate in the creation, production, management or distribution of cultural goods in the digital environment'. However, identification systems typically lack the structure of taxonomies and ontologies, that is, they do not indicate relationships, other than that of mutual exclusion, between the entities they identify. This is an important difference, as the capacity to record values that relate to each other enables users of such vocabularies to provide descriptions that transcend the individual resource. Indeed, it is this ability that may be critical when metadata specialists lay claim to their professional future, as we shall discuss in the remaining chapter.

References

AGROVOC, http://aims.fao.org/standards/agrovoc/about.

Aitchison, J., Gomersall, A. and Ireland, R. (1969) *Thesaurofacet*, English Electric Co. Ltd.

Art and Architecture Thesaurus Online, www.getty.edu/research/tools/vocabularies/aat.

Bélair, J.-A., Bourdon, F. and Mingam, M. (2005) The Répertoire de Vedettes-Matière and RAMEAU: two indexing languages in French: a necessary luxury? In *World Library and Information Conference: 71st IFLA General Conference and Council*, http://archive.ifla.org/IV/ifla71/papers/145e-Belair_Bourdon_Mingam.pdf.

Bibliothèque nationale de France, *Répertoire d'autorité matière encyclopédique et alphabétique unifié*, http://rameau.bnf.fr.

Blackburn, B. (2006) Taxonomy Design Types, *AIIM E-Doc*, **20** (3), 14–16.

Bliss Classification Association, www.blissclassification.org.uk.

Boggs, S. W. and Lewis, D. C. (1945) *The Classification and Cataloging of Maps and Atlases*, Special Libraries Association.

Book Industry Standards and Communications, *BISAC Subject Headings*, www.bisg.org/what-we-do-20-73-bisac-subject-headings-2011-edition.php.

British Museum Materials Thesaurus, www.collectionslink.org.uk/assets/thesaurus_bmm/matintro.htm.

British Standards Institution (2005a) *Structured Vocabularies for Information Retrieval: guide. Definitions, Symbols and Abbreviations* (8723-1).

British Standards Institution (2005b) *Structured Vocabularies for Information Retrieval: guide. Thesauri* (8723–2).

Chan, L. M. and O'Neill, E. T. (2010) *FAST: Faceted Application of Subject Terminology: principles and applications*, Libraries Unlimited.

Coates, E. J. (1960) *The British Catalogue of Music Classification*, Council of the British National Bibliography.

Connelly, J. (2007) Eight Steps to Successful Taxonomy Design, *The Information Management Journal*, **41** (6), 40–6.

Dewey Decimal Classification, www.oclc.org/dewey.

Dunsire, G. and Nicholson, D. (2010) Signposting the Crossroads: terminology web services and classification-based interoperability, *Knowledge Organization*, **37** (4), 280–6.

Eerola, J. and Vakkari, P. (2008) How a General and a Specific Thesaurus Cover Expression in Patients' Questions and Physicians' Answers, *Journal of Documentation*, **64** (1), 131–42.

Escrig-Giminéz, M. and Giminéz-Chornet, V. (2011) Designing a Thesaurus to Give Visibility to the Historical Archives in the Archivo del Reino in Valencia, *Knowledge Organization*, **38** (2), 154–66.

Fitch, K. (2002) Taking RDF and Topic Maps Seriously: what happens when you drink kool aid. In *AusWeb 02*, http://ausweb.scu.edu.au/aw02/papers/refereed/fitch2/paper.html.

Gabriel, C. (2002) Subject Access to Archives and Manuscript Collections: an historical overview, *Journal of Archival Organization*, **1** (4), 53–63.

Gašević, D. and Hatala, M. (2006) Ontology Mappings to Improve Learning Resource Search, *British Journal of Educational Technology*, **37** (3), 375–389.

Gilchrist, A. (2003) Thesauri, Taxonomies and Ontologies: an etymological note, *Journal of Documentation*, **59** (1), 7–18.

Gruninger, M. et al. (2008) Ontology Summit 2007: ontology, taxonomy, folksonomy: understanding the definitions, *Applied Ontology*, **3** (3), 191–200.

Heiner-Freiling, M. (2000) Survey on Subject Heading Languages Used in National Libraries and Bibliographies, *Cataloging and Classification Quarterly*, **29** (2), 53–71.

Hjørland, B. (2007) Semantics and Knowledge Organization, *Annual Review of Information Science and Technology*, **41** (1), 367–405.

Institution of Electrical Engineers (2007) *Inspec Thesaurus*.

Integrated Public Services Vocabulary, http://doc.esd.org.uk/IPSV.

International Federation of Library Associations and Institutions (2009) *Guidelines for Multilingual Thesauri*, http://archive.ifla.org/VII/s29/pubs/Profrep115.pdf.

International Organization for Standardization (2011) *Thesauri and Interoperability with Other Vocabularies. Part 1, Thesauri for Information Retrieval* (25964-1).

International Organization for Standardization (2012) *International Standard Name*

Identifier (ISNI) (27729).

ISO/IEC (International Organization for Standardization and International Electrotechnical Commission) (2003) *SGML Applications: topic maps* (13250).

International Patent Classification, www.wipo.int/classifications/ipc/en.

J. Paul Getty Trust, *Art and Architecture Thesaurus*, www.getty.edu/research/tools/vocabularies/aat.

J. Paul Getty Trust, *Getty Thesaurus of Geographic Names*, www.getty.edu/research/tools/vocabularies/tgn.

J. Paul Getty Trust, *Union List of Artist Names*, www.getty.edu/research/tools/vocabularies/ulan.

Joint Steering Committee for Development of RDA (2010) *RDA: Resource Description and Access*, American Library Association.

Kwaśnik, B. H. (2010) Semantic Warrant: a pivotal concept for our field, *Knowledge Organization*, **37** (2), 106–10.

Landry, P. (2004) Multilingual Subject Access: the linking approach of MACS, *Cataloging & Classification Quarterly*, **37** (3/4), 177–91.

Library of Congress (2007) *Library of Congress Subject Headings*, 30th edn.

Library of Congress (2008-) *Subject Headings Manual*.

Library of Congress (2011) *Library of Congress Subject Headings*, 33rd edn.

Library of Congress, *Library of Congress Clssification*, www.loc.gov/catdir/cpso/lcc.html.

Library of Congress, *Thesaurus for Graphic Materials I: subject terms*, www.loc.gov/rr/print/tgm1.

Library of Congress, *Thesaurus for Graphic Materials II: genre and physical characteristic terms*, www.loc.gov/rr/print/tgm2.

MacEwan, A. (1996) LCSH and the British Library: an international subject authority database? *Catalogue & Index*, **120**, 1–6.

Moys, E. M. (2001) *Moys Classification and Thesaurus for Legal Matters*, 4th edn, K. G. Saur.

National Archives of Australia, *Australian Government Interactive Functions Thesaurus*, www.naa.gov.au/records-management/publications/agift.

National Library of Medicine, *Medical Subject Headings*, www.nlm.nih.gov/mesh.

National Library of Medicine, *NLM Classification*, www.nlm.nih.gov/class.

Pettee, J. (1967) *Classification of the Library of Union Theological Seminary in the City of New York*, Rev. and enl. ed., Union Theological Seminary.

Ranganathan, S. R. (2006) *Colon Classification*, 6th edn, Ess Ess Publications.

Regeln für den Schlagwortkatalog (2010), 3., überarb. und erw. Aufl., Deutsche National Bibliothek.

Répertoire de vedettes-matières, https://rvmweb.bibl.ulaval.ca.

Satija, M. P. (1997) The Revision and Future of Colon Classification, *Knowledge Organization,* **24** (1), 18–23.

Sears List of Subject Headings (2010) 20th edn, H. H. Wilson.

Slavic, A. (2008) Use of the Universal Decimal Classification: a world-wide survey, *Journal of Documentation,* **64** (2), 211–28.

Text Encoding Initiative, www.tei-c.org.

UDC Consortium, www.udcc.org.

UNESCO, *UNESCO Thesaurus,* http://databases.unesco.org/thesaurus.

Virtual International Authority File, http://viaf.org.

W3C, *SKOS: Simple Knowledge Organization System,* www.w3.org/2004/02/skos.

W3C, *Web Ontology Language,* www.w3.org/TR/owl-ref.

WebDewey, www.oclc.org/dewey/versions/webdewey.

Will, L. (2002) Thesauri in the Age of the Internet: HILT and related projects, *Catalogue & Index,* **146**, 8–11.

Yi, M. (2008) Information Organization and Retrieval Using a Topic Maps-based Ontology: results of a task-based evaluation, *Journal of the American Society for Information Science and Technology,* **59** (12), 1898–911.

Zeng, M. L. and Chan, L. M. (2003) Trends and Issues in Establishing Interoperability among Knowledge Organization Systems, *Journal of the American Society for Information Science and Technology,* **55** (5), 377–95.

9

The future of metadata

Introduction

It is clear that people will use metadata to find, identify, select and obtain information resources, and to navigate collections of information resources, for a long time to come. When we consider the future of metadata, then, the question is not whether there is a future, but what that future might look like. There are several aspects to this question, associated with aspects of the metadata we have discussed in the preceding chapters. To what extent will metadata be used in future information retrieval systems, given the rise of content-based retrieval? What kind of metadata will be needed in future information environments? Who will be creating and managing this metadata? What value will we place on it? How will metadata be shared across systems? Will metadata become more, or less, standardized? All these questions are interrelated, of course, and can be answered only by considering the future of the information environment as a whole.

Three approaches

In today's online world, access to information resources can be provided by taking one or more of three general approaches. First, there is the approach which bypasses metadata altogether and uses computers to analyse the content of information resources to retrieve those most likely to be relevant to users' needs. Second, there is the 'Web 2.0' approach, in which end-users, contributors and authors provide the metadata. Third, there is the 'traditional' approach, in which resources are organized and described by information professionals, in the ways that they deem most effective for their clients. We can address the questions posed above by examining the prospects for each of these approaches.

Ultimately, approaches to information retrieval reflect different perspectives on the nature of information resources themselves. In the first chapter, we observed that every information resource contains a *message*. This can be viewed 'objectively', that is, as an independent object, and analysed by a third party without reference to either creator or recipient. Although the third party could be a person, such as an information professional, this perspective is most clearly adopted by *content-based* retrieval systems. Alternatively, the message can be viewed and analysed according to the meaning intended (or thought to be intended) by its creator. This perspective is reflected in metadata supplied by authors and publishers. Again, the message can be viewed and analysed according to its utility, a perspective frequently associated with user-generated metadata.

While computers may not be so good at determining intentions or needs, information professionals might adopt any of the three perspectives outlined above. It would seem, however, that ideally they should serve as a 'bridge' between author and user, identifying aspects of the message that the user may not be aware of and, conversely, identifying aspects of the message the author may not have thought of. Accordingly, whereas the field of information retrieval has increasingly focused on the computer processing of content, the field of information organization has developed tools and standards with reference to content and carriers, authors and users.

Two major traditions of information organization established prior to the emergence of 'information retrieval' (in the narrower sense) are that of library cataloguing, which emphasizes the importance of the collection and literary warrant, and the 'documentation' tradition, from which emanate vocabularies based on a combination of literary and user warrant. Products of the first tradition include AACR and LCSH; those of the second tradition include UDC and the thesaurofacet. The two traditions have, to some extent, merged; the result is a body of theory and practice that exerts considerable influence on a range of information domains, although perhaps not as much as content-based information retrieval nowadays does. We shall consider the future of information organization as a profession later in the chapter. First, we shall consider the progress that has been made in content-based information retrieval, and then look at the prospects for 'social' information organization.

Content-based information retrieval

When it comes to analysing the content of information resources, computers have some obvious advantages over humans. They can be programmed to process vast amounts of content very thoroughly and very consistently, and can do so very rapidly. They are thus able to find resources much faster than people can when using, say, a card index. Computers retrieve not only records but also, very often, the resources themselves. By ranking the resources in order of probable relevance, they also assist with selection. Content-based retrieval systems are very scalable, as the likes of Google have shown, and very accommodating of additional resources. Moreover, they generally cost less than information professionals do.

Although some retrieval algorithms do attempt to take account of users' needs, most centre around the 'bags' of words or other components of content. In many contexts, this has proved quite effective, and many experiments over the years have indicated that 'keyword searching' can produce results at least as good as those based on structured metadata and controlled vocabularies. There are, however, limits to what even a computer can do with a bag of words, and results in basic text retrieval appear to have reached a plateau (Rasmussen, 2004). Furthermore, they become less impressive as the amount of content decreases. For instance, automatically generated book indexes compare poorly with those produced by professional indexers working at the level of individual pages.

Content-based systems are also not so good, thus far, at dealing with non-verbal information, which is often more ambiguous. The message of a picture, for example, might be interpreted in many different ways, even if it depicts objects that can be readily identified (Hughes and Rafferty, 2011). A picture of a house, say, may not be about a house, but about 'dereliction' or 'modernity', or a host of other concepts. Yet even at the level of object, computers struggle because the content they are processing does not comprise the language (i.e. words) in which people mostly express their information needs. While content-based image retrieval (CBIR) systems are able to deal with 'primitive' aspects of pictures, such as colour, texture and shade, they appear to be some way off from achieving reliable results at the higher 'denotative' and 'connotative' levels (Chen, Fu and Huang, 2010; Beaudoin, 2007). Similarly, content-based music retrieval is still in its infancy. In fact, it is not even clear here what the unit of meaning is (Byrd and Crawford, 2002). When does a melody start and finish? Some researchers consider musical meaning to be beyond the scope of automated systems, and instead limit themselves to matching physical phenomena (Lippincott, 2002). Manual, text-based description of audiovisual resources continues to have the predominant role to play in their retrieval.

Moreover, content-based systems have also been less effective in contexts where users are unsure of what it is they want. In such cases, independent summaries could well assist users with their selections, yet attempts at automatic summarization have been largely unconvincing. Similarly, computers are less well placed to create structured overviews of whole collections of resources for users to navigate. As Lancaster (2003, 335) observes, 'while some progress has certainly been made in applying computers to various tasks related to information retrieval, little evidence exists that automatic procedures can yet outperform humans in such intellectual tasks as indexing, abstracting, thesaurus construction, and the creation of search strategies'.

While content-based retrieval systems are often good at finding and obtaining information resources, they are not, therefore, always so good at supporting the tasks of selection and navigation. Nor do they necessarily support the task of identification, since people often identify resources through various non-content attributes (as we discussed in Chapter 2). The problem, essentially, is that computers cannot draw on external knowledge of the world to the extent that humans can. Thus, they can learn how to classify resources into pre-defined schemes, or cluster resources according to similar content, but they have been notably unsuccessful in building knowledge structures that are 'logical' and make sense to users. In the open web environment, this may not be practicable, but in closed environments such structures may well be worth the human effort. For example, Barnum et al. (2004, 186) compared full-text searching of books and the use of a manually created index, and found that readers were generally better off starting with the index, even though it was not always their preference. The researchers concluded that 'the day when machines replicate the intellectual processes that human indexers provide isn't foreseeable anytime soon. The question, then, is "Where should the dividing line be for human indexing and information retrieval by machine?"' We shall return to this question shortly.

Social metadata

We now turn to the second approach to information retrieval, namely, for end-users, contributors and other 'lay' people to provide the metadata, sometimes referred to as 'social'. The contemporary online environment empowers the general public to directly contribute both resources and resource descriptions. The obvious advantage that social metadata has over that produced by professionals is that it costs less (though it still has to be managed). It is also, potentially, far more scalable than professional description. The question, then, is whether it is good enough.

It is still fairly early days, but some evaluations have been carried out and the results are mixed. Those who advocate that metadata should be based on end-users' needs might argue that nothing can be more user-centric than that which is produced by end-users themselves. Certainly, users can provide valuable insights into a resource's utility, while resource creators are in a particularly good position to shed light on attributes relating to a resource's origins.

The enthusiasm for social metadata, even amongst information professionals, needs to be tempered, however, by careful consideration of the issues involved. First, there is the issue of consistency. Different users inevitably have different perspectives and different needs. Accommodating these different users does allow for greater recall than professional description tends to do. Nevertheless, the resulting inconsistency also leads to lower precision for any given user. Studies comparing professional and social indexing have generally confirmed this trade-off.

The reasons for the lower precision are quite straightforward. Unless predefined schemas and vocabularies are used, the 'synonym' problem will emerge, as will the 'homonym' problem; there is also likely to be analytical inconsistency, with users indexing at different conceptual levels (Spiteri, 2007). Whether the reduction in precision is worth the increased recall really all depends on the search context. Many of the retrieval systems using social tagging deal with images, video, imaginative works and other resources in which the interpretation of content is an especially 'subjective' matter. In such contexts, with so many interpretations even amongst indexers, recall could well be a more important consideration than precision (Hughes and Rafferty, 2011; Saarti, 2002).

Another issue is that of representation. Social tagging may not necessarily be representative of users' views. In practice, not all users will provide metadata, and those who do, for any given resource, could well be biased in some way or other. It has been shown, for instance, that the LibraryThing folksonomies tend to be USA-centric (Bates and Rowley, 2011). Statistically, the chance of misrepresentation diminishes as the number and proportion of social taggers increases, but the description provided by a professional with a good knowledge of their audience as a whole might, in some cases, be more representative.

Moreover, it can be argued that 'users' may not always know how, and in what way, a given resource might help them. This claim does not represent professional arrogance; rather, it highlights the important distinction between potential use and actual use. Information organization exists to help the prospective user, whereas social metadata is invariably created by those who have already used the resource. There could well be reasons for which a resource could potentially be used, other than those reflected in user tagging. Even if social metadata is representative of users' views, it may not fully reflect the utility of resources.

Another critical question is a practical one: will users provide rich and accurate metadata when they are not being paid to do so? Someone with a personal connection to a resource is more likely to tag, though they are also more likely to provide misleading metadata (whether deliberately or not). For social metadata to represent the 'wisdom of the crowd', however, people with less of an attachment to the resource need to be persuaded to tag too. Managers of digital collections therefore need to foster an environment that encourages tagging, for example, by making it easy or fun. Thus far, librarians have not enjoyed all that much success at getting patrons to tag, or even rate, their loaned items. Many borrowers are probably too far removed from both system and resource.

Even when non-professionals do make the effort (and an honest effort), their metadata may suffer from carelessness to a greater degree than professional description does. If they are expected to use controlled vocabularies, it may also suffer from a lack of technical expertise. As Wilson (2007, 26) points out, 'the onus is on the metadata community to build systems and interfaces that harvest contributor semantic content ... leveraging a contributor's discipline knowledge'.

However, the value of folksonomies may actually lie in their lack of control. In the main, controlled vocabularies do not keep up with linguistic or conceptual developments as well as people do. Nor are they always so inclusive, either linguistically or conceptually. Studies have found that LCSH, for example, fails to cover a quarter of subject queries and about a third of user tags (Carlyle, 1989; Mering and Nowick, 2003; Lund, Ng and Pera, 2009). While efforts are under way to make folksonomies more structured, either *pre-hoc* (by restricting tagging to a controlled vocabulary) or *post-hoc* (by mapping the results onto a controlled vocabulary), they may well be missing the point (Chan and Yi, 2009; Hunter, 2009).

Folksonomies can supplement controlled indexing with little extra cost, but may be too unreliable to replace it (Rolla, 2009). According to Bates and Rowley (2011, 445), 'folksonomy should thus not be viewed as a quick-fix solution to the creation of an organic, dynamic and inclusive OPAC resource discovery tool'. Instead, social tagging and professionally applied controlled vocabularies can be seen as complementary. The question then becomes one of how a system should *integrate* the two approaches. Different ways of doing it are currently being tried out, and the answer is not yet clear.

Professional description

The interest shown in both content-based retrieval and social metadata often has more to do with the bottom line than with their relative effectiveness. The metadata specialist's salary may still be viewed as a good investment when the information environment is contained and the resources are critical, but many information agencies now find themselves dealing with huge amounts of content that are forcing hard decisions. Nowhere have these been more keenly felt than in library cataloguing.

Many cataloguers are wondering what the future has in store for them (Sanchez, 2011). Some are tentative, some are pessimistic. For Yee (2009, 75), 'it appears that the [American Library Association] is now dominated by library administrators with shrinking budgets who know very little about the complexities of bibliographic control (other than its expense) and who wonder if the fact that undergraduates are in love with Google might not provide an excuse for libraries to dispense with the information organization part of their budget entirely'. There have, of course, always been some library administrators less sympathetic to cataloguing theory than others, while economics has shaped the direction of practice for well over 100 years. Cutter himself lamented how the introduction of the LC's card distribution service, at the turn of the 20th century, had ended the 'golden days of cataloguing'. The cataloguing code reforms in the middle of the 20th century were likewise spurred on by anxiety over backlogs.

Nevertheless, it is the case that cataloguing has become a highly concentrated activity, with most record creation (if not editing) carried out within the confines of a small number of 'elite' libraries. Consequently, cataloguing is now covered only minimally in many of the professional curricula. In 2006, LC announced that it would no longer control (most) series titles. In the same year, it commissioned a report which questioned the need for LCSH, in the light of undergraduate use of search engines such as Google

(Calhoun, 2006). Many cataloguers saw, and can still see, a slippery slope.

It might be argued that cataloguers have only themselves to blame. Despite repeated calls to change, some have continued to strive for the 'perfect' record, regardless of budgetary realities (Steinhagen and Moynahan, 1998). On the other hand, some administrators may also be missing the point. It is not that cataloguers are resistant to change per se; rather, it is the kind of change that they are not so keen on (Gross, 2008). Cataloguers are no different from other people: they do not like being made redundant. Neither do they wish to see the marginalization of the OPAC. Instead, they advocate for changes that would enhance the catalogue and make better use of the bibliographic data they provide.

We shall soon see if RDA will convince library administrators more than have LCSH and MARC21. Unfortunately, the message from cataloguers themselves is mixed. Gorman (2007, 65) argues that RDA has gone too far, that it 'seeks to find a third way between standard cataloguing (abandoning a slew of international agreements and understandings) on the one hand and the metadata crowd and boogie-woogie Google boys on the other. The sad thing is that betraying the former has not managed to appease the latter.'

However, RDA is designed to be applied to the description of library resources, not to everything covered by Google. As Banush and LeBlanc (2007, 102) ask, 'if we embrace the assumption that today's students and researchers seldom use library catalogs, except perhaps as finding aids to facilitate delivery of known library assets, then to what extent are these information seekers really library "users"? When much of the information world is digitized, will anyone need the library at all? And what exactly do they need now?' The answer is that for some patrons, at least, the first one or two pages of resources via Google is not sufficient; rather, they require a collection of quality resources. Library cataloguing is there to support the use of this collection, not the use of the web. Danskin (2007, 207) suggests that 'there is a degree of hysteria attached to the idea that because it is impossible to catalogue the web it is no longer necessary to catalogue anything'.

Whether the 'metadata crowd' will ever be able to engineer their vision of the Semantic Web is unclear (as we shall shortly discuss), but to distinguish cataloguing from metadata, as Gorman does, is surely retrograde. Metadata schemas, such as RDA, and vocabularies, such as LCSH, provide structures that support the navigation of collections, something that neither content-based retrieval nor uncontrolled folksonomies can do. As Danskin (2007) points out, library catalogues do not merely provide access to resources, they create maps of knowledge, highlighting relationships between them. This does not mean, though, that libraries and other information agencies should build walls around their collections and ignore the rest of the information universe. On the contrary, they need to ensure that their collections are as integrated as possible into the ever-expanding online world, which means making their systems interoperable and linking their metadata to other metadata.

This need for integration is why cataloguing needs to become metadata. It is the reason why, quite apart from economics, the next-generation OPACs may also be the last generation of OPACs. Increasingly, the interfaces of catalogues are being hidden behind discovery layers that provide access to a far greater range of resources than the traditional OPAC ever did. This should not make cataloguers fearful; rather, it affords an opportunity for them to expand their job scope, without changing their core function, that is, to organize information.

It appears likely that library cataloguers will increasingly become metadata librarians, and not just in name. They may still create metadata, but they may also spend a good deal of time managing it, and managing systems that use it. Metadata librarians are probably going to need to address more directly a wider range of information organization considerations. Chapman (2007) has identified four 'roles' which define their positions: collaboration, research, education and development. These roles require new skills, such as programming, project management and training. The trend towards a broader skill base is mirrored in the experiences of other contemporary metadata specialists. Indexers, for instance, are looking to fill new roles as 'vocabulary creators, planners and checkers' (Browne and Jermey, 2007, 198). Nevertheless, they will still need many of the same core attributes that they have benefited from up until now, such as 'good general knowledge, the ability to grasp new concepts quickly, curiosity, attention to detail, interest in logistic issues, and the ability to see things from somebody else's point of view' (Browne and Jermey, 2007, 2).

These trends do not mean that those who specialize in creating metadata, including bibliographic data, will disappear. It is unlikely to be left entirely to authors and end-users. However, they may well find themselves working in different environments. Libraries are increasingly outsourcing their cataloguing services, for instance (Primary Research Group, 2011). There is also likely to be more use of computers to extract metadata for cataloguers to verify.

Metadata specialists will likewise be challenged by what they describe, as new kinds of information resource emerge. Already, social media are being employed by scientists and other knowledge workers in the course of their professional routines; these resources need to be organized in much more systematic ways than they are at present (Das et al., 2008). Online information will become even more dynamic and even more difficult to pin down. This will make the FRBR concept of 'work' harder to apply, but all the more relevant.

For sure, professionals will not be employed to describe everything. The description of resources deemed of lesser informational value, if it is done at all, may be left to others. This is often already the case, of course. Even when metadata specialists are employed, they may need to provide more limited descriptions for certain resources. The decisions that will have to be made will not be new, although the contexts will be. In all cases, policy should be made with reference to users, and with a full appreciation of the benefits that quality metadata provides them.

Controlled vocabularies

Naturally, metadata specialists apply standards far more than authors and users do. Although non-specialists might use standard structures for their descriptions, they are less likely to use standard vocabularies. Of course, many of these vocabularies, particularly if they are presented in a straightforward way, can be applied by non-professionals (after all, they may well be searched on by non-professionals), but in many situations this is not going to happen. Furthermore, we have already noted that folksonomies' lack of control can be their strength.

We have discussed how standardized values can solve the homonym problem, so that a given value consistently represents a particular concept; this increases precision. Controlled vocabularies can also help to solve the synonym problem, with cross-references to the preferred value for a given concept; this increases recall. In these ways, controlled vocabularies can support the finding function of a retrieval system.

However, it is in their support for the navigation of resource collections that controlled vocabularies really come into their own. While they can be criticized for representing just a single perspective, or at best a 'unified' perspective, it is a perspective that can nevertheless help the information seeker to work out what they need. Neither precision nor recall can be achieved until the user has determined what is relevant. Although this can and does occur through the inspection of uncontrolled metadata, and through inspection of the resources themselves, it can also be facilitated by organizing resources or their metadata as a whole, and in a way that is logical. While end-users can describe resources in ways that may be logical, they rarely do so with reference to a larger collection; conversely, computers may be able to analyse all the resources of a collection, but are not good at mapping out collections in a way that reflects people's knowledge structures. Thus controlled vocabularies *scaffold* information seeking (as well as indexing), helping users to drill down to what they want; they provide *context*, which can form a backdrop for browsing or can be more deliberately and systematically explored through navigation, pre- or post-search.

Various commentators have identified contextualization as the distinguishing feature of vocabulary control. Jacob (2004, 538) highlights the difference between categorization and classification: it is the latter that contextualizes, that establishes 'relationships between classes that are stable and meaningful'. This can be particularly helpful when the user is unsure of a knowledge domain, or unsure of what exactly they are looking for (Golub, 2006). As Mann (2008, 162–3) argues, 'keyword inquiries – no matter how the words are weighed, ranked, massaged, or manipulated – essentially give you only those results having the terms you've been able to specify in advance. They do not bring to your attention, except by chance, conceptual options that are slightly different in their focus. They do not allow you to recognize related sources whose terms you cannot think of beforehand.' Shiri and Revie (2006) found that a subject thesaurus can provide many search terms that would otherwise not have been thought of. The researchers also found that once users had been introduced to the thesaurus tool, many resolved to continue using it.

Vocabulary control has its drawbacks. The stability of the system becomes a barrier when the user does not share the ontology provided. It is the potential disconnect between system and user that concerns many who advocate for a post-modern approach, as represented by social tagging and folksonomies. They argue that everyone's view of a resource is equally valid and that there is no 'essence' to be described. Mai (2011) thus characterizes the application of controlled vocabularies as 'modernist' in outlook, whereby the indexer attempts to describe documents 'objectively', fitting them into a predefined conceptual structure.

However, the use of a predefined structure does not in itself make the indexer an 'essentialist'. Indeed, most indexing primers emphasize the user's perspective. For example, Lancaster (2003, 9) advises that 'effective subject indexing involves deciding not only what a document is about but also why it is likely to be of interest to a particular group of users'. Although a given controlled vocabulary could be regarded as *the* knowledge structure, most professional indexers realize that it represents only one way of looking at things. It is not used to impose a particular view of knowledge on users, but to improve consistency between indexer and searcher, and to *guide* users.

To minimize disconnect with users, vocabularies need to be updated on an on-going basis, with reference to both user and literary warrant. In the past, 'it was assumed that meaning became more stable and consensus firmer as the evidence mounted and the idea withstood the test of time' (Kwaśnik, 2010, 108). Early classificationists such as Dewey aimed to build relatively permanent structures; the authors' messages were thought to reflect an external reality (Hjørland, 2007). However, it is now widely accepted that both the authors' messages and the interpretations of these messages change over time. Controlled vocabularies need to change correspondingly. Of course this is easier said than done, even in the digital environment. It requires very considerable amounts of intellectual effort, particularly when coupled with the problem of re-applying a changing vocabulary to pre-existing resources. Applying a controlled vocabulary is itself an expensive business. Nevertheless, it can also be a very profitable one, from an information seeker's perspective.

So will LCSH still be applied in tomorrow's libraries? Some librarians look instead to content-based retrieval as e-books overtake the printed codex, supplemented by user tagging. This may suffice for many subject queries, but it will not provide a systematic overview of a collection and it will not help users to formulate their queries. The more work the metadata specialist does to prepare the ground pre-search, the more likely it is that the user will reach their destination. McCutcheon (2009, 62) concludes that keyword and controlled vocabulary search 'each has its strengths and weaknesses, that in practice they are complementary to one another, and that the best results are achieved by using the two in combination: in other words, they who have the most tools win'.

Semantic Web technologies

Standardized metadata does not only help human seekers of information. It is also critical for computers, as we noted in earlier chapters. They need data, including metadata, to be encoded in a format that they can process. However, the vision of the Semantic Web is for computers not only to process data but to make sense of it. For this to happen, metadata schemas and vocabularies also need to be standardized. Information professionals who wish to connect their resources to the Semantic Web are working to align existing standards for information resource description with the generic standards, such as RDF, on which the new Semantic Web technologies are based.

The concept of the Semantic Web can be grasped by differentiating it from the two 'webs' with which we are now quite familiar. The original Web (1.0) may be thought of as a gigantic collection of resources hyperlinked to each other in all sorts of ways, some might say in a tangled web. The Social Web (2.0) has not replaced this web, but supplemented it with applications that allow for more user input. Today's web has become much more interactive as a result, with blogs, wikis, tags and so on. The Semantic Web is a vision, mostly unrealized as yet, that transforms the web from a collection of resources handled by humans to a collection of *data* that can be processed by computers (i.e. a database). Again, the Semantic Web would not replace the existing web; instead, it would make its content 'meaningful' not only to humans, but also to computers. Table 9.1 outlines how Semantic Web technologies could revolutionize our information environment.

Just like any other database, the Semantic Web needs to be organized in systematic ways. It is also dependent on metadata created by humans, who 'tell' the computer what the data is about. This metadata is linked together, through devices such as namespaces, as we saw in Chapter 7. Computers (i.e. Semantic Web 'agents') can then follow these links to explore the context of the data, thereby making 'sense' of it and allowing for its analysis. This mirrors, of course, the way in which human information seekers might use predefined structures to navigate resource collections.

The comparison and synthesis of online information has, up till now, been largely performed by humans. In theory, Semantic Web technologies could potentially save them enormous amounts of time and effort. They could be used to analyse all sorts of resources, not just information resources. Schemas and vocabularies are thus being developed to describe a wide range of things – even people. The resulting structures are intended to represent 'our' various knowledge domains, but expressed in a way that computers can process.

The field of information organization is contributing its fair share of Semantic Web standards. We have noted, for example, how the RDA elements can be expressed using RDF/XML. In 2009, the Library of Congress launched

Table 9.1 *Three generations of the world wide web (source: Ding et al., 2009)*			
	Traditional Web (Web 1.0)	Social Web (Web 2.0)	Semantic Web (Web 3.0)
User	Browsing	Browsing Publishing Organizing	Browsing Publishing Organizing Interacting
Communication style	One-way (e.g., reading a book)	One way Human-to-human (e.g. sharing)	One way Human-to-human Human-to-machine (e.g. query answering)
Data	Resources (syntactic data): • content and format mixed • documents hyperlinked	Resources, tags, metadata: • content and format separated • data are linked	Resources, tags, metadata: • content and format separated • ontological data • data are semantically linked
Data contributor	Webmaster or experienced user	Average user	Average user and web agents
Linking data	Hyperlinks	Different types of hyperlinks	Semantic links
Adding data	Composing HTML pages	Online publishing tagging	Online publishing tagging machine-generated data and metadata

its Authorities and Vocabularies service, which 'provides access to Library of Congress standards and vocabularies as Linked Data'. There is also a W3C Library Linked Data Incubator Group (www.w3.org/2005/Incubator/lld), whose mission is 'to help increase global interoperability of library data on the Web, by bringing together people involved in Semantic Web activities – focusing on Linked Data – in the library community and beyond, building on existing initiatives, and identifying collaboration tracks for the future'. Similar initiatives are underway in other parts of the information organization fraternity.

Semantic Web applications, however, are for the most part still in research mode. As Legg (2007, 413) observes, 'the Semantic Web has not yet enjoyed the rapid, seemingly inexorable uptake of the original Web'. She cites four key challenges still to be surmounted. First, there is the problem of *inferential tractability*, that is, for computers to be able to make inferences from data across the whole web, rather than small parts of it. Different vocabularies might be joined together in patchwork fashion (though even mapping relatively simple vocabularies is a lot of work), but at the expense of inferential power. 'Universal' ontologies, such as CycL, developed in the Cognitive Science Laboratory at Stanford University, which could serve as 'spines' for this mapping work, have not yet yielded very convincing results. Second, there is the need for *logical consistency*. Unfortunately, statements can be true or false in different contexts. Third, the web is ever changing, and so data structures will need to be constantly updated. Fourth, there is the question of political will: ultimately, it is humans who have to create and maintain these structures.

It is perhaps this last problem that is the Semantic Web's biggest sticking point. If controlled vocabularies are considered expensive by library administrators, what are the chances that they will be applied across the entire web, or even a large section of it? In certain closed environments there may be sufficient 'will' for the development of systems that realize elements of the Semantic Web vision, but it seems unlikely that Semantic Web technology will become pervasive in the foreseeable future. Does this make 'linked data' a waste of time? Even if this data does not end up supporting many Semantic Web applications, information professionals should remind themselves that controlled vocabularies provide context not only for computers, but also for people.

Conclusion

Each of the three approaches to the provision of information access has its merits, and each has its shortcomings. The approaches support the five functions of information retrieval systems (finding, identifying, selecting, obtaining, navigating) in different ways and to varying degrees. They are more or less effective, depending on the nature of the information sought and how, and to what extent, this information is conceived. Ultimately, they complement each other. Content-based systems have revolutionized the way we retrieve information, and often yield very good results. They are not so good, however, at attending to the *actual* needs of the user. In this respect, user tagging can be very helpful, representing the needs of fellow users, if not the user in question. Professional indexers can also consider what those actual needs might be, and can help users to work their needs out for themselves by providing structures that scaffold their searching.

To some extent, the three approaches serve different purposes, making comparison problematic. Anderson and Pérez-Carballo (2001) point out the difficulties involved in controlling the many variables that surround human and machine indexing. Furthermore, the traditional measures of recall and precision are based on a concept of relevance that often does not apply to the reality of information seeking. Different people will see things differently, and some people will not see things at all. Systems and tools need to be provided to help everyone, not just a particular person with a very specific notion of what it is they are looking for.

Some commentators view the rise of the search engine as part of an increasingly 'post-modern' information environment, in which context is constructed *post-search* (Enser, 2008). Information will become ever more atomized, they theorize, rather than standardized. This assumes, however, that people are becoming increasingly autonomous, that they consider their judgements to necessarily be as valuable as anyone else's. Is this really the case? Do they not appreciate the commentary that others, including metadata specialists, can provide? Mai (2011) calls for information professionals to stop imposing their cognitive authority on users, as represented by 'their' metadata, but perhaps users value this cognitive authority, just as they value the opinions of other professionals. Everyone makes their own value judgements, but these include judgements about the judgements of others. Should they trust commercial search engines, or even their fellow users, more than the metadata specialists whose professional reputation, and perhaps job, is on the line? Search engines are obviously very popular, but the more they are used, the more risk there is of their results being distorted by those wishing to 'optimize' them. In other words, the more reason there will be not to trust them.

Clearly, the depth and breadth of professional description will be constrained by economic considerations, as it has always been. As non-specialists become increasingly involved in metadata creation, their appreciation of effective information resource description becomes all the more important. It is unlikely, however, that their growing expertise will make the professional indexer redundant. Many people can cook, yet there are still professional chefs.

If all three approaches to the provision of information access are to be embraced, the question then becomes one of how they should be combined. Much more research needs to be carried out in this area, particularly in combining folksonomies and controlled vocabularies. In Peterson's view (2008), 'a database that truly integrates the two systems does not seem feasible at this time. Since traditional cataloguing is rule-bound and limiting, while folksonomy is open-ended and relative to each user, the two remain distinct, self-contained systems of subject analysis.'

Haynes (2004, 178) predicted that the following five features of metadata would continue into the future:

- It is here to stay.
- Metadata will be an integral part of information systems.
- Metadata will be invisible to most users.
- Metadata development will progress through co-operation between communities of interest.
- There is a need for a universal model for metadata to encourage further development of this subject.

These are surely sound predictions. FRBR has laid some of the groundwork for a 'universal model', particularly if a fifth function of metadata – to navigate – is added. Of course, the FRBR model limits itself to metadata for 'information access' purposes. It also remains largely untested and needs to be supplemented by studies of users' conceptualizations of, for example, 'works' and 'expressions'.

A universal model for metadata must take into account both the process of user–system interaction and its context. Similarly, the two strands of indexing research identified by Ellis and Ford (1998, 36), focusing around cognition, on the one hand, and users, on the other, provide equally valuable insights: 'indexing is not concerned simply with the distillation of some "objective" content, but takes place in a framework of assumptions concerning the potential interests of users, the sort of information they tend to require, and the total acquisition policy of the database'.

The human aspects of information retrieval make it impossible for any system to achieve perfection. As Lancaster observes (2003, 283), 'the information retrieval problem, then, can be considered essentially one of trying to match approximations of information needs with approximations of message. Small wonder that the results are not always completely satisfactory.' Retrieval systems need all the help they can get, and this would certainly include quality metadata. What makes for quality metadata nevertheless varies across information domains and search contexts. Each domain needs to be studied, each context analysed, as the information environment continues to evolve.

Will quality metadata be valued accordingly, in the systems of the future? Ultimately, this question depends on how we view information itself. There are many things we value in modern-day life: access to health care, housing, employment, the ballot box, to name but few; access to information is surely another. How much we value it is up to us, as citizens, as well as information professionals, to say.

References

Anderson, J. D. and Pérez-Carballo, J. (2001) The Nature of Indexing: how humans and machines analyse messages and texts for retrieval. Part I: research, and the nature of human indexing, *Information Processing and Management*, **37** (2), 231–54.

Banush, D. and LeBlanc, J. (2007) Utility, Library Priorities, and Cataloging Policies, *Library Collections, Acquisitions, & Technical Services*, **31** (2), 96–109.

Barnum, C. et al. (2004) Index versus Full-text Search: a usability study of user preference and performance, *Technical Communication*, **51** (2), 185–206.

Bates, J. and Rowley, J. (2011) Social Reproduction and Exclusion in Subject Indexing: a comparison of public library OPACs and LibraryThing folksonomy, *Journal of Documentation*, **67** (3), 431–48.

Beaudoin, J. E. (2007) Visual Materials and Online Access: issues concerning content representation, *Art Documentation*, **26** (2), 24–8.

Browne, G. and Jermey, J. (2007) *The Indexing Companion*, Cambridge University Press.

Byrd, D. and Crawford, T. (2002) Problems of Music Information Retrieval in the Real World, *Information Processing and Management*, **38** (2), 249–72.

Calhoun, K. (2006) *The Changing Nature of the Catalog and its Integration with Other Discovery Tools: final report*, Library of Congress, www.loc.gov/catdir/calhoun-report-final.pdf.

Carlyle, A. (1989) Matching LCSH and User Vocabulary in the Library Catalog, *Cataloging and Classification Quarterly*, **10** (1/2), 37–63.

Chan, L. M. and Yi, K. (2009) Linking Folksonomy to Library of Congress Subject Headings: an exploratory study, *Journal of Documentation*, **65** (6), 872–900.

Chapman, J. W. (2007) The Roles of the Metadata Librarian in a Research Library, *Library Resources & Technical Services*, **51** (4), 279–85.

Chen, H., Fu, T. and Huang, C. (2010) Text-based Video Content Classification for Online Video-sharing Sites, *Journal of the American Society for Information Science and Technology*, **61** (5), 891–906.

Danskin, A. (2007) Tomorrow Never Knows: the end of cataloguing? *IFLA Journal*, **33**, 205–9.

Das, S. et al. (2008) Building Biomedical Web Communities Using a Semantically Aware Content Management System, *Briefings in Bioinformatics*, **10** (2), 129–38.

Ding, Y. et al. (2009) Perspectives on Social Tagging, *Journal of the American Society for Information Science and Technology*, **60** (12), 2388–2401.

Ellis, D. and Ford, N. (1998) In Search of the Unknown User: indexing, hypertext and the World Wide Web, *Journal of Documentation*, **54** (1), 28–47.

Enser, P. G. B. (2008) Visual Image Retrieval, *Annual Review of Information Science and Technology*, **42**, 1–42.

Golub, K. (2006) Automated Subject Classification of Textual Web Documents, *Journal of Documentation*, **62** (3), 350–71.

Gorman, M. (2007) RDA: imminent debacle, *American Libraries*, December, 64–5.

Gross, T. (2008) Who Moved My Pinakes? In Roberto, K. R. (ed.), *Radical Cataloging: essays at the front*, McFarland.

Haynes, D. (2004) *Metadata for Information Management and Retrieval*, Facet Publishing.

Hjørland, B. (2007) Semantics and Knowledge Organization, *Annual Review of Information Science and Technology*, **41** (1), 367–405.

Hughes, A. V. and Rafferty, P. (2011) Inter-indexer Consistency in Graphic Materials Indexing at the National Library of Wales, *Journal of Documentation*, **67** (1), 9–32.

Hunter, J. (2009) Collaborative Semantic Tagging and Annotation Systems, *Annual Review of Information Science and Technology*, **43** (1), 1–84.

Jacob, E. K. (2004) Classification and Categorization: a difference that makes a difference, *Library Trends*, **52** (3), 515–40.

Kwaśnik, B. H. (2010) Semantic Warrant: a pivotal concept for our field, *Knowledge Organization*, **37** (2), 106–10.

Lancaster, F. W. (2003) *Indexing and Abstracting in Theory and Practice*, 3rd edn, Facet Publishing.

Legg, C. (2007) Ontologies on the Semantic Web, *Annual Review of Information Science and Technology*, **41** (1), 407–51.

Lippincott, A. (2002) Issues in Content-based Music Information Retrieval, *Journal of Information Science*, **28** (2), 137–42.

Lund, W., Ng, Y.-K. and Pera, M. S. (2009) A Sophisticated Library Search Strategy Using Folksonomies and Similarity Matching, *Journal of the American Society for Information Science and Technology*, **60** (7), 1392–406.

Mai, J.-E. (2011) Folksonomies and the New Order: authority in the digital order,

Knowledge Organization, **38** (2), 114–22.

Mann, T. (2008) Will Google's Keyword Searching Eliminate the Need for LC Cataloging and Classification? *Journal of Library Metadata*, **8** (2), 159–68.

McCutcheon, S. (2009) Keyword vs Controlled Vocabulary Searching: the one with the most tools wins, *The Indexer*, **27** (2), 62–5.

Mering, M. and Nowick, E. A. (2003) Comparisons between Internet Users' Free-Text Queries and Controlled Vocabularies: a case study in water quality, *Technical Services Quarterly*, **21** (2), 62–5.

Peterson, E. (2008) Parallel Systems: the coexistence of subject cataloguing and folksonomy, *Library Philosophy and Practice*, April, www.webpages.uidaho.edu/~mbolin/e-peterson3.htm.

Primary Research Group (2011) *Academic Library Cataloging Practices Benchmarks.*

Rasmussen, E. (2004) Information Retrieval Challenges for Digital Libraries. In Chen, Z. et al. (eds) *Digital Libraries: international collaborations and cross-fertilization*, Springer.

Rolla, P. J. (2009) User Tags versus Subject Headings: can user-supplied data improve subject access to library collections? *Library Resources & Technical Services*, **53** (3), 174–84.

Saarti, J. (2002) Consistency of Subject Indexing of Novels by Public Library Professionals and Patrons, *Journal of Documentation*, **58** (1), 49–65.

Sanchez, E. R. (ed.) (2011) *Conversations with Cataloguers in the 21st Century*, Libraries Unlimited.

Shiri, A. and Revie, C. (2006) Query Expansion Behaviour within a Thesaurus-enhanced Search Environment: a user-centred evaluation, *Journal of the American Society for Information Science and Technology*, **57** (4), 462–78.

Spiteri, L. F. (2007) The Structure and Form of Folksonomy Tags: the road to the public library catalog, *Information Technology and Libraries*, September, 13–24.

Steinhagen, E. N. and Moynahan, S. A. (1998) Catalogers Must Change! Surviving between a rock and a hard place, *Cataloging & Classification Quarterly*, **26** (3), 3–20.

Wilson, A. J. (2007) Toward Releasing the Metadata Bottleneck: a baseline evaluation of contributor-supplied metadata, *Library Resources & Technical Services*, **51** (1), 16–28.

Yee, M. M. (2009) Wholly Visionary: the American Library Association, the Library of Congress, and the card distribution program, *Library Resources & Technical Services*, **53** (2), 68–78.

Further reading

Abbas, J. (2009) *Structures for Organizing Knowledge: exploring taxonomies, ontologies, and other schemas*, Neal-Schuman.

Aitchison, J., Bawden, D. and Gilchrist, A. (2000) *Thesaurus Construction and Use: a practical manual*, 4th edn, Aslib.

Alasem, A. (2009) An Overview of e-Government Metadata Standards and Initiatives Based on Dublin Core, *Electronic Journal of e-Government*, **7** (1), 1–10.

Anderson, J. D. and Pérez-Carballo, J. (2005) *Information Retrieval Design: principles and options for information description, organization, display, and access in information retrieval databases, digital libraries, catalogs, and indexes*, Ometeca Institute.

Baca, M. (ed.) (2008) *Introduction to Metadata*, 2nd edn, Getty Research Institute.

Baeza-Yates, R. and Ribeiro-Neto, B. (2011) *Modern Information Retrieval: the concepts and technology behind search*, 2nd edn, Addison Wesley.

Boll, J. J. and Olson, H. A. (2001) *Subject Analysis in Online Catalogs*, 2nd edn, Libraries Unlimited.

Breeding, M. (2010) *Next-gen Library Catalogs*, Facet Publishing.

Brooks, T. A. (2002) The Semantic Web, Universalist Ambition and Some Lessons from Librarianship, *Information Research*, **7** (4), http://InformationR.net/ir/7-4/paper136.html.

Broughton, V. (2012) *Essential Library of Congress Subject Headings*, Facet Publishing.

Broughton, V. (2006) *Essential Thesaurus Construction*, Facet Publishing.

Browne, G. and Jermey, J. (2007) *The Indexing Companion*, Cambridge University Press.

Caplan, P. (2003) *Metadata Fundamentals for all Librarians*, American Library Association.

Chan, L. M. (1999) *A Guide to the Library of Congress Classification*, 5th edn, Libraries Unlimited.

Chan, L. M. (2005) *Library of Congress Subject Headings: principles and application*, 4th edn, Libraries Unlimited.

Chan, L. M. (2007) *Cataloging and Classification: an introduction*, 3rd edn, Scarecrow Press.

Chan, L. M. and Mitchell, J. S. (2003) *Dewey Decimal Classification: principles and application*, 3rd edn, OCLC.

Chowdhury, G. G. (2010) *Introduction to Modern Information Retrieval*, 3rd edn, Facet Publishing.

Chowdhury, G. G. and Chowdhury, S. (2007) *Organizing Information: from the shelf to the web*, Facet Publishing.

Chu, H. (2010) *Information Representation and Retrieval in the Digital Age*, 2nd edn, American Society for Information Science and Technology.

Cleveland, A. D. and Cleveland, D. B. (2001) *Introduction to Indexing and Abstracting*, 3rd edn, Libraries Unlimited.

Cox, R. J. (2007) Revisiting the Archival Finding Aid, *Journal of Archival Organization*, **5** (4), 5–32.

Coyle, K. (2010) Understanding the Semantic Web: bibliographic data and metadata, *Library Technology Reports*, **46** (1), 5–13.

Croft, W. B., Metzler, D. and Strohman, T. (2010) *Search Engines: information retrieval in practice*, Addison-Wesley.

Dickey, T. J. and Connaway, L. S. (2010) *The Digital Information Seeker: report of the findings from selected OCLC, RIN and JISC user behaviour projects*, HEFCE, www.jisc.ac.uk/publications/reports/2010/digitalinformationseekers.aspx.

Dunsire, G. and Nicholson, D. (2010) Signposting the Crossroads: terminology web services and classification-based interoperability, *Knowledge Organization*, **37** (4), 280–6.

Eden, D. B. (2008) *Information Organization Futures*, Emerald Group Publishing Limited.

Foulonneau, M. and Riley, J. (2008) *Metadata for Digital Resources: implementation, systems design and interoperability*, Chandos Publishing.

Fox, M. J. and Wilkerson, P. L. (1998) *Introduction to Archival Organization and Description*, Getty Information Institute.

Fried Foster, N. et al. (eds) (2011) *Scholarly Practice, Participatory Design and the eXtensible Catalog*, ACRL.

Harpring, P. (2010) *Introduction to Controlled Vocabularies: terminology for art, architecture, and other cultural works*, Getty Research Institute.

Haynes, D. (2004) *Metadata for Information Management and Retrieval*, Facet Publishing.

Hider, P. and Harvey, R. (2008) *Organising Knowledge in a Global Society: principles and practice in libraries and information centres*, Centre for Information Studies, Charles Sturt University.

Hillmann, D. I. and Westbrooks, E. L. (2004) *Metadata in Practice*, American Library Association.

Hopkinson, A. (1999) Traditional Communication Formats: MARC is far from dead, *International Cataloguing and Bibliographic Control*, **28** (1), 17–21.

Intner, S. S., Lazinger, S. S. and Weihs, J. R. (2006) *Metadata and its Impact on Libraries*, Libraries Unlimited.

Joint Steering Committee for Development of RDA, www.rda-jsc.org.

Joudrey, D. N. and Taylor, A. G. (2009) *The Organization of Information*, 3rd edn, Libraries Unlimited.

Kilner, K. (2005) The AustLit Gateway and Scholarly Bibliography: a specialist implementation of the FRBR, *Cataloging & Classification Quarterly*, **39** (3/4), 87–102.

Lambe, P. (2007) *Organising Knowledge: taxonomies, knowledge and organizational effectiveness*, Chandos Publishing.

Lancaster, F. W. (2003) *Indexing and Abstracting in Theory and Practice*, 3rd edn, Facet Publishing.

Landry, P. et al. (eds) (2011) *Subject Access: preparing for the future*, De Gruyter Saur.

Lesk, M. (2005) *Understanding Digital Libraries*, 2nd edn, Elsevier.

Liu, J. (2007) *Metadata and its Applications in the Digital Library: approaches and practices*, Libraries Unlimited.

Lopez-Huertas, M. J. E. (ed.) (2002) *Challenges in Knowledge Representation and Organization for the 21st Century: integration of knowledge across boundaries*, Ergon.

Ma, J. (2007) *Metadata*, Association of Research Libraries.

Mann, T. (2008) The Peloponnesian War and the Future of Reference, Cataloging, and Scholarship in Research Libraries, *Journal of Library Metadata*, **8** (1), 53–100.

Maxwell, R. L. (2008) *FRBR: a guide for the perplexed*, American Library Association.

McIlwaine, I. C. (2000) *The Universal Decimal Classification: a guide to its use*, UDC Consortium.

Miles, A. and Perez-Aguera, J. R. (2007) SKOS: simple knowledge organisation for the Web, *Cataloging & Classification Quarterly*, **43** (3/4), 69–83.

Moffat, M. (2006) Marketing with Metadata: how metadata can increase exposure and visibility of online content, *New Review of Information Networking*, **12** (1–2), 23–40.

Morville, P. and Rosenfeld, L. (2007) *Information Architecture for the World Wide Web: designing large-scale web sites*, 3rd edn, O'Reilly.

Mulvany, N. C. (2005) *Indexing Books*, University of Chicago Press.

Oliver, C. (2010) *Introducing RDA: a guide to the basics*, Facet Publishing.

Park, J.-R. and Tosaka, Y. (2010) Metadata Quality Control in Digital Repositories and Collections: criteria, semantics, and mechanisms, *Cataloging & Classification Quarterly*, **48** (8), 696–715.

Qin, J. and Zeng, M. L. (2008) *Metadata*, Facet Publishing.

Riley, J. (2010) *Seeing Standards: a visualization of the metadata universe*, www.dlib.indiana.edu/~jenlrile/metadatamap/seeingstandards.pdf.

Roberto, K. R. (ed.) (2008) *Radical Cataloging: essays at the front*, McFarland & Co.

Rowley, J. and Hartley, R. (2007) *Organizing Knowledge: an introduction to managing access to information*, 4th edn, Ashgate.

Sanchez, E. R. (ed.) (2011) *Conversations with Cataloguers in the 21st Century*, Libraries Unlimited.

Šauperl, A. (2002) *Subject Determination during the Cataloging Process*, Scarecrow Press.

Schilling, V. (2010) The Catalogers' Revenge: unleashing the Semantic Web, *PNLA Quarterly*, **74** (3), 9–23.

Schwartz, C. (2001) *Sorting out the Web: approaches to subject access*, Ablex.

Search Engine Watch, http://searchenginewatch.com.

Shepherd, E. and Yeo, G. (2003) *Managing Records: a handbook of principles and practice*, Facet Publishing.

Svenonius, E. (2000) *The Intellectual Foundation of Information Organization*, MIT Press.

Taylor, A. G. (2006) *Introduction to Cataloging and Classification*, 10th edn, Libraries Unlimited.

Tennant, R. (2002) MARC Must Die, *Library Journal*, 15 October, www.libraryjournal.com/article/CA250046.html.

Trant, J. (2009) Studying Social Tagging and Folksonomy: a review and framework, *Journal of Digital Information*, **10** (1), http://journals.tdl.org/jodi/article/view/269/278.

UKOLN, www.ukoln.ac.uk.

Welsh, A. and Batley, S. (2012) *Practical Cataloguing: AACR, RDA and MARC 21*, Facet Publishing.

Yi, K. (2007) Automatic Text Classification Using Library Classification Schemes: trends, issues, and challenges, *International Cataloguing and Bibliographic Control Journal*, **36** (4), 78–82.

Zhang, Y. and Salaba, A. (2009) *Implementing FRBR in Libraries: key issues and future directions*, Neal-Schuman.

Metadata standards

Archival description and recordkeeping

Bureau of Canadian Archivists (2008) *Rules for Archival Description*, 2nd edn.

Cook, M. and Procter, M. (2000) *Manual of Archival Description*, 3rd edn, Gower.

Hensen, S. L. (1989) *Archives, Personal Papers, and Manuscripts: a cataloging manual for archival repositories, historical societies, and manuscript libraries*, 2nd edn, Society of American Archivists.

Hensen, S. L. (2007) *Describing Archives: a content standard*, Society of American Archivists

International Council on Archives (2000) *ISAD(G): General International Standard Archival Description*, 2nd edn, www.icacds.org.uk/eng/ISAD%28G%29.pdf.

International Council on Archives (2004) *ISAAR (CPF): International Standard Archival Authority Record for Corporate Bodies, Persons and Families*, 2nd edn, www.icacds.org.uk/eng/ISAAR%28CPF%292ed.pdf.

International Organization for Standardization (2006) *Records Management Processes: metadata for records. Part 1, Principles* (23081-1).

International Organization for Standardization (2009) *Records Management Processes: metadata for records. Part 2, Conceptual and Implementation Issues* (23081-2).

International Organization for Standardization (2011) *Records Management Processes: metadata for records. Part 3, Self-Assessment Method* (23081-3).

Cataloguing and bibliographic description

American Library Association (1878) *Condensed Rules for Cataloging*, Library Journal, 3, 12–19.

American Library Association (1941) *ALA Catalog Rules, Author and Title Entries*.

American Library Association (1949) *ALA Cataloging Rules for Author and Title Entries*, 2nd edn, American Library Association.

American Library Association (1967) *Anglo-American Cataloging Rules*, Library

Association, 1967.

American Library Association (1980) *ALA Filing Rules*.

Baca, M. et al. (2006) *Cataloguing Cultural Objects: a guide to describing cultural works and their images*, ALA Editions.

Cutter, C. A. (1904) *Rules for a Dictionary Catalog*, 4th edn, USGPO.

Gorman, M. (2004) *The Concise AACR2*, 4th edn, American Library Association, Canadian Library Association, Chartered Institute of Library and Information Professionals.

Instruktionen für die Alphabetischen Kataloge der Preußischen Bibliotheken (1899), Asher.

International Federation of Library Associations (1971) *ISBD(M): International Standard Bibliographic Description for Monographic Publications*.

International Federation of Library Associations and Institutions (2001) *Guidelines for Authority Records and References*, 2nd edn, K. G. Saur, www.ifla.org/files/cataloguing/garr/garr.pdf.

International Federation of Library Associations and Institutions (2011) *ISBD: International Standard Bibliographic Description*, Consolidated edn, De Gruyter Saur.

International Organization for Standardization (2010) *Guidelines for Bibliographic References and Citations to Information Resources* (690).

Joint Steering Committee for Development of RDA (2010) *RDA: Resource Description and Access*, American Library Association.

Joint Steering Committee for Revision of AACR (1978) *Anglo-American Cataloguing Rules*, 2nd edn, American Library Association.

Joint Steering Committee for Revision of AACR (2005) *Anglo-American Cataloguing Rules*, 2nd edn, 2002 revision, 2005 update, American Library Association.

Library Association (1881) *Cataloguing Rules of the Library Association of the United Kingdom*.

Library Association and American Library Association (1908) *Cataloguing Rules: author and title entries*, Library Association.

Library of Congress (1949) *Rules for Descriptive Cataloging in the Library of Congress*.

Library of Congress (2000) *Archival Moving Image Materials: a cataloging manual*, 2nd edn.

Library of Congress (2010) *Library of Congress Rule Interpretations*.

Panizzi, A. (1841) Rules for the Compilation of the Catalogue. In *Catalogue of Printed Books in the British Museum*, vol. 1.

Regeln für Alphabetische Katalogisierung (1977), Reichert.

Guidelines for cataloguing rules

Anderson, D. and Chaplin, A. H. (eds) (1963) *International Conference on Cataloguing Principles, Paris, 9th–18th October 1961: report*, K.G. Saur.

International Federation of Library Associations and Institutions (1998) *Functional Requirements for Bibliographic Records: final report*, K. G. Saur.

International Federation of Library Associations and Institutions (2009) IFLA *Cataloging Principles: the Statement of International Cataloguing Principles*, K. G. Saur.

International Federation of Library Associations and Institutions (2009) *Functional Requirements for Authority Data: a conceptual model*, K. G. Saur.

International Federation of Library Associations and Institutions (2011) *Functional Requirements for Subject Authority Data (FRSAD): a conceptual model*, K. G. Saur.

Indexing and abstracting standards

ANSI/NISO (American National Standards Institute and National Information Standards Organization) (1997) *Guidelines for Abstracts* (Z39.14).

International Organization for Standardization (1985) *Methods for Examining Documents, Determining their Subjects, and Selecting Indexing Terms* (5963).

International Organization for Standardization (1996) *Guidelines for the Content, Organization and Presentation of Indexes* (999).

Style manuals

American Psychological Association (2010) *Publication Manual of the American Psychological Association*, 6th edn.

Iverson, C. et al. (2007) *AMA Manual of Style: a guide for authors and editors*, 10th edn, Oxford University Press.

Modern Language Association of America (2008) *MLA Style Manual and Guide to Scholarly Publishing*, 3rd edn.

University of Chicago Press (2010) *The Chicago Manual of Style*, 16th edn.

Schemas

ANZLIC, www.anzlic.org.au.

Baca, M. and Harpring, P. (eds) (2009) *Categories for Descriptions of Works of Art*, www.getty.edu/research/publications/electronic_publications/cdwa/index.html.

Bibliographic Ontology, http://bibliontology.com.

Canadian Heritage Information Network, www.pro.rcip-chin.gc.ca.

CanCore, www.cancore.ca.

DataCite, *DataCite Metadata Schema Repository*, http://schema.datacite.org.

Data Documentation Initiative, www.ddialliance.org.

Dublin Core Metadata Initiative, http://dublincore.org.

Dublin Core Metadata Initiative, *DC-Education Application Profile*, http://dublincore.org/educationwiki/DC_2dEducation_20Application_20Profile.

EDItEUR, *ONIX*, www.editeur.org/8/ONIX.

Education Network Australia, http://edna.edu.au, http://apps-new.edna.edu.au/ edna_retired/edna/go.html.

e-Government Metadata Standard, www.esd.org.uk/standards/egms.

Encoded Archival Context, http://eac.staatsbibliothek-berlin.de/index.php.

European Commission on Preservation and Access, *SEPIADES*, www.ica.org/7363/paag-resources/sepiades-recommendations-for-cataloguing-photographic-collections.html.

Gateway, www.thegateway.org.

Government Information Locator Service, www.archives.gov/records-mgmt/policy/gils.html.

Institute of Electrical and Electronics Engineers, *Learning Object Metadata*, http://ltsc.ieee.org/wg12.

International Council of Museums, International Committee for Documentation (1995) *International Guidelines for Museum Object Information: the CIDOC information categories*.

International Imaging Industry Association, *DIG35*, www.i3a.org/technologies/digitalimaging/metadata.

International Organization for Standardization (2006) *A Reference Ontology for the Interchange of Cultural Heritage Information* (21127).

International Organization for Standardization (2009) *Geographic Information: metadata* (19115).

International Press Telecommunications Council, *IPTC Core & Extension*, www.iptc.org/site/Photo_Metadata/IPTC_Core_&_Extension.

Library of Congress, *Encoded Archival Description*, www.loc.gov/ead.

Library of Congress, *Metadata Authority Description Schema*, www.loc.gov/standards/mads.

Library of Congress, *Metadata Object Description Schema*, www.loc.gov/standards/mods.

McKemmish, S. et al. (2000) *Australian Recordkeeping Metadata Schema*, www.infotech.monash.edu.au/research/groups/rcrg/projects/spirit/deliverables/au strkms-schemes.html.

McKenna, G. and Patsatzi, E. (2005) *SPECTRUM: the UK museum documentation standard*, 3rd edn, MDA.

Moving Picture Experts Group, *MPEG-7*, http://mpeg.chiariglione.org/standards/mpeg-7/mpeg-7.htm.

Music Ontology, http://musicontology.com.

National Archives of Australia, *AGLS Metadata Standard*, www.agls.gov.au.

PBCore, www.pbcore.org.

Taxonomic Databases Working Group, *Darwin Core*, http://rs.tdwg.org/dwc/index.htm.

Text Encoding Initiative, www.tei-c.org.

US Federal Geographic Data Committee, *Content Standard for Digital Geospatial Metadata*, www.fgdc.gov/metadata/csdgm.

Visual Resources Association, *VRA Core*, www.loc.gov/standards/vracore.

Alphabetical vocabularies

AGROVOC, http://aims.fao.org/standards/agrovoc/about.

Aitchison, J., Gomersall, A. and Ireland, R. (1969) *Thesaurofacet*, English Electric Co. Ltd.

Art and Architecture Thesaurus Online, www.getty.edu/research/tools/vocabularies/aat.

Bibliothèque nationale de France, *Répertoire d'autorité matière encyclopédique et alphabétique unifié*, http://rameau.bnf.fr.

Book Industry Standards and Communications, *BISAC Subject Headings*, www.bisg.org/what-we-do-20-73-bisac-subject-headings-2011-edition.php.

British Museum Materials Thesaurus, www.collectionslink.org.uk/assets/thesaurus_bmm/matintro.htm.

Education Resources Information Center, *ERIC Thesaurus*, www.eric.ed.gov/ERICWebPortal/thesaurus/thesaurus.jsp.

Institution of Electrical Engineers (2007) *Inspec Thesaurus*.

Integrated Public Services Vocabulary, http://doc.esd.org.uk/IPSV.

J. Paul Getty Trust, *Art and Architecture Thesaurus*, www.getty.edu/research/tools/vocabularies/aat.

J. Paul Getty Trust, *Getty Thesaurus of Geographic Names*, www.getty.edu/research/tools/vocabularies/tgn.

J. Paul Getty Trust, *Union List of Artist Names*, www.getty.edu/research/tools/vocabularies/ulan.

Library of Congress (2011) *Library of Congress Subject Headings*, 33rd edn.

Library of Congress, *Thesaurus for Graphic Materials I: subject terms*, www.loc.gov/rr/print/tgm1.

Library of Congress, *Thesaurus for Graphic Materials II: genre and physical characteristic terms*, www.loc.gov/rr/print/tgm2.

National Archives of Australia, *Australian Government Interactive Functions Thesaurus*, www.naa.gov.au/records-management/publications/agift.

National Library of Medicine, *Medical Subject Headings*, www.nlm.nih.gov/mesh.

Répertoire de vedettes-matières, https://rvmweb.bibl.ulaval.ca.

Sears List of Subject Headings (2010) 20th edn, H. H. Wilson.

UNESCO, *UNESCO Thesaurus*, http://databases.unesco.org/thesaurus.

Virtual International Authority File, http://viaf.org.

Guidelines for vocabularies

British Standards Institution (2005a) *Structured Vocabularies for Information Retrieval: guide. Definitions, Symbols and Abbreviations* (8723-1).

British Standards Institution (2005b) *Structured Vocabularies for Information Retrieval: guide. Thesauri* (8723–2).

International Federation of Library Associations and Institutions (2009) *Guidelines for Multilingual Thesauri*, http://archive.ifla.org/VII/s29/pubs/Profrep115.pdf.

International Organization for Standardization (2011) *Thesauri and Interoperability with Other Vocabularies. Part 1, Thesauri for Information Retrieval* (25964-1).

Library of Congress (2008-) *Subject Headings Manual*.

Regeln für den Schlagwortkatalog (2010), 3., überarb. und erw. Aufl., Deutsche National Bibliothek.

Classification schemes

Bliss Classification Association, www.blissclassification.org.uk.

Boggs, S. W. and Lewis, D. C. (1945) *The Classification and Cataloging of Maps and Atlases*, Special Libraries Association.

Coates, E. J. (1960) *The British Catalogue of Music Classification*, Council of the British National Bibliography.

Dewey Decimal Classification, www.oclc.org/dewey.

Library of Congress, *Library of Congress Classification*, www.loc.gov/catdir/cpso/lcc.html.

International Patent Classification, www.wipo.int/classifications/ipc/en.

Moys, E. M. (2001) *Moys Classification and Thesaurus for Legal Matters*, 4th edn, K. G. Saur.

National Library of Medicine, *NLM Classification*, www.nlm.nih.gov/class.

Pettee, J. (1967) *Classification of the Library of Union Theological Seminary in the City of New York*, Rev. and enl. ed., Union Theological Seminary.

Ranganathan, S. R. (2006) *Colon Classification*, 6th edn, Ess Ess Publications.

UDC Consortium, www.udcc.org.

Identifiers

American National Standards Institute and National Information Standards Organization (1996) *Serial Item and Contribution Identifier* (Z39.56).

International DOI Foundation, *The DOI System*, www.doi.org.

International Organization for Standardization (2002) *International Standard Audiovisual Number* (15706).

International Organization for Standardization (2005) *International Standard Book Number* (2108).

International Organization for Standardization (2007) *International Standard Serial Number* (3297).

International Organization for Standardization (2009) *International Standard Music Number* (10957).

International Organization for Standardization (2009) *International Standard Text Code* (21047).

International Organization for Standardization (2012) *International Standard Name Identifier* (ISNI) (27729).

Encoding and transmission standards

ANSI/NISO (2010) *The OpenURL Framework for Context-Sensitive Services* (Z39.88).

International Federation of Library Associations and Institutions, *UNIMARC*, www.unimarc.net.

International Organization for Standardization (1998) *Information Retrieval (Z39.50): application service definition and protocol specification* (23950).

International Organization for Standardization (2008) *Format for Information Exchange* (2709).

International Organization for Standardization and International Electrotechnical Commission (2003) *SGML Applications: topic maps* (13250).

Library of Congress, *MARC21*, www.loc.gov/marc.

Library of Congress, *Metadata Encoding and Transmission Standard*, www.loc.gov/standards/mets.

Library of Congress, *Search/Retrieval by URL*, www.loc.gov/standards/sru.

Open Archives Initiative, *Protocol for Metadata Harvesting*,
    www.openarchives.org/OAI/openarchivesprotocol.html.

The Bath Group (2004) *The Bath Profile: an international Z39.50 specification for library applications and resource discovery*, release 2.0,
    www.collectionscanada.gc.ca/bath/91/tp-bath2-e.pdf.

W3C, *Resource Description Framework*, www.w3.org/RDF.

W3C, *SKOS: Simple Knowledge Organization System*, www.w3.org/2004/02/skos.

W3C, *Web Ontology Language*, www.w3.org/TR/owl-ref.

Registries

Dublin Core Metadata Initiative, *The Dublin Core Metadata Registry*,
    http://dcmi.kc.tsukuba.ac.jp/dcregistry.

Open Metadata Registry, http://metadataregistry.org.

Schemapedia, http://schemapedia.com.

Index